Communications
in Computer and Information Science

2833

Series Editors

Gang Li, *School of Information Technology, Deakin University, Burwood, VIC, Australia*
Joaquim Filipe, *Polytechnic Institute of Setúbal, Setúbal, Portugal*
Zhiwei Xu, *Chinese Academy of Sciences, Beijing, China*

Rationale
The CCIS series is devoted to the publication of proceedings of computer science conferences. Its aim is to efficiently disseminate original research results in informatics in printed and electronic form. While the focus is on publication of peer-reviewed full papers presenting mature work, inclusion of reviewed short papers reporting on work in progress is welcome, too. Besides globally relevant meetings with internationally representative program committees guaranteeing a strict peer-reviewing and paper selection process, conferences run by societies or of high regional or national relevance are also considered for publication.

Topics
The topical scope of CCIS spans the entire spectrum of informatics ranging from foundational topics in the theory of computing to information and communications science and technology and a broad variety of interdisciplinary application fields.

Information for Volume Editors and Authors
Publication in CCIS is free of charge. No royalties are paid, however, we offer registered conference participants temporary free access to the online version of the conference proceedings on SpringerLink (http://link.springer.com) by means of an http referrer from the conference website and/or a number of complimentary printed copies, as specified in the official acceptance email of the event.

CCIS proceedings can be published in time for distribution at conferences or as post-proceedings, and delivered in the form of printed books and/or electronically as USBs and/or e-content licenses for accessing proceedings at SpringerLink. Furthermore, CCIS proceedings are included in the CCIS electronic book series hosted in the SpringerLink digital library at http://link.springer.com/bookseries/7899. Conferences publishing in CCIS are allowed to use Online Conference Service (OCS) for managing the whole proceedings lifecycle (from submission and reviewing to preparing for publication) free of charge.

Publication process
The language of publication is exclusively English. Authors publishing in CCIS have to sign the Springer CCIS copyright transfer form, however, they are free to use their material published in CCIS for substantially changed, more elaborate subsequent publications elsewhere. For the preparation of the camera-ready papers/files, authors have to strictly adhere to the Springer CCIS Authors' Instructions and are strongly encouraged to use the CCIS LaTeX style files or templates.

Abstracting/Indexing
CCIS is abstracted/indexed in DBLP, Google Scholar, EI-Compendex, Mathematical Reviews, SCImago, Scopus. CCIS volumes are also submitted for the inclusion in ISI Proceedings.

How to start
To start the evaluation of your proposal for inclusion in the CCIS series, please send an e-mail to ccis@springer.com.

Hugo Rios-Neto · Pieter Robberechts ·
Maaike Van Roy · Albrecht Zimmermann

Editors

Machine Learning and Data Mining for Sports Analytics

12th International Workshop, MLSA 2025
Porto, Portugal, September 15, 2025
Revised Selected Papers

 Springer

Editors
Hugo Rios-Neto
Universidade Federal de Minas Gerais
Belo Horizonte, Brazil

Pieter Robberechts
Katholieke Universiteit Leuven
Leuven, Belgium

Maaike Van Roy
Katholieke Universiteit Leuven
Leuven, Belgium

Albrecht Zimmermann
University of Caen Normandie
Caen, France

ISSN 1865-0929 ISSN 1865-0937 (electronic)
Communications in Computer and Information Science
ISBN 978-3-032-15164-3 ISBN 978-3-032-15165-0 (eBook)
https://doi.org/10.1007/978-3-032-15165-0

This Springer imprint is published by the registered company Springer Nature Switzerland AG
The registered company address is: Gewerbestrasse 11, 6330 Cham, Switzerland

If disposing of this product, please recycle the paper.

Preface

The Machine Learning and Data Mining for Sports Analytics workshop aims to bring together a diverse set of researchers working on Sports Analytics in a broad sense. In particular, it aims to attract interest from researchers working on sports from outside of machine learning and data mining. The 12th edition of the workshop was co-located with the European Conference on Machine Learning and Principles and Practice of Knowledge Discovery 2025.

Sports Analytics has been a steadily growing and rapidly evolving area over the last decade, both in US professional sports leagues and in European football leagues. The recent implementation of strict financial fair-play regulations in European football will definitely increase the importance of Sports Analytics in the coming years. In addition, there is the popularity of sports betting. The developed techniques are being used for decision support in all aspects of professional sports, including but not limited to:

- Match strategy, tactics, and analysis
- Player acquisition, player valuation, and team spending
- Training regimens and focus
- Injury prediction and prevention
- Performance management and prediction
- Match outcome and league table prediction
- Tournament design and scheduling
- Betting odds calculation

The interest in the topic has grown so much that there is now an annual conference on Sports Analytics at the MIT Sloan School of Management, which has been attended by representatives from over 70 professional sports teams in eminent leagues such as Major League Baseball, National Basketball Association, National Football League, National Hockey League, Major League Soccer, English Premier League, and the German Bundesliga. Furthermore, sports data providers such as Hudl/Statsbomb, Stats Perform, and Wyscout have started making performance data publicly available to stimulate researchers who have the skills and vision to make a difference in the sports analytics community. Moreover, the National Football League has sponsored a Big Data Bowl where they release data and a concrete question to try to engage the analytics community.

There has been growing interest in the Machine Learning and Data Mining community about this topic, and the 2025 edition of MLSA built on the success of prior editions at ECML PKDD 2013, ECML PKDD 2015 – ECML/PKDD 2024.

Both the community's on-going interest in submitting to and participating in the MLSA workshop series, and the fact that you are reading the seventh volume of MLSA proceedings show that our workshop has become a vital venue for publishing and presenting sports analytics results. While other researchers occasionally organize workshops co-located with other conferences, and sports analytics papers appear more often at major conferences, MLSA remains a primary venue for publishing sports analytics research from a machine learning and data mining perspective.

In fact, when discussion turned to whether there was interest in continuing the series, participants were overwhelmingly in favor, with several volunteering to take on organizational tasks. The 2025 edition of MLSA is an example of this, with three regular participants taking on the role of organizers for the first time, guided by an experienced organizer.

This year's edition of the workshop received 24 submissions, in line with historical trends, of which 13 were selected after a single-blind reviewing process involving at least two program committee members per paper. One of the accepted papers was withdrawn from publication in the proceedings; another paper was an extended abstract based on a journal publication. In terms of the sports represented, this year's workshop was again heavily dominated by soccer, but also contained a mix of other reoccurring sports such as basketball, table tennis, and ultimate frisbee. Notably, a paper on speedway (i.e., a motorsport) was presented for the first time. Topics included tactical analysis, outcome predictions, data acquisition, performance optimization, and player evaluation.

Deviating from past years, the workshop was held during half a day. To accommodate the large number of high-quality submissions, yet limited amount of time, a poster session was organized for the first time. The workshop started off with a mix of full-length presentations and concluded with poster spotlight presentations and a poster session, which the attendees seemed to enjoy.

Further information about the workshop can be found on the workshop's website at https://dtai.cs.kuleuven.be/events/MLSA25/.

November 2025

Hugo Rios-Neto
Pieter Robberechts
Maaike Van Roy
Albrecht Zimmermann

Organization

Workshop Co-chairs

Hugo Rios-Neto	Universidade Federal de Minas Gerais, Brazil & Orlando City SC, USA
Pieter Robberechts	KU Leuven, Belgium
Maaike Van Roy	KU Leuven, Belgium
Albrecht Zimmermann	Université de Caen Normandie, France

Program Committee

Gennady Andrienko	Fraunhofer IAIS, Germany
Harish S. Bhat	University of California, Merced, USA
Henrik Biermann	German Sports University Cologne, Germany
Lotte Bransen	KU Leuven, Belgium
Ulf Brefeld	Leuphana University of Lüneburg, Germany
Lorenzo Cascioli	KU Leuven, Belgium
Jesse Davis	KU Leuven, Belgium
Arie-Willem de Leeuw	The Hague University of Applied Sciences, Netherlands
Martin Eastwood	UK
Keisuke Fujii	Nagoya University, Japan
Matthias Kempe	University of Vienna, Austria
Hyunsung Kim	Korea Advanced Institute of Science & Technology, South Korea
John Komar	Nanyang Technological University, Singapore
Patrick Lambrix	Linköping University, Sweden
Jakub Michalczyk	Leuphana University of Lüneburg, Germany
Tim Op De Beéck	Runeasi, Belgium
Konstantinos Pelechrinis	University of Pittsburgh, USA
Marc Plantevit	EPITA, France
Pegah Rahimian	Uppsala University, Sweden
François Rioult	GREYC CNRS UMR6072 - Université de Caen Normandie, France
Yannick Rudolph	Leuphana University of Lüneburg, Germany
Jan Van Haaren	KU Leuven & Club Brugge, Belgium
Steven Verstockt	University of Ghent, Belgium

Contents

Other Team Sports

Individual Sports

Analysis of Service Returns in Table Tennis

Riad Attou[1(✉)] [ID], Marin Mathé[1] [ID], Aymeric Eradès[1,2] [ID],
and Romain Vuillemot[1,2] [ID]

[1] École Centrale de Lyon, Écully, France
attou.rd@gmail.com
[2] LIRIS CNRS UMR 5205, Lyon, France

Abstract. This article explores the relationship between received serves and returns in table tennis by combining statistical and visual analyses. Our key findings highlight concrete patterns: for instance, **F. Zhendong** exhibits a strong dependence between serve clusters and return zones ($p < 0.001$), while **A. Lebrun** and **F. Lebrun** show no such coupling ($p = 0.176$ and $p = 0.61$ respectively). Additionally, **F. Lebrun** adapts his returns to domination phases ($p = 0.013$) and pressure levels ($p = 0.039$), and return choices are significantly associated with point outcomes for both **A. Lebrun** ($p = 0.078$) and **F. Zhendong** ($p = 0.044$). These results provide precise insights into tactical decision-making and lay the groundwork for predictive performance models.

Keywords: Sports Analytics · Table Tennis · Returns · Clustering

1 Introduction

In table tennis, service returns are the initial response by the receiver to the serves. This aspect of the game is often overlooked despite its strategic importance [7]. Unlike serves, where the player has complete control over the stroke, the receiver is constrained: they must react quickly and adapt their response based on several factors (e.g. spin, speed, and placement of the ball) within a very short time frame to influence the course of the rally.

There are various ways to respond to a serve, whether by returning in identified zones or by making a specific striking technique. While these tactical choices are crucial, they remain underdocumented in the scientific literature. Existing studies focus on serve dynamics [6], stroke biomechanics [18], or general tactics that include service returns [1], but without specifically addressing them. More in-depth tactical studies directly focus on the analysis of sequences of several strokes [15,19]. More recently, [5] conducted a study on specific striking techniques and took serves as a study case for analysis, but none on returns. The question of how players adjust their returns based on the nature of the serves or the match context remains largely unexplored.

© The Author(s), under exclusive license to Springer Nature Switzerland AG 2026
H. Rios-Neto et al. (Eds.): MLSA 2025, CCIS 2833, pp. 3–18, 2026.
https://doi.org/10.1007/978-3-032-15165-0_1

This article aims to explore these interactions in depth by identifying recurring patterns and tactical choices related to service returns. It provides an exploratory analysis of a substantial dataset and presents the results of statistical tests. These analyses have enabled us to identify player profiles, meaning a list of actions frequently executed in similar situations. This information serves as a foundation for developing strategies and refining players' gameplay.

2   Background and Related Work

In this section, we introduce the concept of a rally, describe and illustrate the phases of the service return in table tennis (Fig. 1), and survey prior work on quantitative analyses and return strategies in racket sports.

Definition 1 (Stroke). *A stroke S occurs when a player strikes the ball validly over the net to the opponent.*

Definition 2 (Return). *A return S_1 is the stroke made by the receiver in response to the serve (S_0), in which the player strikes the ball over the net into the server's court in a valid manner.*

Definition 3 (Rally). *A rally $R = S_0, S_1, \ldots, S_n$ is a finite sequence of valid strokes per Definition 1, where S_0 is the serve and S_1 the service return. The rally concludes with S_n, after which a new rally begins.*

Definition 4 (Anticipation and reaction phase). *The anticipation and reaction phase begins slightly before the server's strike (S_0), when the receiver uses pre-impact kinematic cues to predict the ball's trajectory, and lasts until immediately after the ball's first bounce. During this interval the receiver not only formulates an early prediction of the trajectory but also adjusts their movements in response to updated sensory information [16].*

Definition 5 (Adjustment phase). *The adjustment phase covers the interval between the first and second bounces, when the receiver refines posture and footwork to optimize positioning for the return.*

Definition 6 (Decision and execution phase). *The decision and execution phase is the period from the second bounce of S_0 to the moment of contact with the ball for S_1, during which stroke selection and racket alignment are finalized.*

Serves vary along four main dimensions—length, speed, spin and side—each of which constrains the receiver's options (Table 1). Different return strokes reflect strategic intentions:

- **Push**: A defensive stroke executed by slicing under the ball resulting in a backspin. Used on backspin serves when the player cannot attack.
- **Flip**: An offensive stroke on a short ball. Applying speed and topspin.
- **Topspin**: An offensive stroke on long ball with a lot of speed and spin.

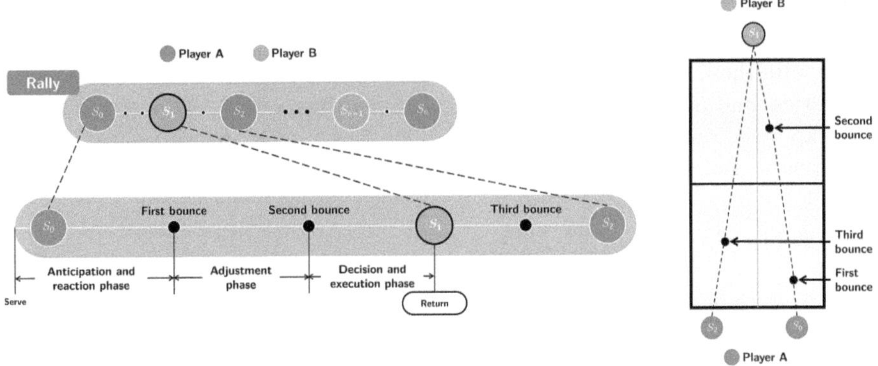

Fig. 1. Phases of the service return (left) and spatial layout of serve S_0 and return S_1 (right). Note that in this study we focus specifically on the return S_1. The anticipation and reaction phase extends from just before the serve S_0 until the ball's first bounce. The adjustment phase takes place between the first and second bounces. Finally, the decision and execution phase occurs between the second bounce and contact with the ball S_1.

Table 1. Serve types and their influence on the return.

Serve Characteristic	Effect on Return
Short	Restricts attacking strokes; favors controlled pushes
Long	Enables offensive topspin returns
Spin (any)	Alters ball trajectory and increases difficulty of return
Side	Limits the player's forehand/backhand options.

Quantitative analysis in racket sports has evolved from foundational biomechanical studies to sophisticated tactical and sequence-aware modeling. Early research emphasized biomechanics, examining the physical determinants of stroke performance—for instance, trunk and wrist coordination in table tennis [18]. Subsequent work introduced spatial occupation models to assess court coverage and tactical intent [4,20]. With the availability of richer datasets, dataâĂŘ-driven methods became central to performance analysis: clustering techniques such as k-means were explored for pattern discovery [12], subgroup discovery methods enabled the extraction of conditional tactical rules [3], and new metrics for shot dominance and diversity were introduced to quantify serving strategies [2]. Recent advances focus on sequenceâĂŘaware models that capture shot dependencies and tactical transitions using visual analytics tools for multi-shot sequences [15,19]. These approaches align with broader insights emphasizing anticipation and adaptation as key components of competitive play [8,9].

In table tennis, service return analysis has gained attention due to its strategic complexity: elite players exhibit greater variability and adaptability in returns [13], and a clustering-based taxonomy of serves has been proposed [6]. However, many studies still model returns in isolation, neglecting the dynamic interplay between strokes [5].

Despite these advancements, few works integrate rebound position, spin characteristics, and adaptive behavior into a unified framework. This study bridges that gap by combining clustering, tactical metrics, and sequence-aware modeling to deliver a comprehensive analysis of table tennis service returns.

3   Methods

We introduce several methods to enrich the dataset by generating clusters of return behaviors with k-means and defining two key metrics—domination, which captures transient momentum shifts via a time-decayed aggregation of past point outcomes, and pressure, which quantifies each point's contextual importance by combining factors such as score gap and match-critical situations. Using the same dataset as [5], which comprises 1,195 returns from 15 unique players, we first apply k-means clustering to categorize return patterns into distinct behavioral groups. We then define the domination and pressure metrics (presented in Sects. 3.3 and 3.4 respectively) and finally apply the χ^2 test to assess the dependence between return clusters and these metrics. These steps underpin our exploratory analysis and the subsequent interpretation of how players adapt their returns to evolving match dynamics.

3.1   Clustering via K-Means

We objectively compare players' spatial return placement strategies by first segmenting rebound impact locations into distinct zones. For this purpose, we apply the k-means algorithm to the two-dimensional coordinates of return rebounds to identify spatial return zones [10,11]. To determine the optimal value of k, we applied the elbow method to the combined match data for each studied player (**A. Lebrun, F. Lebrun**, and **F. Zhendong**), using the same value of k for all matches, which identifies the point where intra-cluster inertia stops decreasing significantly as the number of clusters increases. This analysis led us to select $k = 4$ as the optimal value for each player, which will be maintained throughout the study (see Fig. 9 in Appendix for **A. Lebrun**'s case as an example). Clustering is repeated over 200 random initializations as explained in Sect. 3.5.

The visualization of these clusters provides insights into emerging trends for each player and allows us to observe differences in playing styles. An example of such a comparison is shown in Fig. 2. In these figures, the server is always positioned at the bottom of the table, while the receiver is at the top. Consequently, the second bounces of the serves are represented in the upper half of the table, and the bounce of the service return in the lower half.

3.2   Chi-Square Test of Independence

As part of this study, we aim to observe and analyze the service returns of table tennis players. To do so, it is essential to test whether return placement

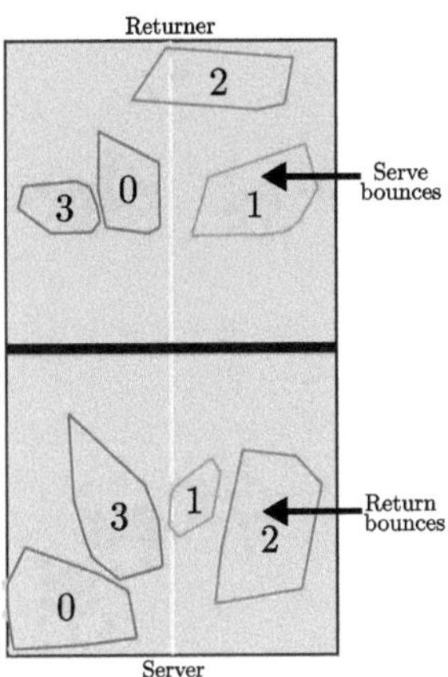

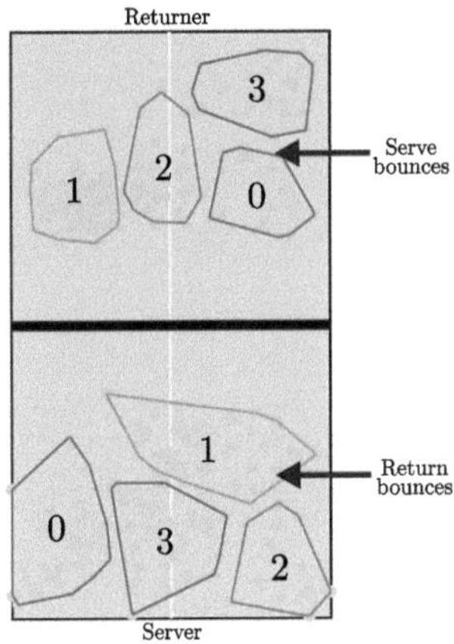

(a) All service returns from matches of **F. Lebrun**. Returns by **F. Lebrun** at the bottom, serves received by **F. Lebrun** at the top.

(b) All service returns from matches of **F. Zhendong**. Returns by **F. Zhendong** at the bottom, serves received by **F. Zhendong**at the top.

Fig. 2. Comparison of all returns by **F. Lebrun** on the left and **F. Zhendong** on the right. It can be observed that **F. Lebrun** is less likely to play short compared to **F. Zhendong** and tends to avoid playing long balls to the opponent's forehand.

depends on various factors. In line with previous work on k-means clusters and χ^2 testing [14,17].

The χ^2 test is a statistical method used to determine whether two variables are dependent or not. It measures whether the observed frequencies (derived from the data) differ significantly from the expected frequencies (those that would be observed if there were no relationship between the variables).

The threshold α was set at 0.1, which is higher than the conventional value commonly used in the literature (typically 0.05). This choice is motivated by the fact that strong or clear-cut trends are rare in human behavior, and our goal is to detect even subtle patterns of effect or dependency.

3.3   Domination

A domination indicator at the scale of a set or match—taking into account tactical, physical, and psychological dimensions over an entire rally or set—has been proposed [2]. In contrast, we define a local indicator D_t depending solely on the sequence of previous point outcomes, focusing on the immediate point-by-point dynamics. This metric quantifies momentum shifts during a match, offering insight into player behavior on returns. Indeed, table tennis matches feature key moments where one player dominates—imposing rhythm, scoring consecutively, and pressuring the opponent. Capturing these phases with a performance indicator would help analyze return behavior in relation to momentum shifts.

We define a local domination indicator D_t to capture transient control during a match. For a match between player A and player B at time t:

$$D_t = \sigma\left(\sum_{i=1}^{t-1} \beta_{t-i} V_{t-i}\right), \quad \beta_j = \frac{5 \cdot j^p}{\sum_{i=0}^{t-1} i^p}, \quad \sigma(x) = \frac{1}{1 + e^{-x}},$$

where $V_j = +1$ if A won point j (else -1), and weights β_j decrease with time to emphasize recent points. We categorize $D_t > 0.6$ as A dominating, $D_t < 0.4$ as B dominating, else neutral. A significant χ^2 test on the contingency of "dominant player" vs. return cluster indicates if players adapt returns to domination phases.

3.4 Pressure

During a table tennis match, certain points carry particular significance. For example, a set point is far more critical to defend than a simple point played when the score is 5–3 and one player is already leading by 2 sets to 0.

To capture such nuances, we model point-by-point pressure by combining sub-indicators:

$$\text{pressure}_{\text{score}} = \frac{1}{1 + \text{score\_gap}},$$

$$\text{pressure}_{\text{set\_end}} = \frac{1}{1 + |10 - \min(10, \max(s_A, s_B))|},$$

$$\text{pressure}_{\text{key\_moments}} = \begin{cases} 1, & \text{if set/match point with gap} < 2 \\ 0, & \text{otherwise} \end{cases},$$

$$\text{pressure}_{\text{set}} = \frac{1}{1 + \text{set\_gap}},$$

$$\text{pressure}_{\text{decisive\_set}} = \begin{cases} 1, & \text{in decisive set} \\ 0, & \text{otherwise} \end{cases},$$

with s_A and s_B representing the scores of players A and B, respectively. These combine as

$$\text{pressure}_{\text{total}} = \sum_{i=1}^{5} \alpha_i \cdot \text{sub\_indicator}_i,$$

with $(\alpha_1, \alpha_2, \alpha_3, \alpha_4, \alpha_5) = (2.25, 2.25, 2.25, 0.75, 2.50)$. We then test independence between pressure-level bins and return clusters via χ^2.

3.5 Initialization Robustness

To ensure that our k-means results are not sensitive to centroid seeds, we repeat the clustering procedure over 200 independent random initializations.

The choice of 200 initializations was established after analyzing the convergence of characteristic metrics (mean, variance, and confidence interval bounds at 95%) as a function of the number of iterations. We observed that beyond 200 initializations, these metrics showed negligible variation, ensuring the stability and reliability of the obtained results.

4   Exploratory Analysis

Figure 3 provides a visual summary of the data, with players sorted based on the percentage of topspin returns. It shows the proportion of different return shot types—topspin (red), flip (blue), push slice (green), and block (orange)—used by each player. While this visualization provides an overview of shot preferences, interpreting it requires caution due to several contextual factors.

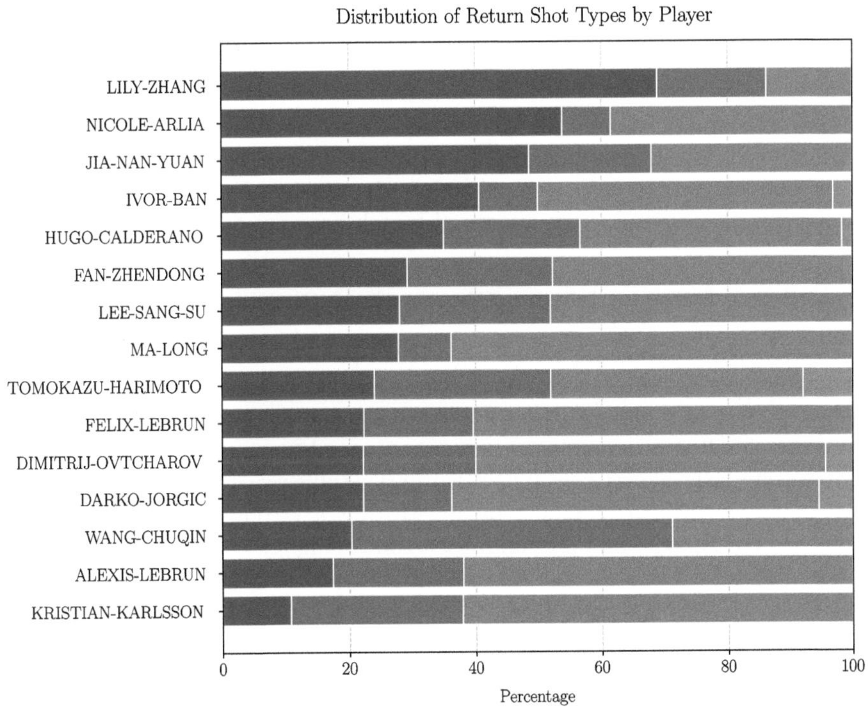

Fig. 3. Distribution of return types by player. **Lily Zhang** executes the most topspin shots, while **Kristian Karlsson** executes the fewest. Meanwhile, **Wang Chuqin** performs the most flip shots.

For instance, **Wang Chuqin** uses a high proportion of flips compared to other players. However, this statistic alone does not indicate effectiveness, as many of these flips may have occurred in unfavorable conditions forced by the opponent's serves. Specifically, certain types of serves can compel a player to flip under pressure or from a less advantageous position, reducing the success rate of these returns. Thus, integrating win/loss statistics on points following each shot type would be critical to evaluate the true tactical value of these shots.

Players with a higher proportion of blocks might be reacting to long serves that surprise them, limiting their options to a defensive block. Understanding whether these blocks are predominantly responses to long serves could provide insights into the effectiveness of serving strategies targeting specific return zones. Distinguishing between long and short pushes would enhance this analysis, as each imposes different tactical constraints and demands different return techniques.

Overall, the figure reveals shot-type tendencies but requires complementary data—such as the location and spin of serves and the outcome of the points—to fully interpret how these return types relate to the players' strategic responses and match dynamics.

5 Results

We now report our main findings through four complementary analyses: the dependence between serve placement and return zones; the relationship between return clusters and point outcomes; the adaptation of return choices during domination phases; and the influence of match pressure on return behavior.

Dependence between Return Clusters and Received Service Clusters

We constructed contingency tables of received-serve cluster versus return-cluster assignments for three players (**A. Lebrun, F. Lebrun, F. Zhendong**) and applied χ^2 test of independence with $\alpha = 0.10$. For **A. Lebrun**, $p = 0.176$ indicating no significant dependence between serve placement and return zone. **F. Lebrun** similarly shows $p = 0.61$, also non-significant. In contrast, **F. Zhendong**'s test returns $p < 0.001$, demonstrating a strong strategic association between serve clusters and chosen return zones (Fig. 4).

The figure illustrates the spatial distribution of return positions (right) depending on the combination of serve and return clusters, summarized in the contingency table (left). On the court diagram, colored regions represent the different return clusters, each marked by a number (0–3). These clusters are distinct from the serve clusters, which are also labeled 0–3, indicating that return positioning is influenced by serve patterns but follows its own clustering logic.

It is important to note that the numbering of serve clusters (rows) and return clusters (columns) are independent—cluster 1 for serves is not the same as cluster 1 for returns. The table shows the number of points observed for each combination of serve and return clusters. A particularly notable pattern appears for Serve cluster 1 and Return cluster 1: this combination accounts for 33 points—by far the highest frequency in the matrix. This indicates a strong relationship: when the serve falls into cluster 1, which is a short serve in the forehand of **F. Zhendong**, the returner tends to respond from within return cluster 1, which is a short return which is a cross-court return. This spatial and tactical alignment suggests a predictable return behavior influenced by the serve's characteristics.

Dependence between Point Winners and Return Clusters

To determine which return zones favor point wins, we analyze contingency tables of winners versus return clusters. **A. Lebrun**'s test yields $p = 0.078$, indicating dependence: his most effective zone is cluster 3 (23 vs. 19 wins), whereas cluster 2 under-performs (16 vs. 20) (Fig. 5). **F. Lebrun**'s $p = 0.645$ shows no significant association, reflecting uniform effectiveness across clusters. **F. Zhendong**'s $p = 0.044$ confirms a significant relationship: clusters 2 (8 vs. 4) and 0 (21 vs. 15) are most successful, while cluster 1 yields fewer wins (18 vs. 23) (Fig. 6).

Dependence between Domination and Return Clusters

This analysis tests whether a player's domination phase (self, opponent, or neither) affects the choice of return cluster. We construct contingency tables of domination status versus return clusters.

For **A. Lebrun**, $p = 0.858$ indicates no significant dependence, suggesting his return zones remain stable across domination phases. **F. Lebrun** shows $p = 0.013$, revealing a significant association: he favors cluster 1 when dominating (16 occurrences) and cluster 2 when dominated (22) (Fig. 7). **F. Zhendong**'s $p = 0.285$ likewise indicates no dependence, implying his return choices are unaffected by who is dominating.

These findings demonstrate that only **F. Lebrun** adapts his return zones according to domination dynamics, whereas **A. Lebrun** and **F. Zhendong** maintain consistent placement regardless of match control. Notably, when **F. Lebrun** is under pressure, he tends to select cluster 2, which corresponds to a short zone on the opponent's forehand side (assuming a right-handed opponent), likely to avoid a backhand flip—typically more effective and easier to execute than a forehand flip.

Dependence between the Pressure and the Return Clusters

We examine whether the level of pressure influences return–cluster choices by constructing contingency tables and applying Pearson's chi-square test at $\alpha = 0.10$. For **A. Lebrun**, $p = 0.92$ indicates no significant dependence, suggesting his return selections remain consistent across pressure levels. In contrast, **F. Lebrun**'s $p = 0.039$ reveals a significant association: he favors cluster 1 under low or medium pressure (12 and 20 occurrences, respectively) and reduces risk under high pressure by choosing shorter returns in clusters 0 and 2 (Fig. 8). Finally, **F. Zhendong** yields $p = 0.12$, showing no statistical dependence, although he tends toward long-body returns when pressure peaks. Only **F. Lebrun** demonstrates a pressure-driven adaptation in return zones.

Summary of Independence Results

Table 2 summarizes the statistical independence results presented in the previous sections.

Table 2. Independence test results (p-values and interpretation) for each player and for each test

Player	Service ↔ Return	Winner ↔ Return	Dominance ↔ Return	Pressure ↔ Return
F. Lebrun	$p = 0.61$ Independence	$p = 0.645$ Independence	$p = 0.013$ **Dependence**	$p = 0.039$ **Dependence**
A. Lebrun	$p = 0.176$ Independence	$p = 0.078$ **Dependence**	$p = 0.858$ Independence	$p = 0.92$ Independence
F. Zhendong	$p < 0.001$ **Dependence**	$p = 0.044$ **Dependence**	$p = 0.285$ Independence	$p = 0.12$ Independence

Activity-Centered Interpretation

Beyond the statistical relationships uncovered through χ^2 tests, we propose a complementary reading based on the activity-centered approach, commonly used in sports science to interpret athlete behavior in terms of motor adaptation, strategic learning, and individual predispositions.

For example, **F. Zhendong**'s strong dependence between serve and return clusters may reflect a form of expertise developed through targeted and repeated training of fixed serve–return sequences. Such consistency suggests a highly internalized tactical schema reinforced through structured practice. This aligns with the common perception of Chinese players as highly regular and efficient, favoring reliable and optimized routines over variability.

In contrast, **A. Lebrun** and **F. Lebrun** exhibit no significant dependence at the match level ($p = 0.176$ and 0.61, respectively), which could indicate a more flexible or unpredictable return strategy. This is consistent with their reputation for creative play—often deliberately avoiding repetition and seeking to vary their responses point after point. Rather than reflecting a lack of structure, this variability appears to be a deliberate tactical approach, integral to their playing identity.

When considering contextual dynamics, **F. Lebrun** shows significant variation in his return choices depending on whether he is dominating or under pressure. This suggests an adaptive behavior that may stem from a natural tactical sensitivity—often described as "game sense" or an instinctive feel for the game. Interestingly, this context-dependent adaptation contrasts with his otherwise variable style, suggesting that **F. Lebrun** modulates his creativity in response to match situations.

By contrast, **A. Lebrun** and **F. Zhendong** do not significantly modify their return zones under pressure or domination, which may reflect a more stable tactical model—potentially the result of deliberate training routines aimed at ensuring consistency regardless of context. In that sense, **F. Lebrun** appears to rely more heavily on in-the-moment adjustments, dynamically adapting his behavior to the flow of the match, which may reflect a different kind of expertise— less standardized, and more emergent.

From an activity-based viewpoint, the observed return behaviors can be interpreted as the result of two complementary forces: structured training protocols (consistent, rehearsed responses) and innate or cultivated abilities (creative, intuitive adjustments). These findings highlight not only individual differences but also stylistic choices that are deeply embedded in each player's tactical philosophy.

6   Conclusion

We contributed to novel insights on service returns in table tennis, by employing statistical methods and clustering techniques such as k-means. The findings reveal that the relationship between the type of serve and subsequent return varies notably across players. For instance, while **F. Zhendong** exhibits a clear and predictable correlation between service clusters and his return behavior— indicative of a highly calculated approach—**A. Lebrun** and **F. Lebrun** display more diverse or context-dependent return patterns. Moreover, the investigation into the influence of match pressure and domination phases further underscores how situational dynamics can shape the tactical responses. Our code and data are publicly released[1] for transparency and reproducibility purposes.

These results not only enhance our understanding of the underlying strategies but also pave the way for developing predictive models aimed at optimizing players' performance. Future research could build upon these findings by incorporating additional variables and exploring inter-individual differences in greater depth.

---

[1] https://github.com/centralelyon/table-tennis-returns.

Appendix

Serve \ Return	0	1	2	3
0	14	2	0	2
1	8	33	10	19
2	6	5	0	2
3	8	1	2	3

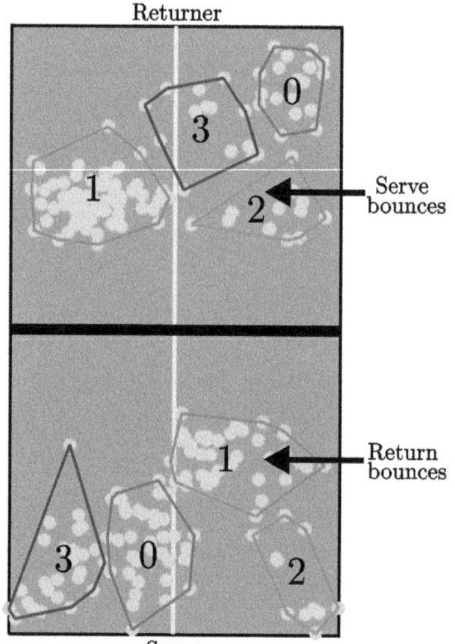

Fig. 4. On the left, the contingency table shows the relationship between serve and return clusters for **F. Zhendong**. On the right, all his service returns are displayed, with returns positioned at the bottom and received serves at the top.

Winner \ Return	0	1	2	3
A. Lebrun	18	28	16	23
Opponent	18	30	20	19

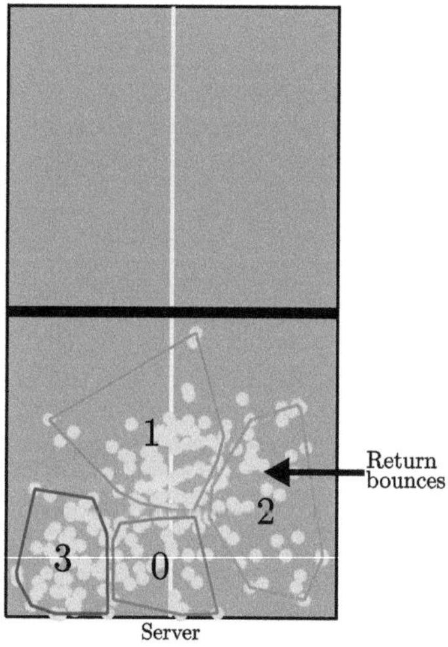

Fig. 5. On the left, contingency table representing the data used to study the dependence between return clusters and point winners for **A. Lebrun** on return. On the right, all service returns from matches of **A. Lebrun**.

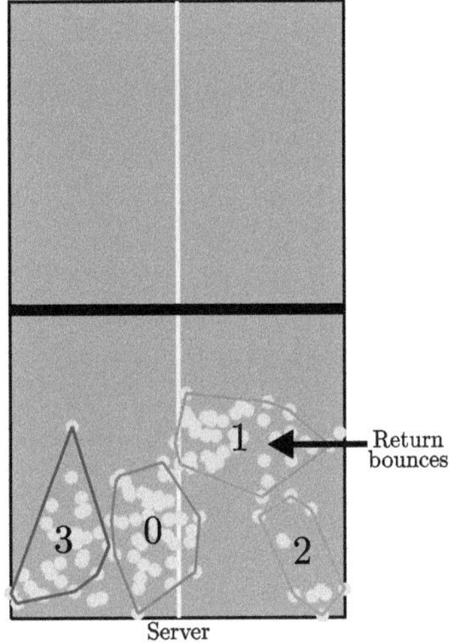

Winner \ Return	0	1	2	3
F. Zhendong	21	18	8	15
Opponent	15	23	4	11

Fig. 6. On the left, contingency table representing the data used to study the dependence between return clusters and point winners for **F. Zhendong** on return. On the right, all service returns from matches of **F. Zhendong**.

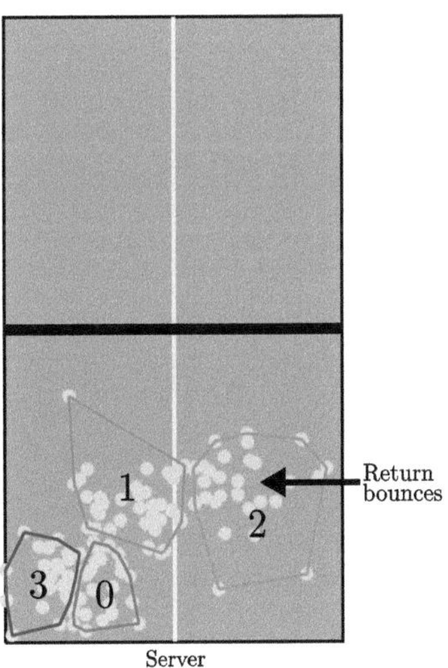

Dominant \ Return	0	1	2	3
F. Lebrun	9	16	6	7
Opponent	11	17	22	7
Nobody	5	6	4	11

Fig. 7. On the left, contingency table representing the data used to study the dependence between return clusters and the player in a phase of domination for **F. Lebrun** on return. On the right, all service returns from matches of **F. Lebrun**.

Pressure \ Return	0	1	2	3
Low	7	12	5	12
Medium	9	20	4	2
Fairly High	11	9	4	2
High	6	5	1	5

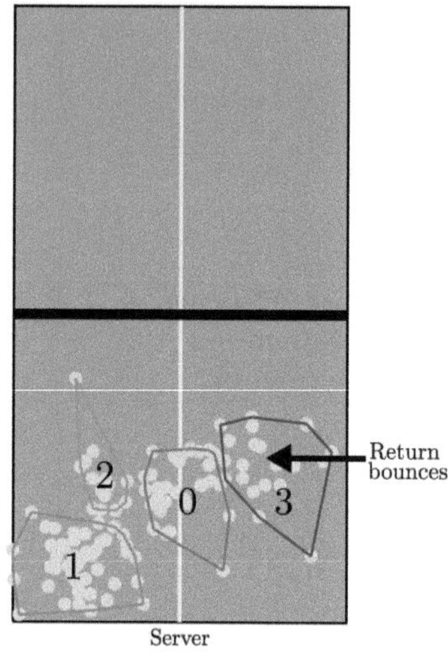

Fig. 8. On the left, contingency table representing the data used to study the dependence between return clusters and pressure for **F. Lebrun** on return. On the right, all service returns from matches of **F. Lebrun**.

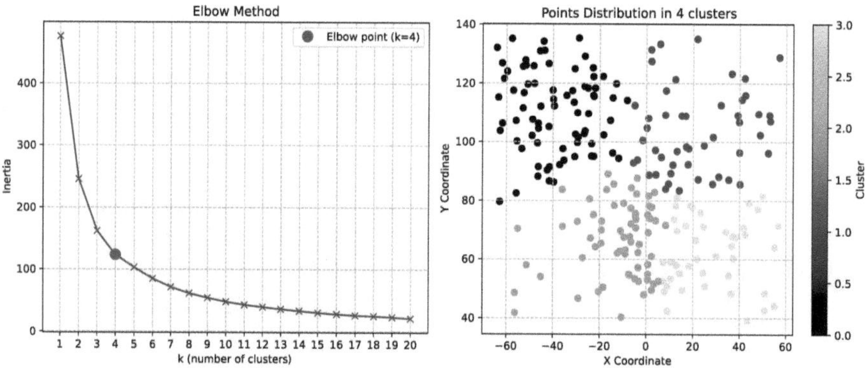

Fig. 9. Analysis of **A. Lebrun**'s service returns clustering using the elbow method. Left: Evolution of inertia as a function of the number of clusters (k), showing the elbow point that suggests the optimal number of clusters. Right: Spatial distribution of service return points colored by their assigned cluster, after outlier removal and coordinate normalization. Each cluster represents a distinct pattern in **A. Lebrun**'s return strategy.

References

1. Calandre, J., Péteri, R., Mascarilla, L., Tremblais, B.: Extraction et analyse de trajectoires de balle de tennis de table à partir d'une seule caméra pour l'aide à la performance sportive. In: Reconnaissance des Formes, Image, Apprentissage et Perception (RFIAP), Vannes, France (2020). https://hal.science/hal-02975085
2. Calmet, G., Eradès, A., Vuillemot, R.: Exploring table tennis analytics: domination, expected score and shot diversity. In: Brefeld, U., Davis, J., Van Haaren, J., Zimmermann, A. (eds.) Machine Learning and Data Mining for Sports Analytics. MLSA 2023. Communications in Computer and Information Science, vol 2035. Springer, Cham (2024). https://doi.org/10.1007/978-3-031-53833-9_14
3. Duluard, P., Li, X., Plantevit, M., Robardet, C., Vuillemot, R.: Discovering and Visualizing Tactics in a Table Tennis Game Based on Subgroup Discovery. In: Brefeld, U., Davis, J., Van Haaren, J., Zimmermann, A. (eds.) Machine Learning and Data Mining for Sports Analytics, vol. 1783, pp. 101–112. Springer Nature Switzerland, Cham (2023). https://doi.org/10.1007/978-3-031-27527-2_8, https://link.springer.com/10.1007/978-3-031-27527-2_8
4. Erades, A., Peuch, L., Vuillemot, R.: Investigating control areas in table tennis. In: Schulz, H.J., Villanova, A., (eds.) Sixteenth International EuroVis Workshop on Visual Analytics (EuroVA). The Eurographics Association (2025). https://hal.science/hal-05032405, https://doi.org/10.2312/eurova.20251104, ISSN = 2664-4487, ISBN = 978-3-03868-283-7
5. Erades, A., Vuillemot, R.: Player-Centric Shot Maps in Table Tennis. Computer graphics Forum (Proc. Eurovis) **44**, e70109, p. 10 (2025). https://hal.science/hal-04997867, https://doi.org/10.1111/cgf.70109
6. Eradès, A., Papon, T., Vuillemot, R.: Characterizing Serves in Table Tennis (2024). https://doi.org/10.1007/978-3-031-86692-0_1
7. Hodges, L.: Table Tennis Tactics for Thinkers. CreateSpace Independent Publishing Platform (2013). https://archive.org/details/isbn_9781477643785
8. Krizkova, S., Tomaskova, H., Tirkolaee, E.B.: Sport performance analysis with a focus on racket sports: A review. Appl. Sci. **11**(19), 9212 (2021). https://doi.org/10.3390/app11199212, https://www.mdpi.com/2076-3417/11/19/9212
9. Lees, A.: The evolution of racket sport science - a personal reflection. Ger. J. Exerc. Sport Res. **49**(3), 213–220 (2024). https://doi.org/10.1007/s12662-019-00604-2, https://doi.org/10.1007/s12662-019-00604-2
10. Lloyd, S.: Least squares quantization in PCM. IEEE Trans. Inf. Theory **28**(2), 129–137 (1982). https://doi.org/10.1109/TIT.1982.1056489, https://hal.science/hal-04614938
11. Lloyd, S.P.: Least squares quantization in pcm. Technical note, Bell Telephone Laboratories, Murray Hill, NJ (1982)
12. Mohiuddin, A., Raihan, S., Syed, M.: The k-means Algorithm: A Comprehensive Survey and Performance Evaluation. Electronics **9**(8), 1295 (2020). https://www.mdpi.com/2079-9292/9/8/1295, https://doi.org/10.3390/electronics9081295
13. Nikolakakis, A., Telopoulos, P., Malagoli Lanzoni, I., Mavridis, G.: Comparison of the Service and Reception Between Winning and Defeated High-Level Table Tennis Athletes. J. Hum. Sport Exerc. **18**(3), 670–678 (2023). https://hdl.handle.net/11585/966729, https://doi.org/10.14198/jhse.2023.183.13
14. Sànchez-Alcaraz, B.J., Muñoz, D., Pradas, F., Ramón-Llin, J., Cañas, J., Sánchez-Pay, A.: Analysis of serve and serve-return strategies in elite male and female padel. Appl. Sci. **10**(19) (2020). https://doi.org/10.3390/app10196693, https://www.mdpi.com/2076-3417/10/19/6693

15. Wang, J., Wu, J., Cao, A., Zhou, Z., Zhang, H., Wu, Y.: Tac-Miner: Visual Tactic Mining for Multiple Table Tennis Matches. IEEE Trans. Visual Comput. Graphics **27**(6), 2770–2782 (2021). https://doi.org/10.1109/TVCG.2021.3074576, https://ieeexplore.ieee.org/document/9411869/
16. Wang, J., et al.: Tac-Anticipator: visual analytics of anticipation behaviors in table tennis matches. Comput. Graphics Forum **42**(3), 223–234 (2023). https://doi.org/10.1111/cgf.14825, https://onlinelibrary.wiley.com/doi/abs/10.1111/cgf.14825, _eprint: https://onlinelibrary.wiley.com/doi/pdf/10.1111/cgf.14825
17. Whiteside, D., Reid, M.: Spatial characteristics of professional tennis serves with implications for serving aces: A machine learning approach. J. Sports Sci. **35**, 1–7 (2016). https://doi.org/10.1080/02640414.2016.1183805
18. Wong, D.W.C., Lee, W.C.C., Lam, W.K.: Biomechanics of table tennis: a systematic scoping review of playing levels and maneuvers. Appl. Sci. **10**(15), 5203 (2020)
19. Wu, Y., et al.: iTTVis: interactive visualization of table tennis data. IEEE Trans. Visual Comput. Graphics **24**(1), 709–718 (2018). https://doi.org/10.1109/TVCG.2017.2744218, http://ieeexplore.ieee.org/document/8017600/
20. Ye, S., Chen, Z., Chu, X., Wang, Y., Fu, S., Shen, L., Zhou, K., Wu, Y.: ShuttleSpace: exploring and analyzing movement trajectory in immersive visualization. IEEE Trans. Visual Comput. Graphics **27**(2), 860–869 (2021). https://doi.org/10.1109/TVCG.2020.3030392, https://ieeexplore.ieee.org/document/9222313/

Racing Beyond the Gate: Predicting Speedway Results with Expected Points (xP)

Piotr Kaczorek$^{(\boxtimes)}$, Jędrzej Słupski , Franciszek Kornobis , Michał Zaręba , Tomasz Górecki , and Tomasz Piłka

Faculty of Mathematics and Computer Science, Adam Mickiewicz University, Poznań, Poland
{piokac4,jedslu,frakor}@st.amu.edu.pl,
{michal.zareba,tomasz.gorecki,tomasz.pilka}@amu.edu.pl

Abstract. This study presents a novel predictive framework for individual rider outcomes in the Polish speedway PGE Ekstraliga. Using 2018–2024 data, we introduce the Expected Points (xP) metric and apply feature engineering, including Elo ratings, gate- and track-specific indicators, and rivalry stats. An XGBoost model, optimized with hyperparameter tuning, achieves over 50% accuracy across four classes. Feature importance analysis shows the critical role of long-term rider attributes, dynamic ratings, and contextual variables such as riders' gate preferences. The validated xP sets a benchmark for speedway analytics and enables practical applications in tactical planning, rider evaluation, and talent identification. Future work should explore the integration of telemetry and cross-league data for improved predictions.

Keywords: Speedway racing · Predictive modeling · Machine learning · Classification Methods · Sports analytics

1 Introduction

Speedway racing is among Poland's most popular sports, with the PGE Ekstraliga considered the world's top speedway league [16]. However, quantitative analysis of speedway performance remains limited compared to other sports.

Speedway presents unique analytical challenges due to the complex interplay of rider skill, bike setup, track conditions, and psychology. Accurate rider performance prediction could provide significant competitive advantages in team selection and tactics, and enhance the fan experience.

In Polish speedway, the primary competition format is the league match, consisting of 15 heats each. Every heat features four riders, who start simultaneously from four gates in a stationary position on 500cc motorcycles. Heat line-ups follow the official race schedule, although team managers may make tactical substitutions when their team is at least six points behind. Riders (see Fig. 1) then race four laps on a 300–400 m long oval track, reaching speeds up

H. Rios-Neto et al. (Eds.): MLSA 2025, CCIS 2833, pp. 19–31, 2026.
https://doi.org/10.1007/978-3-032-15165-0_2

to 140 km/h. Each heat lasts 55–70 s, depending on track length[1]. Points are awarded as follows: 3 to the winner, 2 for second place, 1 for third, and none for the last rider.

Fig. 1. Speedway riders in action during FIM Speedway Grand Prix round at National Stadium in Warsaw, Poland, 14th May 2022 (author: Wojciech Tarchalski)

In speedway, each heat features four riders competing for points, generating twelve permutations of rider pairs. Our model predicts the winner of each pair and extracts the win probabilities, which are later aggregated into the xP (expected points) metric for each rider in a heat. Inspired by football's xG (expected goals) [12], xP shares some similarities: it quantifies the likelihood of each scoring opportunity (in this case, a rider's heat score) and relates directly to match points. Crucially, unlike xG, calculated post-event [2], xP is calculated pre-race, offering strategic foresight.

This study makes three key contributions: a systematic analysis of factors affecting rider scoring in the PGE Ekstraliga, the development and comparison of predictive models, and the quantification of the importance of key variables in predicting race outcomes. To the best of our knowledge, this is the first comprehensive machine learning application for predicting individual heat results in speedway, providing a foundation for future research. The xP metric also has practical uses: enhancing TV broadcasts with pre-race expected points, supporting coaches in tactical decisions, and enabling objective post-match evaluation by comparing xP to actual scores.

2 Background and Literature Overview

While sports analytics have rapidly evolved, motorsports – particularly speedway – have lagged in advanced statistical applications. Recent work in motorsports

---

[1] https://www.youtube.com/watch?v=BcKkrC_E6F8 (accessed on July 26, 2025).

analytics, such as that by Van Kesteren and Bergkamp [17], which provided Bayesian insights into Formula 1 race outcomes, has established foundational methodologies for assessing driver and team effects. Heilmeier et al. [6] employed neural networks for strategic decision-making in motorsport, while Więckowski et al. [20] successfully predicted Formula 1 lap times using machine learning. Peng et al. [14] further extended these predictive approaches into broader racing contexts, proposing advanced rank position forecasting methods for car racing.

In team and individual sports such as tennis and basketball, sophisticated predictive models are already well-established. Kovalchik [8] introduced statistical methods for predicting tennis outcomes [17], and similarly, the hybrid neural network model known as MambaNet [7] demonstrated significant success in forecasting NBA playoff outcomes. These studies underscore the effectiveness of machine learning-based predictive modeling across various sports, highlighting the potential for analogous advancements in motorsports.

Speedway-specific literature has primarily focused on isolated elements rather than comprehensive predictive modeling. Martin et al. [11] identified the crucial impact of starting gate selection and initial positioning, while Markowski et al. [10] emphasized reaction times and rider experience as influential factors. Additionally, Williamson [18] addressed systematic gate position biases. However, these works did not explore predictive modeling for individual heat outcomes or incorporate dynamic skill ratings.

Our research addresses these gaps by introducing the Expected Points (xP) metric for speedway. By integrating the Elo rating system [5], updated dynamically after each heat, we establish a robust, skill-based metric superior to traditional point averages. This innovation significantly enhances prediction accuracy and provides tactical foresight. Unlike prior studies, our model utilizes comprehensive pairwise rivalry features, gate- and track-specific indicators, and systematically engineered rider attributes. This holistic and dynamic approach sets our research apart, creating a benchmark framework for predictive analytics in speedway racing and aligning speedway analytics with advancements seen in other sports domains. Moreover, our study introduces rigorous feature selection and validation procedures, systematically identifying the most predictive rider attributes and contextual variables through advanced model interpretability techniques such as SHAP values. This ensures a precise understanding of rider performance factors, a dimension that has often been overlooked or insufficiently explored in previous research. Thus, our approach not only enhances predictive accuracy but also delivers valuable strategic insights for teams, coaches, and stakeholders.

3   Methodology

3.1   Data Collection

Given speedway's limited global popularity, no public datasets exist for the sport. Therefore, a dedicated dataset was constructed using match data from the Polish PGE Ekstraliga[2] covering all matches from the 2018âĂŞ2024 seasons. Collected information includes:

---

[2] https://www.ekstraliga.pl/.

- Information about match (date, starting time, referee, track).
- Teams participating in a match with their line-ups.
- Single heat results (starting gates, substitutions, and rider points, representing also riders' positions).

3.2 Data Preprocessing

In each speedway heat (assuming no exclusions, falls, and engine failures), riders earn points by position: 3 (1st), 2 (2nd), 1 (3rd), and 0 (4th). A bonus point, not affecting match results but included in salaries, rewards riders finishing directly behind a teammate ahead of an opponent, designed to prevent intra-team rivalry [15]. The raw data underwent cleaning procedures detailed in Fig. 2 before dataset creation.

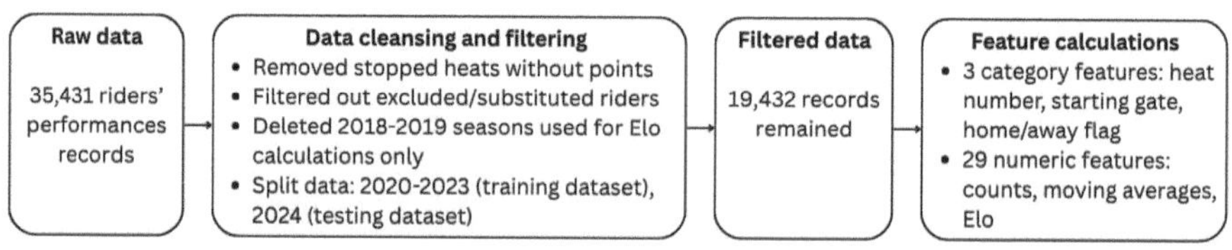

Fig. 2. The process of preparing the dataset

As shown in Fig. 3, the dataset contains data on the performances of 19,432 riders in 5,004 races and 336 competitions, as well as information on 158 riders recorded in the database.

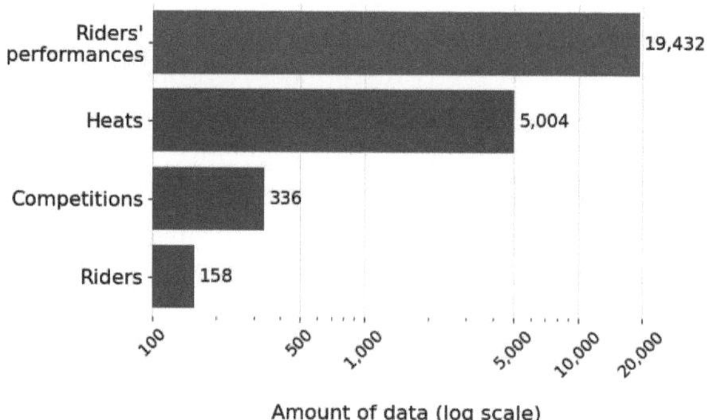

Fig. 3. Dataset summary

3.3 Performance Metrics

Mean Absolute Error (MAE) was used for error quantification due to its interpretability and direct proportionality to xP values [19]. Given balanced classes, standard accuracy sufficed for classification evaluation without error weighting.

Standard accuracy requires an exact match between predicted and actual points. However, due to the bonus point rule in speedway, some predictions may be considered accurate, even though they were initially counted as inaccurate. When a rider finishes directly behind a teammate and at least one opponent is behind them, a bonus point is awarded to the latter. This point does not affect the match result, only the rider's salary. The rule was introduced to limit intra-team rivalry and adds a tactical aspect to specific heats. In bonus point situations, the front rider often focuses on overtaking, while the latter adopts more defensive tactics to avoid being overtaken by rivals. Therefore, we introduced an Accuracy with bonuses metric: predictions are also considered correct if a bonus point is awarded. For n predictions, the formula for Accuracy with bonuses is:

$$\text{Accuracy}_B := \frac{\sum\limits_{i=0}^{3} (T_i + F_{i;B})}{n} \cdot 100\%,$$

where T_i is the number of correctly classified i-point gains, $F_{i;B}$ are the total cases of falsely predicted i-point gains, in a bonus point situation.

4 Approach Dilemma

4.1 Heat Approach

Speedway riders compete in four-rider heats, making heat context crucial for point prediction. To capture this, a quadruple merge was performed on the dataset. As a result, each row contains not only the target rider's features but also those of the three competitors in the heat, thereby contextualizing target rider data concerning all opponents. This methodology, referred to as the Heat Approach, provides comprehensive modeling of the competitive environment of the heat. During development, multiple algorithms were compared to select the top-performing model for the dataset, with XGBoost [3] achieving the best results (MAE = 0.786, Accuracy$_B$ = 47.04), as detailed in Table 1.

Table 1. Results of tested models

Model	MAE	Accuracy$_B$
Bayesian Ridge	0.792	46.87
LightGBM	0.787	45.78
Random Forest	0.806	44.88
SVM	0.791	46.77
XGBoost	**0.786**	**47.04**

4.2 Pair Approach

Speedway is a dangerous and unpredictable (engine failures, crashes, false starts) sport, what often leads to rider exclusions, preventing them from participating in re-runs and complicating predictions where excluded riders features influence predictions. The Pair Approach addresses this by decomposing heats into rider duels, with each record containing paired rider-opponent features and four new metrics, capturing the dynamics of the rivalry between each pair.

Mirroring the Heat Approach methodology, a double merge was applied to preserve competitive context while excluding inactive riders, appending the in-pair opponent's features to each row. This ensures each row contains complete rider-opponent data without exclusion artifacts.

Heat-level predictions aggregate duel results: predicted points equal duel wins, and xP sums duel win probabilities, as shown in Table 2.

Table 2. Conversion from duels results to heat results for one rider (R1)

Rider1	Rider2	Rider1 prob	Rider2 prob
R1	R2	0.696	0.304
R1	R3	0.425	0.575
R1	R4	0.881	0.119

$\Longrightarrow$

Rider	xP	Duels won
R1	2.002	2

Duels   **Heat**

5 Variables Considered in Pair Model

5.1 Feature Engineering

After switching to the Pair Approach, the newly-trained model underwent extensive feature engineering using Shapley Additive exPlanations (SHAP) [9] to identify significant predictors of rider performance. Features were retained if either the rider's or opponent's SHAP values exceeded an absolute threshold of 0.1. For features below this threshold, the difference between rider and opponent statistics was evaluated for predictive power. If so, the differential feature was retained and the individual rider/opponent components were removed (as an example shows in Fig. 4); otherwise, all were discarded.

This process resulted in 46 essential features capturing rider-opponent dynamics (36 of which were calculated for both the rider and his opponent, and the remaining 10 represented the differences between corresponding attributes of the rider and his opponent). The calculated and considered features are described in Table 3. Key findings:

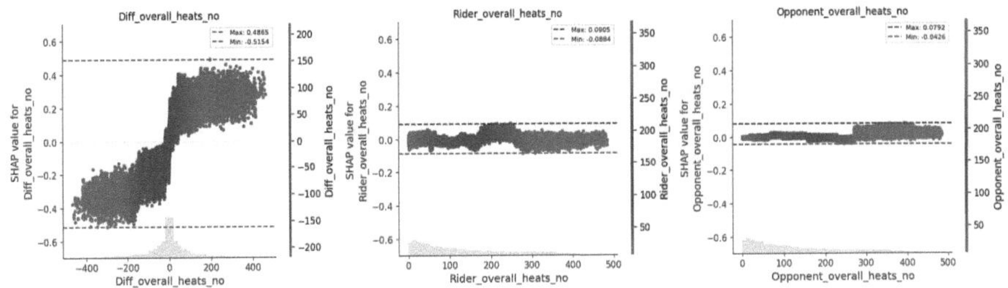

Fig. 4. Example of feature salvage: `Rider_overall_heats_no` and `Opponent_overall_heats_no` showed insufficient individual significance, but their difference demonstrated predictive power

- Match-specific averages (e.g., rider's points per match) showed low predictive value, while cumulative heat points within the game proved highly informative.
- Gate performance statistics gained significance when calculated over multi-season periods.
- Transient factors (previous heat results, team score sums, and differentials) had minimal impact.

Table 3. Overview of feature categories employed in the xP predictive model

Features category and quantity	Description
Categorical variables (4)	Indicators of the rider's starting gate assignment and whether the heat is contested on their home track. Those two features, calculated for both riders, capture positional and venue-related contextual factors.
Rider characteristics (14)	Quantitative measures of individual form and efficacy, including cumulative point totals, season-long and career averages, and short-term moving averages (last 3 and 5 matches), computed for both the focal rider and their opponent to enable relative class assessment.
Track-related statistics (16)	Performance metrics stratified by track and gate combinations, such as point averages and win ratios, together with the number of heats elapsed since the track's most recent grading, reflecting venue-specific proficiency.
Duel statistics (3)	Head-to-head encounter data encompassing the total number of pairwise duels, individual win counts for each rider, and the resultant winâĂŞloss balance, thus quantifying direct competitive history.
Difference-based features (9)	Derived variables representing the differential between rider and opponent across key statistics (e.g., average points, total points, track/gate performance), serving to model relative competitive advantage.

5.2   Elo Rating

To enhance the input feature set for our predictive models, it has become apparent that there is a need to include an additional variable that captures the skill level of riders, beyond their average point performance. For this purpose, the Elo rating system [4] was adopted.

Each heat is treated as a set of six independent pairwise match-ups (duels) between riders. Within-team duels are ignored. Therefore, each race results in four pairwise match-ups between riders from opposing teams. The probability that rider i beats rider j is calculated using the standard Elo formula:

$$E_{i,j} = \frac{1}{1 + 10^{\frac{R_j - R_i}{400}}},$$

where R_i and R_j represent the Elo ratings of riders i and j. The constant value 400 from the original Elo system was used, as it helps to maintain the interpretability of the rating differences. After each heat, the ratings are updated according to the following formula:

$$R_i' = R_i + K \cdot (S_{i,j} - E_{i,j}),$$

where R_i' is the updated rating of the rider i, K is the sensitivity factor, $S_{i,j}$ is the actual result (1 if i wins, 0 if j wins), and $E_{i,j}$ is the expected probability of i winning.

In practice, the ratings are not updated immediately after each heat. Instead, rating changes are accumulated in a temporary buffer during the competition and applied to each rider at the end of the event. This ensures all duels within a competition are evaluated using the same pre-competition ratings. The selection of the K factor and thresholds was based on empirical evaluation. Eight different Elo rating variants were generated, each based on a different combination of K values and heat thresholds. For each variant, a predictive model was trained and evaluated using the corresponding Elo ratings as input features. The lowest mean absolute error was obtained with K set to 40 for riders with fewer than 75 heats, 30 for riders with 75 to 150 heats, and 20 for riders with more than 150 heats, thereby reducing volatility and stabilizing the position of the experienced rider. This configuration was therefore adopted due to its superior predictive performance.

6   Results

The final XGBoost model, developed using the Pair Approach and trained on data from the 2020–2023 seasons, demonstrated strong predictive performance on the 2024 test set. Hyperparameter tuning was conducted with Optuna [1], and the parameter ranges considered during optimization with best values found are listed in Table 4. Results are presented in Table 5 and visualized in Fig. 5.

Table 4. XGBoost model hyperparameter search ranges with values found for best model

Hyperparameter	Range	Best values found
`learning_rate`	[0.001, 0.3]	0.289
`max_depth`	[3, 10]	5
`subsample`	[0.1, 1.0]	0.886
`colsample_by_tree`	[0.1, 1.0]	0.862
`min_child_weight`	[1, 20]	2

Table 5. Final results of XGBoost model with the Pair Approach

Model	MAE	Accuracy$_B$
XGBoost	**0.7387**	**50.112**

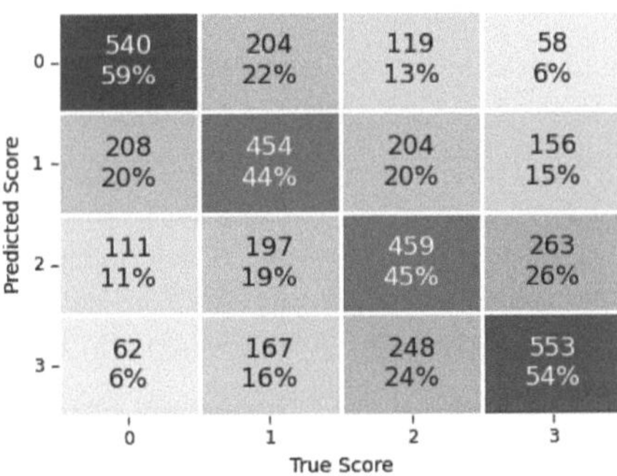

Fig. 5. Confusion Matrix of XGBoost model with the Pair Approach

The final model achieves the highest accuracy for classes corresponding to 0 and 3-point outcomes. This result aligns with expectations, as predicting intermediate positions —- 2nd and 3rd place —- proves more challenging. In many heats, the first and last positions are more distinct, and the competition for middle positions tends to be more balanced.

6.1   Feature Importance Analysis

XGBoost feature importance analysis was conducted using permutation importance calculation [13]. Although individual importance scores exhibit some stochastic variation, Elo ratings and rolling sums of points in the current match consistently emerged as the strongest predictors. Figure 6 shows these results.

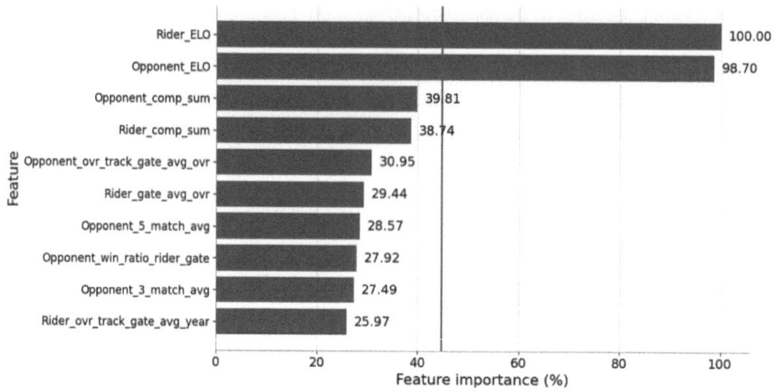

Fig. 6. The top 10 most important features (permutation importance). The red vertical line represents the mean feature importance for the top 10 features. (Color figure online)

These results confirm that the new Speedway Elo Rating is an excellent indicator of riders' performance level, as both `Rider_ELO` and `Opponent_ELO` exhibit the highest permutation importance, surpassing other features by a considerable margin. The high importance of the `*_comp_sum` features (cumulative points already scored in the current match) indicates that a rider's overall performance throughout the game, as reflected by total points accumulated so far, is a strong predictor of their expected performance in the upcoming heat.

7   Discussion

This study demonstrates that long-term historical features outperform short-term form indicators in predicting speedway rider performance. The Elo rating – computed over a fixed two-season window – emerged as the most significant predictor, despite not being used in practice, while the seasonal heat average ranked substantially lower. Moreover, feature differences, particularly the difference in seasonal averages between competitors, yielded stronger predictive signals than individual metrics.

The predictive model achieved very satisfactory overall accuracy but exhibited two systematic biases. First, debuting riders with limited historical data (e.g., 2024 entrants Cook and Jepsen Jensen) incurred higher MAE values (1.120 and 0.956 compared to the 0.7387 average). Second, prediction errors followed a U-shaped dependence on Elo rating, indicating greater volatility among mid-tier riders. Extreme scores (0 and 3 points) were forecasted more accurately than intermediate outcomes (Figs. 5 and 7).

8   Conclusions

The results indicate that XGBoost successfully captures the complex relationships underlying speedway performance. Despite the inherent randomness of the

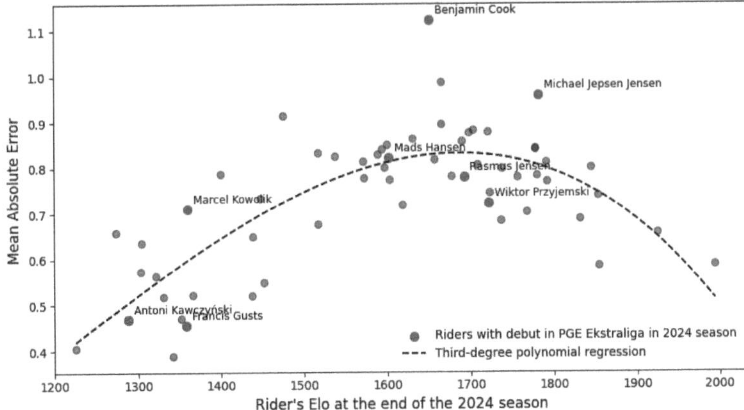

Fig. 7. Relationship between riders' Elo at the end of the 2024 season and prediction error (MAE). Each dot represents a rider with more than 20 appearances in the 2024 season. The dashed curve is a third-degree polynomial regression fitted to the data. Riders debuting in the 2024 season are shown in red and labelled.

data, the model achieved 50% accuracy with bonuses in a challenging four-class prediction task. Longitudinal rider profiles and contextual features, particularly those summarizing extended historical performance, proved to be the strongest determinants of predictive success.

To further improve model accuracy, future research should adapt the Elo framework to reflect speedway-specific dynamics (e.g., gate position and track characteristics) and disentangle individual contributions from team effects. Incorporating results from lower divisions could significantly improve initial skill estimates for newcomers, provided appropriate weighting schemes are developed. Finally, expanding the feature set to include telemetry data – such as reaction times, first-corner performance, acceleration, and racing lines – may further enhance predictive accuracy and support advanced decision-support tools for team managers.

References

1. Akiba, T., Sano, S., Yanase, T., Ohta, T., Koyama, M.: Optuna: a next-generation hyperparameter optimization framework. In: Proceedings of the 25th ACM SIGKDD International Conference on Knowledge Discovery & Data Mining, pp. 2623–2631. KDD '19, Association for Computing Machinery, New York, NY, USA (2019). https://doi.org/10.1145/3292500.3330701
2. Berrar, D., Lopes, P., Davis, J., Dubitzky, W.: Guest editorial: special issue on machine learning for soccer. Mach. Learn. **108**(1), 1–7 (2019). https://doi.org/10.1007/s10994-018-5763-8

3. Chen, T., Guestrin, C.: XGBoost: a scalable tree boosting system. In: Proceedings of the 22nd ACM SIGKDD International Conference on Knowledge Discovery and Data Mining, pp. 785–794 (2016). https://doi.org/10.1145/2939672.2939785

4. Elo, A.E.: The proposed USCF rating system, its development, theory, and applications. Chess life **22**(8), 242–247 (1967)

5. Elo, A.E.: The Rating of Chessplayers. Past and Present. Arco Publishing, New York (1978)

6. Heilmeier, A., Thomaser, A., Graf, M., Betz, J.: Virtual strategy engineer: using artificial neural networks for making race strategy decisions in circuit motorsport. Appl. Sci. **10**(21), 7805 (2020). https://doi.org/10.3390/app10217805

7. Khanmohammadi, R., Saba-Sadiya, S., Esfandiarpour, S., Alhanai, T., Ghassemi, M.M.: MambaNet: a hybrid neural network for predicting the NBA playoffs. SN Comput. Sci. **5**(5) (2024). https://doi.org/10.1007/s42979-024-02977-0

8. Kovalchik, S.A.: Searching for the goat of tennis win prediction. J. Quant. Anal. Sports **12**(3), 127–138 (2016). https://doi.org/10.1515/jqas-2015-0059

9. Lundberg, S.M., Lee, S.I.: A unified approach to interpreting model predictions. In: Proceedings of the 31st International Conference on Neural Information Processing Systems, pp. 4768–4777. NIPS'17, Curran Associates Inc., Red Hook, NY, USA (2017). arxiv preprint arxiv:1705.07874

10. Markowski, M., Szczepan, S., Zatoń, M., Martin, S., Michalik, K.: The importance of reaction time to the starting signal on race results in elite motorcycle speedway racing. PLoS ONE **18**(1), e0281138 (2023). https://doi.org/10.1371/journal.pone.0281138

11. Martin, S., Starbuck, C., Coyle, M.: The relationship between heart rate and positioning in speedway racers. J. Sports Sci. **32**(sup2), s47–s48 (2014). https://doi.org/10.1080/02640414.2014.968386

12. Mead, J., O'Hare, A., McMenemy, P.: Expected goals in football: improving model performance and demonstrating value. PLOS ONE **18**(4), 1–29 (2023). https://doi.org/10.1371/journal.pone.0282295

13. Molnar, C.: Interpretable Machine Learning. 3 edn. (2025). https://christophm.github.io/interpretable-ml-book. Accessed 14 June 2025

14. Peng, B., Li, J., Akkas, S., Araki, T., Yoshiyuki, O., Qiu, J.: Rank position forecasting in car racing. In: Proceedings of the IEEE International Parallel and Distributed Processing Symposium (IPDPS), pp. 724–733 (2021). https://doi.org/10.1109/IPDPS49936.2021.00082

15. Polish Automobile and Motorcycle Federation: Regulations (in Polish). https://pzm.pl/zuzel/regulaminy-i-druki. Accessed 14 June 2025

16. Speedway Media: About Poland's Infatuation With Speedway Racing. https://speedwaymedia.com/2024/04/29/about-polands-infatuation-with-speedway-racing/. Accessed 14 June 2025

17. Van Kesteren, E.J., Bergkamp, T.: Bayesian analysis of formula one race results: disentangling driver skill and constructor advantage. J. Quant. Anal. Sports **19**(4), 273–293 (2023). https://doi.org/10.1515/jqas-2022-0021

18. Williamson, C.A.: Reducing starting position bias in the Speedway Grand Prix. J. Sports Anal. **6**(2), 99–109 (2020). https://doi.org/10.3233/JSA-200453

19. Willmott, C.J., Matsuura, K.: Advantages of the mean absolute error (MAE) over the root mean square error (RMSE) in assessing average model performance. Climate Res. **30**(1), 79–82 (2005). https://doi.org/10.3354/cr030079
20. Więckowski, J., Paradowski, B., Kizielewicz, B., Shekhovtsov, A., Sałabun, W.: Decision support system based on MLP: formula one (F1) grand prix study case. In: Proceedings of the 30th Neural Information Processing International Conference (ICONIP), pp. 265–276 (2023). https://doi.org/10.1007/978-981-99-8079-6_21

Soccer

Contextual Evaluation of Individual Contributions from Pressing Situations in Football

Minho Lee[1,5], Geonhee Jo[2,5], Miru Hong[2,5], Pascal Bauer[3,4], and Sang-Ki Ko[2,5(✉)]

[1] Institute for Sports and Preventive Medicine, Saarland University, Saarbrücken, Germany
minho.lee@uni-saarland.de
[2] Department of Artificial Intelligence, University of Seoul, Seoul, South Korea
{geonhee,miru,sangkiko}@uos.ac.kr
[3] Chair for Sports Analytics, Saarland University, Saarbrücken, Germany
pascal.bauer@uni-saarland.de
[4] Deutscher Fussball-Bund (DFB), Frankfurt am Main, Germany
[5] Korea AI Research Society for Sports, Seoul, South Korea

Abstract. Pressing is a key tactic in football for disrupting opponents' strategies and creating advantageous opportunities. However, existing studies often rely on static, rule-based definitions, overlooking the dynamic evolution of pressing sequences and each player's contribution. To address these limitations, this paper introduces exPressV2, a novel framework that uses a physics-informed 'Pressing Intensity' metric to dynamically identify high-pressure events from continuous tracking data. Our spatio-temporal architecture, combining a Gated Recurrent Unit (GRU) and a Graph Attention Network (GAT), then analyzes the sequence leading up to a press to predict the probability of regaining possession. The proposed framework was validated using 7,800 pressing situations from 36 *K League 1* matches and demonstrated superior performance to baseline models with an ROC AUC of 0.731. This framework offers practical applications that translate the model's predictive power into objective tools for both individual player evaluation and tactical simulation. The source code is publicly available at https://github.com/leemingo/express-v2.

Keywords: Football Analytics · Pressing Analysis · Machine Learning · Deep Learning · Graph Neural Network

1 Introduction

The availability of tracking and event data has transformed football analytics, enabling studies of advanced metrics and complex tactical patterns far beyond

---

M. Lee and G. Jo—These authors contributed equally to the paper.

H. Rios-Neto et al. (Eds.): MLSA 2025, CCIS 2833, pp. 35–47, 2026.
https://doi.org/10.1007/978-3-032-15165-0_3

the traditional focus on goals, assists, and passes [23,25,33]. While much of this work has focused on on-ball offensive actions like shooting [2,4], passing [3,12, 32,35,38], and possession value models [15,16,37], the focus has increasingly shifted to more complex off-ball dynamics. This includes analyzing set-pieces [8, 36], team formations [7,20,22,26], learning player representations from tracking data [10,14,27], and models of space control [15,29] (Fig. 1).

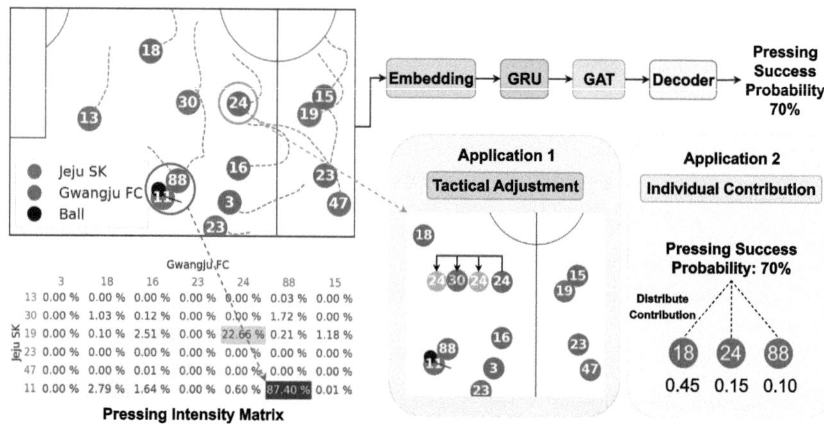

	3	18	16	23	24	88	15
13	0.00 %	0.00 %	0.00 %	0.00 %	0.00 %	0.03 %	0.00 %
30	0.00 %	1.03 %	0.12 %	0.00 %	0.00 %	1.72 %	0.00 %
19	0.00 %	0.10 %	2.51 %	0.00 %	22.66 %	0.21 %	1.18 %
23	0.00 %	0.00 %	0.00 %	0.00 %	0.00 %	0.00 %	0.00 %
47	0.00 %	0.00 %	0.01 %	0.00 %	0.00 %	0.00 %	0.00 %
11	0.00 %	2.79 %	1.64 %	0.00 %	0.60 %	87.40 %	0.01 %

Fig. 1. Overview of the exPressV2 framework, where a GRU-GAT model processes graph-represented tracking data to predict pressing success probability, enabling applications in tactical simulation and individual contribution analysis.

Among these topics, the quantitative analysis of pressing dynamics has become an important research topic [5,11,17,19,21,30]. The foundational work by Andrienko et al. [1] introduced a rule-based metric to measure pressure using static player positions and angles. This line of research has expanded to distinguish between high-pressing and deep-defending strategies [30], analyze defensive principles for successful ball recovery [18,21], and even create individual 'Pressure Matrices' from 3D body motion data [24]. Bekkers [9] introduced 'Pressing Intensity', a physics-informed metric that incorporates player velocities and directions, offering a more dynamic alternative to the static rules.

Beyond measuring pressure, another critical line of research evaluates the effectiveness and outcomes of these actions. Frameworks such as the Valuing Pressure decisions by Estimating Probabilities (VPEP) [34] and its extensions [31] established a risk-reward methodology to quantify the value of pressing decisions. Risk-reward contemplations have also been conducted in counterpressing, a special tactical pressing pattern [6]. Similarly, the exPress framework [28] specifically connected player positioning to a probabilistic outcome, offering an explainable approach through counterfactual analysis. However, its reliance on static, event-based snapshot data fundamentally limited its ability to capture the full temporal dynamics of a coordinated press or the contributions of all players involved.

This study addresses these gaps, building on [28] by introducing our new framework, exPressV2, which makes two major adjustments: (1) We use high-frequency tracking data that provides the positions of all players, enabling us to capture the full dynamics of pressing actions and comprehensively analyze player contributions. (2) We leverage the physics-informed pressing intensity metric [9] to dynamically identify high-pressure events instead of manually collected pressing events. To analyze the sequence of events leading up to a press, we employ a spatio-temporal architecture that combines a Gated Recurrent Unit (GRU) [13] to capture temporal dynamics with a Graph Attention Network (GAT) [39] to model the complex spatial interactions between players. A key aspect of our framework is its end-to-end learning directly from raw player coordinates. This design, distinct from models that rely on handcrafted spatial features, enables our two key practical applications: simulating positional adjustments to evaluate pressing effectiveness and attributing the predicted success to individual player contributions.

To develop and validate this framework, we utilize a comprehensive real-world dataset of tracking and event data from 36 matches of the 2024 *K League* season. We particularly demonstrate the practical utility of our approach through an in-depth analysis of Gwangju FC, a team renowned for its modern and effective pressing tactics. The results show our framework provides a more granular and dynamic understanding of pressing, bridging the gap between advanced data analysis and practical, player-specific tactical insights.

2   Proposed Framework

This section details our framework by first explaining how we define and prepare pressing situations for analysis—from identifying pressing events to constructing input sequences and labels (Sect. 2.1–2.3). We then describe the architecture of the spatio-temporal model (Sect. 2.4) and the method for attributing its predictions to individual players (Sect. 2.5).

2.1   Dynamic Identification of Pressing Situations

Instead of relying on manually annotated events, our framework begins by dynamically identifying pressing situations using a physics-informed metric. We build upon the Pressing Intensity metric [9], which quantifies the pressure exerted on a target by calculating the time required for defenders to intercept it, a concept introduced in previous work [38]. The metric is based on the probability of a successful interception $(p_{i,j})$, which is derived from the time to intercept $(T_{i,j})$—the physically calculated time for a defender i to reach a moving target j. This probability is calculated as follows:

$$p_{i,j}(t) = \left[1 + \exp\left(-\frac{\pi}{\sqrt{3}\sigma}\left(T - T_{i,j}(t)\right)\right)\right]^{-1}.$$

All physical values are set following the respective standards [9].[1] Using this metric, we define a "pressing frame" as any moment where the calculated $p_{i,j}$ from at least one defender on the ball carrier exceeds a high threshold of 0.9. This value was determined through preliminary experiments with various thresholds and was chosen to selectively filter for moments of intense pressure, while excluding more ambiguous, low-intensity defensive actions.

2.2   Construction of Spatio-Temporal Input Sequences

Once the pressing frames are identified, the next step is to construct a meaningful input representation for our spatio-temporal model. Instead of analyzing each pressing frame in isolation, our framework aims to capture the full temporal context leading up to the high-pressure moment.

Let $\mathcal{F}_P = \{f_1, f_2, \ldots, f_N\}$ be the set of all *pressing frames* identified in Sect. 2.1, ordered chronologically by their timestamps $t(f_i)$. We group consecutive frames into *pressing sequences*, that is, we consider f_i begins a new sequence if it is more than 5 s apart from the previous pressing frame f_{i-1}. This five-second threshold is a widely adopted heuristic in football analytics for delineating distinct phases of play [31]. Then, for the first frame (now denoted as f_{start}) of each pressing sequence, we sample a fixed-size sequence of 10 tracking data frames at uniform intervals from the five-second window before its timestamp. The sequence length of 10 was determined experimentally to balance temporal detail with computational cost.

To incorporate the context of on-ball actions, we enrich this sequence using the event data. For each of the 10 sampled tracking frames at a given timestamp t, we find the nearest subsequent event $e^*(t)$, which is formally defined as:

$$e^*(t) = \underset{e \in \mathcal{E},\, t(e) \geq t}{\text{argmin}} \; (t(e) - t).$$

where $\mathcal{E}$ is the set of all recorded events during the match.

We then extract the type of this event $\text{type}(e^*(t))$ and append it as a new categorical feature to the original tracking data tensor for that frame.

This process results in an augmented feature tensor $X(t)$ of shape $[A, F]$ for all A agents at a given sampled timestamp. The final input to our model, $\mathbf{X}_{\text{seq}}$, is the ordered sequence of these 10 augmented state tensors:

$$\mathbf{X}_{\text{seq}} = (X(t_1), X(t_2), \ldots, X(t_{10})),$$

where $\{t_1, \ldots, t_{10}\}$ are the 10 uniformly sampled timestamps preceding the first frame of the pressing sequence.

2.3   Evaluating the Effectiveness of Pressing

To train our model in a supervised manner, we define a binary label, $Y \in \{0, 1\}$, representing the success or failure of each identified pressing sequence. For each

---

[1] $\sigma = 0.45$, $T = 1, 5$, and π is the mathematical constant.

sequence, which begins at a starting frame f_{start}, we analyze the event data within the subsequent five-second window. The press is labeled as successful ($Y = 1$) if the pressing team performs any meaningful action that signifies a clear gain of possession within this window, such as a successful pass, shot, or recovery. Otherwise, it is labeled as a failure ($Y = 0$).

Therefore, the effectiveness of a pressing sequence is quantified by our model's predicted probability of success, $P(Y_t = 1|\mathbf{X}_{\text{seq}})$, which we denote as xPr. A high predicted probability indicates that the model deems the press to be effective.

2.4 Spatio-Temporal Model for Pressing Evaluation

To estimate the xPr value, $P(Y_t = 1|\mathbf{X}_{\text{seq}})$, and predict the success of a pressing sequence, we designed a hierarchical deep learning model that effectively captures both temporal interactions and spatial dynamics.

The process begins with feature enhancement. The categorical event type feature is converted into a dense vector via an embedding layer. This, along with the other kinematic features, is then projected into a higher-dimensional space using a fully-connected (FC) layer, creating a rich representation for each agent at each time step. Next, the model processes temporal dynamics for each agent individually. The sequence of enhanced feature vectors for each agent is fed into a bidirectional GRU network. The GRU processes an agent's entire trajectory to capture their movement patterns as follows: $\mathbf{h}_a = \text{GRU}(\text{FC}(\mathbf{X}_{a,\text{seq}}))$.

Following the temporal encoding, the set of dynamic agent embeddings, $\mathcal{H} = \{\mathbf{h}_1, \dots, \mathbf{h}_A\}$, is used as node features to construct a single graph that represents the collective state of the pressing situation. This graph is then processed by a series of Graph Attention Network (GAT) layers [39], which learn the complex, weighted relationships between players: $\mathcal{H}' = \text{GAT}(\mathcal{H})$.

To produce a single prediction for the entire sequence, a global mean pooling layer first aggregates these updated node embeddings into a single graph-level vector, $\mathbf{z}$. This vector is fed into a single FC layer (the classifier) with a sigmoid activation function (σ) to produce the final pressing success probability, $P(Y = 1|\mathbf{X}_{\text{seq}})$.

2.5 Individual Contribution Attribution

A key contribution of our framework is its ability to move beyond a simple team-level success prediction and attribute the outcome to the individual players involved in the coordinated press. The model's final output, the predicted probability of success xPr, is treated as the total credit, C_{total}, generated by the team's collective pressing action.

To distribute this credit, we first define a contribution weight, w_a, for each pressing player a. This weight represents the total pressure exerted by that player on all opponents, not just the ball carrier. It is calculated as the sum of the individual Pressing Intensity values, $p_{a,o}$, from player a to every opponent player o, that exceed a threshold of 0.5. Let $\mathcal{P}$ be the set of players on the pressing team, and $\mathcal{O}$ be the set of players on the opposing team, as defined below:

$$w_a = \sum_{o \in \mathcal{O} \mid p_{a,o} > 0.5} p_{a,o}.$$

The total credit is then distributed proportionally based on these filtered weights. The final contribution, C_a, for each defending player a is calculated by multiplying the total credit by the player's normalized pressure contribution:

$$C_a = C_{\text{total}} \cdot \frac{w_a}{\sum_{k \in \mathcal{P}} w_k}.$$

This attribution method provides an intuitive and explainable performance metric. It ensures that credit is not only given to the player directly pressuring the ball carrier but also to supporting players who are crucial to the success of a coordinated press. These per-event contribution scores can then be aggregated over a single match or an entire season to produce a robust rating of a player's overall pressing ability.

3 Experiments

3.1 Data

Our framework was developed and validated on a dataset comprising 36 matches from the 2024 *K League 1* season, provided by BEPRO Group Ltd. This dataset includes 30 Hz tracking data (x, y coordinates for all 22 players and the ball) and corresponding event data for discrete on-ball actions. All positional data was normalized to a standard 105×68 m pitch for consistency.

To ensure temporal alignment, all timestamps were synchronized to a uniform 25 Hz (40 ms) grid. From this processed data, we identified a total of 7,800 high-intensity pressing situations, following the methodology described in Sect. 2.1. For our experiments, the 36 matches were partitioned at the match level into training (24 matches), validation (6 matches), and test (6 matches) sets. To ensure a robust evaluation where every part of the training data serves as a test set once, we also employed a 6-fold cross-validation strategy on the training set.

3.2 Implementation Details

The input for our model is a feature vector of 19 channels for each agent (22 players and the ball). The kinematic features within this vector undergo a specific preprocessing pipeline. To smooth the raw positional data and derive robust kinematic features, we first apply a Savitzky-Golay filter to calculate velocity and acceleration. Subsequently, all kinematic data is normalized by scaling positional coordinates to the standard field dimensions and normalizing player and ball kinematics using pre-defined, sport-specific maximums. The remaining features include spatial relationships (distance and angles to the goal and ball) and categorical information (binary indicators for teammates and goalkeepers, and an embedded event type).

Our proposed model, exPressV2, employs a hierarchical architecture that seamlessly processes these features. First, the temporal dynamics of each player's feature sequence are processed individually by a 2-layer bidirectional Gated Recurrent Unit (GRU) with a hidden dimension of 128 and a dropout of 0.4. The resulting player embeddings are then used as node features in a fully connected graph to model their spatial interactions. This graph is processed by a 2-layer Graph Attention Network (GATv2) with 4 attention heads, a hidden dimension of 128, and a dropout of 0.4. The model was trained using the Adam optimizer with a learning rate of 1e-4, a weight decay of 1e-5, and a batch size of 64. We employed gradient clipping at a threshold of 2.0 and utilized a weighted Binary Cross-Entropy loss function to handle class imbalance.

3.3 Experimental Results

Table 1. Performance comparison of exPressV2 and baseline models. The table shows an ablation study on the impact of two key feature sets: positional and velocity features (*Pos.+Vel.*) and contextual (*Event Type*) features.

Model	*Pos.+Vel.*	*Event Type*	AUC ↑	Brier Score ↓	Log Loss ↓
Logistic Regression	✗	✗	0.670	0.228	0.649
	✗	✓	0.683	0.224	0.640
	✓	✗	0.709	0.215	0.623
	✓	✓	0.718	0.212	0.616
Random Forest	✗	✗	0.703	0.182	0.548
	✗	✓	0.710	0.182	0.546
	✓	✗	0.715	0.181	0.545
	✓	✓	0.717	0.181	0.544
XGBoost	✗	✗	0.703	0.220	0.631
	✗	✓	0.709	0.218	0.629
	✓	✗	0.717	0.225	0.642
	✓	✓	0.723	0.216	0.623
exPressV2	✗	✗	0.706	0.190	0.567
	✗	✓	0.710	0.191	0.565
	✓	✗	0.725	0.184	0.548
	✓	✓	**0.731**	**0.179**	**0.546**

To quantitatively evaluate the performance of our proposed model, we compared it against three baseline models: Logistic Regression, XGBoost, and Random

Forest. We used ROC Area Under the Curve (AUC), Brier Score, and Log Loss as our primary metrics. The comprehensive results of our systematic ablation study, with all metrics representing the average of our 6-fold cross-validation, are presented in Table 1.

Our proposed model, exPressV2, demonstrated the best performance across all metrics when all features were included, achieving an AUC of 0.731, a Brier Score of 0.179, and a Log Loss of 0.546, as indicated in the final row of the table.

We also conducted three main ablation studies to understand the impact of different feature sets. Across all baseline models, adding positional and velocity features (*Pos.+Vel.*) provided the most significant performance boost. For our exPressV2 model, the inclusion of these features boosted the AUC from 0.710 to 0.731. The contextual *Event Type* feature also consistently improved performance for all models, though its impact was generally more modest. This highlights the foundational role of player kinematics in this task, with on-ball context providing a valuable secondary signal.

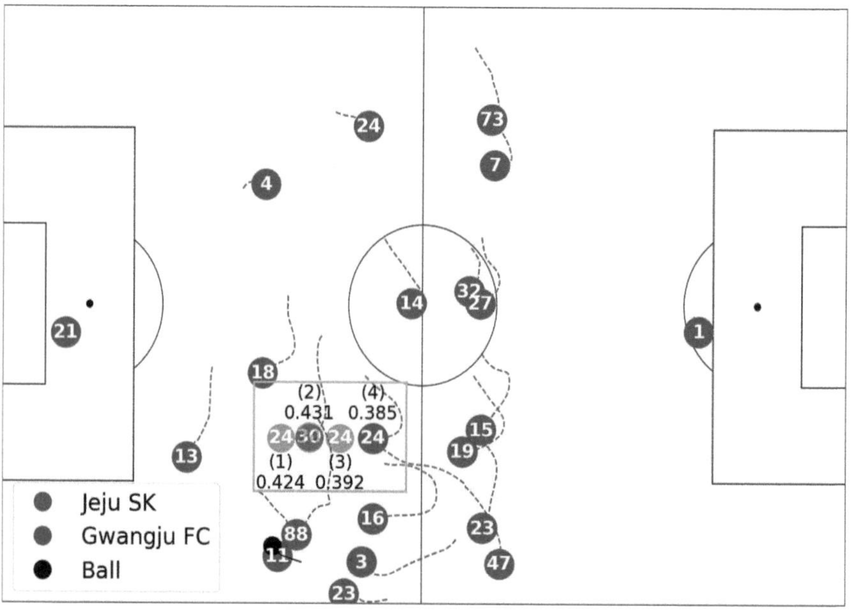

Fig. 2. An application of our framework for evaluating a player's positional decision. The model analyzes alternative locations for the defending player (24) within the spatial channel to an opponent (30). The results table shows that the player's actual position (Location 2) corresponds to the highest predicted pressing success probability ($xP_r = 0.431$), objectively validating his tactical choice.

4 Applications

4.1 Simulating Positional Adjustments for Tactical Optimization

Beyond achieving high predictive accuracy, a key advantage of our framework lies in its ability to serve as a practical tool for tactical analysis. By running counterfactual simulations, the model can move beyond evaluating what happened and begin to explore "what if" scenarios. Figure 2 illustrates this application with a concrete example from a *K League 1* match between Jeju SK and Gwangju FC. The scene captures a moment where Gwangju FC (red) is applying coordinated pressure to disrupt Jeju SK (blue) build-up play. Our analysis focuses on a critical defensive decision: the positioning of Gwangju FC's midfielder (24) tasked with preventing a pass to a potential receiving opponent (30).

To evaluate this player's positioning, we conduct a counterfactual analysis. We first define a one-dimensional spatial channel between the two players and discretize it into four distinct locations. We then simulate four alternative scenarios by hypothetically moving the defending player (24) to each of these locations while keeping all other players in their original positions. For each simulated scenario, we use our trained model to calculate the resulting pressing success probability (xPr).

The results, detailed in the accompanying table, offer a clear validation of the player's tactical intelligence. The analysis reveals that by moving the defender to Location 2, the team's success probability is maximized, yielding the highest predicted value of $xPr = 0.431$. This indicates that a specific positional adjustment could have increased the effectiveness of the press. This application demonstrates how our model can translate a complex model's output into intuitive and actionable feedback, providing objective support for coaching and player development.

4.2 Attributing Pressing Success to Individual Players

Beyond evaluating a single tactical moment, our framework can aggregate the per-event contributions over an entire match to generate a comprehensive rating of a player's pressing performance. By applying the attribution method described in Sect. 2.5, we can move beyond simple event counts to a more nuanced, context-aware evaluation of individual players. This allows us to identify and reward players who may not make the final tackle but are crucial in creating effective, coordinated pressure.

Table 2 showcases this application with a leaderboard of Gwangju FC players, with their performance aggregated across all matches used in this study. The players are ranked by their average xPr contribution score per game from high-pressing situations in the final third. This ranking is then compared against traditional defensive metrics (Recovery and Interception) and physical data (defensive sprints in the final third).

The results reveal how our xPr metric provides a more specialized focus on pressing quality than raw statistics alone. While midfielders like Hoyeon Jeong,

Table 2. Pressing performance of Gwangju FC players over an entire match, ranked by their average xPr contribution score from high-pressing situations in the final third. The ranking is compared with traditional defensive statistics (interceptions and recoveries) and the number of defensive sprints in the final third. Note that the highest value in each column is highlighted in boldface, and the second highest is underlined.

Player	Position	xPr	Intercept.	Recover.	Int.+Rec.	# of Sprints
Jisung Eom	LM	**3.556**	0.14	<u>1.64</u>	1.78	**9.50**
Hoyeon Jeong	CM	<u>3.508</u>	**0.51**	**2.54**	**3.05**	7.38
Huigyun Lee	CF	2.928	0.07	2.03	2.10	5.58
Kunhee Lee	CF	2.725	0.14	0.82	0.96	<u>7.62</u>
Gabriel	RM	2.671	<u>0.23</u>	1.13	1.36	4.66
Kyongrok Choi	CF	2.645	0.12	1.18	1.30	6.84
Beka Mikeltadze	CF	2.539	0.00	0.90	0.90	5.89
Jinho Kim	LB	2.110	<u>0.23</u>	1.62	<u>1.85</u>	4.00
Jasir Asani	RM	2.045	<u>0.23</u>	1.46	1.69	4.62
Alexandar Popovic	CB	1.933	0.08	0.67	0.75	4.22
Average	*–*	*1.492*	*0.11*	*0.80*	*0.91*	*4.53*

who ranks second in both xPr and defensive actions, show a clear correlation between our metric and traditional stats, our model also identifies other types of contributions. For instance, Jisung Eom ranks highest in xPr despite having more moderate defensive event counts, suggesting his value comes from creating pressure that enables teammates, rather than making the final tackle himself. Notably, the high valuation of these players by our metric was reflected in the subsequent transfer market. Following this season, top performers Jisung Eom and Hoyeon Jeong both earned transfers to higher leagues, while Huigyun Lee moved to a top team within the *K League*, providing external validation for our model's findings.

This discrepancy demonstrates the core value of our framework: it does not simply count the final defensive action but rather rewards players for their contribution to effective pressing structures. The effectiveness of this method lies in its ability to contextualize a player's individual effort. While simply summing a player's Pressing Intensity would reward all defensive activity equally, our approach multiplies this effort by the model-predicted success probability (xPr) of the entire situation. Consequently, a player receives significant credit only when their high-intensity actions occur within a tactically advantageous press, effectively distinguishing impactful contributions from futile efforts.

5   Conclusions

In this study, we introduced a spatio-temporal framework that leverages a physics-informed Pressing Intensity metric and a GRU-GAT architecture to offer a holistic evaluation of coordinated pressing sequences, overcoming the limitations of static analysis. Our experiments demonstrated that this approach not only outperforms baseline models in predicting outcomes but also provides actionable insights through counterfactual simulations of player positioning and a more nuanced player contribution model than traditional statistics. Ultimately, our model bridges the gap between advanced data-driven analysis and actionable, player-specific tactical insights, offering a more granular understanding of one of modern football's most critical phases.

Acknowledgements. The authors are grateful to BEPRO Group Ltd for providing the comprehensive *K League* tracking and event data that supported this research.

References

1. Andrienko, G., et al.: Visual analysis of pressure in football. Data Min. Knowl. Disc. **31**(6), 1793–1839 (2017)
2. Anzer, G., Bauer, P.: A goal scoring probability model for shots based on synchronized positional and event data in football (soccer). Front. Sports Active Living **3** (2021)
3. Anzer, G., Bauer, P.: Expected passes: determining the difficulty of a pass in football (soccer) using spatio-temporal data. Data Min. Knowl. Disc. **36**(1), 295–317 (2022)
4. Anzer, G., Bauer, P., Brefeld, U.: The origins of goals in the German Bundesliga. J. Sports Sci. **39**(22), 2525–2544 (2021)
5. Bauer, P.: Automated Detection of Complex Tactical Patterns in Football—Using Machine Learning Techniques to Identify Tactical Behavior. Ph.D. thesis, Universität Tübingen (2022)
6. Bauer, P., Anzer, G.: Data-driven detection of counterpressing in professional football: a supervised machine learning task based on synchronized positional and event data with expert-based feature extraction. Data Min. Knowl. Disc. **35**(5), 2009–2049 (2021)
7. Bauer, P., Anzer, G., Shaw, L.: Putting team formations in association football into context. J. Sports Anal. **9**(1), 39–59 (2023)
8. Bauer, P., Anzer, G., Smith, J.W.: Individual role classification for players defending corners in football (soccer) categorisation of the defensive role for each player in a corner kick using positional data. J. Quant. Anal. Sports **18**(2), 147–160 (2022)
9. Bekkers, J.: Pressing intensity: An intuitive measure for pressing in soccer. arXiv preprint arXiv:2501.04712 (2024)
10. Bialkowski, A., Lucey, P., Carr, P., Yue, Y., Sridharan, S., Matthews, I.: Large-scale analysis of soccer matches using spatiotemporal tracking data. In: IEEE International Conference on Data Mining, pp. 725–730 (2014)
11. Bojinov, I., Bornn, L.: The pressing game: optimal defensive disruption in soccer. In: Proceeding of the 10th MIT Sloan Sports Analytics Conference (2016)
12. Chawla, S., Estephan, J., Gudmundsson, J., Horton, M.: Classification of passes in football matches using spatiotemporal data. ACM Trans. Spatial Algorithms Syst. (TSAS) **3**(2), 1–30 (2017)
13. Cho, K., et al.: Learning phrase representations using RNN encoder-decoder for statistical machine translation. arXiv preprint arXiv:1406.1078 (2014)

14. Decroos, T., Roy, M.V., Davis, J.: SoccerMix: representing soccer actions with mixture models. In: Joint European Conference on Machine Learning and Knowledge Discovery in DDatabases, pp. 459–474 (2020)
15. Fernandez, J., Bornn, L.: Wide open spaces: a statistical technique for measuring space creation in professional soccer. In: Proceeding of the 12th MIT Sloan Sports Analytics Conference (2018)
16. Fernández, J., Bornn, L., Cervone, D.: Decomposing the immeasurable sport: a deep learning expected possession value framework for soccer. In: Proceeding of the 13th MIT Sloan Sports Analytics Conference (2019)
17. Fernandez-Navarro, J., Ruiz-Ruiz, C., Zubillaga, A., Fradua, L.: Tactical variables related to gaining the ball in advanced zones of the soccer pitch: analysis of differences among elite teams and the effect of contextual variables. Front. Psychol. **10**, 3040 (2020)
18. Forcher, L., Beckmann, T., Wohak, O., Romeike, C., Graf, F., Altmann, S.: Prediction of defensive success in elite soccer using machine learning-tactical analysis of defensive play using tracking data and explainable ai. Sci. Med. Football **8**(4), 317–332 (2024)
19. Forcher, L., Forcher, L., Altmann, S., Jekauc, D., Kempe, M.: The success factors of rest defense in soccer-a mixed-methods approach of expert interviews, tracking data, and machine learning. J. Sports Sci. Med. **22**(4), 707–725 (2023)
20. Forcher, L., Forcher, L., Altmann, S., Jekauc, D., Kempe, M.: Is a compact organization important for defensive success in elite soccer?-Analysis based on player tracking data. Int. J. Sports Sci. Coaching **19**(2), 757–768 (2024)
21. Forcher, L., Forcher, L., Altmann, S., Jekauc, D., Kempe, M.: The keys of pressing to gain the ball-characteristics of defensive pressure in elite soccer using tracking data. Sci. Med. Football **8**(2), 161–169 (2024)
22. Forcher, L., et al.: Shedding some light on in-game formation changes in the German Bundesliga: frequency, contextual factors, and differences between offensive and defensive formations. Int. J. Sports Sci. Coaching **18**(6), 2051–2060 (2023)
23. Goes, F., et al.: Unlocking the potential of big data to support tactical performance analysis in professional soccer: a systematic review. Eur. J. Sport Sci. **21**(4), 481–496 (2021)
24. Gu, C., Na, J., Pei, Y., De Silva, V.: Player pressure map–a novel representation of pressure in soccer for evaluating player performance in different game contexts. In: Proceeding of the 18th MIT Sloan Sports Analytics Conference (2024)
25. Herold, M., Goes, F., Nopp, S., Bauer, P., Thompson, C., Meyer, T.: Machine learning in men's professional football: current applications and future directions for improving attacking play. Int. J. Sports Sci. Coaching **14**(6), 798–817 (2019)
26. Kim, H., Kim, B., Chung, D., Yoon, J., Ko, S.K.: SoccerCPD: formation and role change-point detection in soccer matches using spatiotemporal tracking data. In: Proceedings of the 28th ACM SIGKDD Conference on Knowledge Discovery and Data Mining, pp. 3146–3156 (2022)
27. Kim, H., Kim, J., Chung, D., Lee, J., Yoon, J., Ko, S.K.: 6MapNet: representing soccer players from tracking data by a triplet network. In: International Workshop on Machine Learning and Data Mining for Sports Analytics, pp. 3–14 (2021)
28. Lee, M., Jo, G., Hong, M., Bauer, P., Ko, S.K.: exPress: contextual valuation of individual players within pressing situations in soccer. In: Proceeding of the 19th MIT Sloan Sports Analytics Conference (2025)
29. Llana, S., Madrero, P., Fernández, J., Barcelona, F.: The right place at the right time: advanced off-ball metrics for exploiting an opponent's spatial weaknesses in soccer. In: Proceedings of the 14th MIT Sloan Sports Analytics Conference (2020)

30. Low, B., Rein, R., Raabe, D., Schwab, S., Memmert, D.: The porous high-press? An experimental approach investigating tactical behaviours from two pressing strategies in football. J. Sports Sci. **39**(19), 2199–2210 (2021)
31. Merckx, S., Robberechts, P., Euvrard, Y., Davis, J.: Measuring the effectiveness of pressing in soccer. In: International Workshop on Machine Learning and Data Mining for Sports Analytics (2021)
32. Power, P., Ruiz, H., Wei, X., Lucey, P.: Not all passes are created equal: objectively measuring the risk and reward of passes in soccer from tracking data. In: Proceedings of the 23rd ACM SIGKDD Conference on Knowledge Discovery and Data Mining, pp. 1605–1613 (2017)
33. Reep, C., Benjamin, B.: Skill and chance in association football. J. Roy. Stat. Soc. **131**(4), 581–585 (1968)
34. Robberechts, P.: Valuing the art of pressing. In: Proceedings of the StatsBomb Innovation In Football Conference, pp. 1–11. StatsBomb (2019)
35. Robberechts, P., Roy, M.V., Davis, J.: un-xPass: measuring soccer player's creativity. In: Proceedings of the 29th ACM SIGKDD Conference on Knowledge Discovery and Data Mining, pp. 4768–4777 (2023)
36. Shaw, L., Gopaladesikan, S.: Routine inspection: a playbook for corner kicks. In: International Workshop on Machine Learning and Data Mining for Sports Analytics, pp. 3–16 (2020)
37. Spearman, W.: Beyond expected goals. In: Proceedings of the 12th MIT Sloan Sports Analytics Conference (2018)
38. Spearman, W., Basye, A., Dick, G., Hotovy, R., Pop, P.: Physics-based modeling of pass probabilities in soccer. In: Proceeding of the 11th MIT Sloan Sports Analytics Conference (2017)
39. Velickovic, P., Cucurull, G., Casanova, A., Romero, A., Liò, P., Bengio, Y.: Graph attention networks. In: International Conference on Learning Representations (ICLR) (2018)

Beyond Outcome Bias: Incorporating Action Completion Probability and Risk-Return Into Soccer Evaluation Models

Yannik Paul$^{(\boxtimes)}$ iD, Maximilian Klemp iD, and Daniel Memmert iD

Institute of Exercise Training and Sport Informatics, German Sport University of Cologne, 50933 Cologne, Germany
`y.paul@dshs-koeln.de`

Abstract. Current soccer evaluation models such as VAEP or Expected Threat (xT) have advanced performance analysis by quantifying the impact of player actions on future scoring probabilities. However, these models rely on outcome-driven learning, which conflates execution quality with tactical intent. As a result, successful but risky actions are often overrated, while strategically sound actions that fail are undervalued—a distortion known as outcome bias. In this paper, we introduce *xSuccess*, a probabilistic model that estimates the likelihood of successful action completion based on contextual features. We integrate this completion probability into an adjusted action value framework, exemplified using VAEP. Our method isolates completion risk from estimated scoring impact and produces $VAEP_{adjusted}$ values that reflect both reward and uncertainty. Using a public dataset of over 3.6 million on-ball actions, we demonstrate that xSuccess is well-calibrated and the adjusted values align with Expected goals (xG) distributions. Comparative analysis shows that the adjusted model reduces variance caused by rare successful events and offers more realistic valuations. A case study of a goal sequence from Borussia Dortmund illustrates the practical relevance of this framework. Our findings suggest that completion probability is a vital component in soccer analytics, enabling a more accurate and interpretable assessment of player performance under real-game conditions.

Keywords: Decision-making · Probabilistic modeling · Action evaluation · Performance analysis

1 Introduction

Soccer is a low-scoring sport, where a single goal often decides the match outcome [24]. Therefore, match results are frequently reflected by randomness rather than by the true performance of a team or player [15]. As a first step, soccer analytics introduced Expected Goals (xG) [4] to evaluate all shot attempts, extending the evaluative scope to approximately 1% of total actions. Building on this, action

H. Rios-Neto et al. (Eds.): MLSA 2025, CCIS 2833, pp. 48–61, 2026.
https://doi.org/10.1007/978-3-032-15165-0_4

value models such as Expected Threat (xT) [20] or VAEP (Valuing Actions by Estimating Probabilities) [8] aim to quantify the contribution of up to 100% of on-ball actions or game states to the likelihood of scoring. Beyond these, other recent approaches have started to incorporate complementary dimensions such as creativity [19], off-ball spatial advantages [16], or performance under mental pressure [3].

Although current models mark significant progress by shifting evaluation to probabilistic assessments of actions and game states, they share the structural limitation of outcome-driven learning. This introduces a systematic bias: Actions that are successful and lead to goals are consistently valued higher than similar actions that did not, regardless of whether the underlying decision or execution was equally sound [24]. While the Atomic-SPADL representation attempts to mitigate this issue by removing action outcome as a feature component [7], it still lacks interpretability, since shots or passes and the respective outcomes are treated as distinct, disconnected events. Splitting each on-ball event into initiation and reception increases model complexity and disrupts the semantic unity of actions, making it harder to assess intention or outcome—especially for events like risky passes where both parts are tightly linked. It also obscures causal links to long-term outcomes (e.g., goals depend entirely on preceding shots) and reduces interpretability for practitioners, as related segments must be re-aggregated to trace or communicate decision value in scouting or tactical analysis.

This paper introduces a framework that addresses these limitations and enables a more context-aware assessment by separating the completion probability from the estimated contribution of an action to future scoring. In Sect. 2, we further discuss conceptual limitations and introduce psychological theories as a theoretical foundation. Section 3 presents our framework, introducing *xSuccess* as a model to estimate the probability of successful completion for any given action. In Sect. 4, we present an initial implementation, demonstrating how this perspective helps capture risk-return trade-offs in player behavior and enables more robust performance evaluation. Section 5 concludes with a summary and an outlook on future research directions.

2 Theoretical Perspectives on Action Evaluation: Beyond Outcome-Driven Models

This section outlines the current modeling approaches for valuing soccer actions and identifies structural limitations. We then introduce a theoretically grounded alternative based on risk-reward principles, adapted from classical decision theory and motivational psychology.

2.1 Theoretical Considerations of Current Expected Value Models

Modern soccer analytics has made considerable progress by shifting its focus to more comprehensive indicators of player and team performance. Initially, soccer analytics focused on simple event-counting metrics (i.e. goals or shots on target) as primary indicators of performance. To address the inherent randomness of such discrete outcomes, probabilistic models like xG [4] were introduced, estimating the likelihood of a shot resulting in a goal based on large historical datasets. However, this approach remains restricted to shot events, covering only a small fraction of all on-ball actions and assigning value only to the shooter while disregarding the contributions of other involved players. Subsequently, models such as xT [20] and VAEP [8] expanded this methodology to assess all on-ball actions by estimating their contribution to future scoring or conceding. These allow a more nuanced and context-sensitive understanding of tactical behavior and player decision-making across the entire game flow.

Despite their sophistication, these models still rely on a fundamentally outcome-driven learning paradigm: actions are assigned values based on their statistical association with goals or goal-preceding sequences observed in the data. This approach introduces a systematic distortion referred to as *outcome bias*, a tendency to overvalue successful outcomes and undervalue contextually sound decisions that do not lead to scoring [13]. The VAEP developers themselves highlight this issue particularly in the case of shots, noting that: "First, the standard SPADL representation tends to assign shots a value that is the difference between the shot's true outcome and its xG score. Hence, goals or a number of misses, particularly for players who do not take a lot of shots, can have an outsized effect on their VAEP score." [7]. This discrepancy underscores how outcome-driven training can lead to misaligned value estimates, rewarding completion over intent. To formalize this distortion, we can approximate the value that such a model learns for a given action a as follows:

$$\text{xValue}(a) = f(P_{\text{goal}|\text{success}(a)}, P_{\text{success}}(a), ...) \tag{1}$$

where f represents an unknown mapping from completion and impact-related inputs to a scalar value estimate. This illustrates that outcome-driven models implicitly combine the probability of completion with the potential scoring impact of an action, resulting in biased values: risky actions that succeed may be overvalued, while strategic but failed actions are penalized.

2.2 Incorporating Risk and Reward: A Utility-Based Perspective

To address these limitations, we draw on a foundational concept from decision theory and motivational psychology: the trade-off between potential reward and the probability of success. This principle is formalized in the theory of expected utility, introduced by Bernoulli [2] and expanded by von Neumann and Morgenstern [17]. The framework models decision-making under uncertainty as the maximization of weighted outcome utilities. In our simplified context, this translates to balancing the potential value of an action with the probability of its successful completion.

A parallel concept exists in the motivational psychology of achievement. According to Heckhausen and Atkinson [12], motivational strength is shaped by three interacting factors: an individual's motive strength, the subjective probability of success, and the incentive value of the outcome. Their work demonstrates that individuals tend to prefer actions of intermediate difficulty ($P \approx 0.5$), where the combination of risk and reward is perceived as most meaningful—an insight that has been supported by empirical studies across various domains [9].

This trade-off can be meaningfully applied to soccer. Players in high-pressure situations are often faced with choices between a high-value but low-probability action (i.e. a risky through ball) and a safer, less rewarding alternative like a lateral pass. Understanding and modeling how players navigate these decisions is crucial for evaluating their performance, especially when such decisions do not lead to immediate outcomes like goals. A related application of this principle can be found in the work of Power et al. [18], who quantified both the risk and the reward of passes using tracking data to assess pass quality. Building on this conceptual foundation, we argue that soccer action evaluation should reflect both components independently: the contribution to scoring and the likelihood of successful completion. This perspective enables a more faithful representation of decision-making under uncertainty, as it accounts for varying levels of risk tolerance, contextual constraints, and the inherent difficulty of actions. Therefore, we propose a simplified model that forms the theoretical basis of our evaluation framework, by explicitly separating potential reward from completion likelihood:

$$\text{xValue}_{\text{adjusted}}(a) = \text{xValue} \perp P_{\text{success}}(a) \cdot P_{\text{success}}(a) \qquad (2)$$

$\text{xValue} \perp P_{\text{success}}(a)$ denotes the value assigned by an existing model such as xT or VAEP, with completion probability factored out to prevent double-counting. $P_{\text{success}}(a)$ represents the estimated probability of successful completion. The resulting product $\text{xValue}_{\text{adjusted}}(a)$ reflects a risk-aware valuation that integrates both intended impact and completion uncertainty.

In the remainder of this work, we translate this theoretical perspective into a risk-aware modeling approach that separates completion probability from expected value. We show how this can enhance existing evaluation metrics and provide deeper insight into player performance under realistic game conditions.

3   A Risk-Aware Evaluation Framework Based on Action Completion Probability

To operationalize the theoretical separation between action value and completion probability, we extend an existing value model, VAEP, as a concrete example.

3.1   VAEP: Valuing Actions by Estimating Probabilities

To serve as the foundation, we briefly summarize the VAEP model proposed by Decroos et al. [8]. VAEP assigns value to each on-ball action based on its estimated effect on the likelihood of scoring or conceding within the next k actions, derived by computing the change in outcome probabilities between game states before (S_{i-1}) and after (S_i) an action a_i. For each team $x \in \{\text{home}, \text{away}\}$, VAEP estimates the probability that team x will score $(P_{\text{scores}}(a_i, x))$ or concede $(P_{\text{concedes}}(a_i, x))$ within the next k actions. The change in these probabilities between the states before (S_{i-1}) and after (S_i) the action a_i determines the offensive and defensive value:

$$\Delta P_{\text{scores}}(a_i, x) = P_{\text{scores}}(S_i, x) - P_{\text{scores}}(S_{i-1}, x) \tag{3}$$

$$\Delta P_{\text{concedes}}(a_i, x) = P_{\text{concedes}}(S_i, x) - P_{\text{concedes}}(S_{i-1}, x) \tag{4}$$

The total VAEP value of action a_i for team x is then computed as:

$$V(a_i, x) = \Delta P_{\text{scores}}(a_i, x) - \Delta P_{\text{concedes}}(a_i, x) \tag{5}$$

This modeling framework enables action-wise evaluation of all ball-related events, providing tactical insight beyond traditional shot-based metrics.

3.2   xSuccess: Predicting Contextual Completion Success

To complement value-based action evaluation, we introduce *xSuccess*, a model that estimates the completion probability of each individual on-ball action. Unlike VAEP, which relies on scoring-related outcomes, xSuccess focuses solely on whether an action is likely to succeed under the given contextual conditions— independent of its impact on goals. Similar approaches have been proposed for passes, most notably Anzer and Bauer's Expected Passes model [1], which estimates pass completion probabilities using detailed tracking data. Our approach generalizes this concept beyond passes to all on-ball actions.

The success and failure probability $\in [0, 1]$ for a given action a_i and a set of contextual features X describing the game state is defined as:

$$\text{xSuccess} = P_{\text{success}}(a_i, X) = P(a_i \text{ is successful} \mid X) \tag{6}$$

$$P_{\text{failure}}(a_i, X) = 1 - P_{\text{success}}(a_i, X) \tag{7}$$

Each action is labeled binary as successful (1) or unsuccessful (0) based on its direct outcome (e.g., completed pass, won duel), with definitions taken directly from the data provider. This allows the use of a standard binary classifier for predicting the likelihood of success given the observed context.

By estimating completion likelihoods at the action level, this model provides a structured foundation for analyzing decision-making and contextual risk under real match conditions. It can be used to identify high-risk decision patterns, evaluate completion reliability across roles or positions, and quantify situational pressure effects at scale.

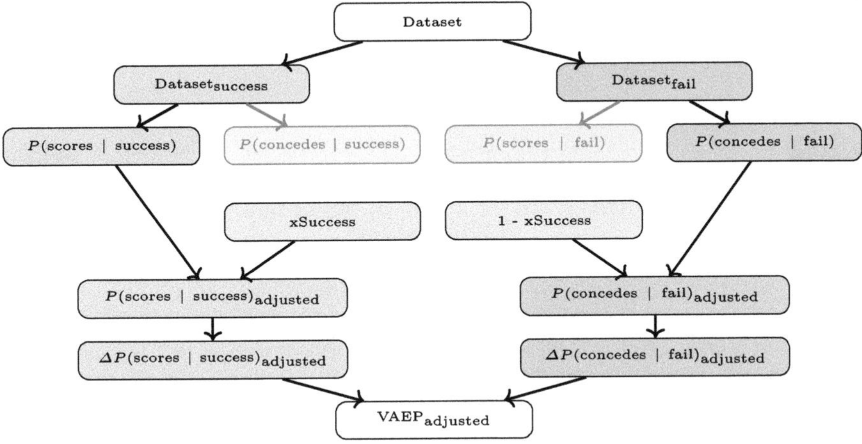

Fig. 1. Overview of the Framework – Incorporating xSuccess into Action Value Modeling (Exemplified with VAEP).

3.3 Framework Structure: Integrating xSuccess Into Action Value Modeling

To realize a more risk-aware evaluation of player actions, we integrate the xSuccess model into the VAEP framework by explicitly decoupling the completion probability from the action value. While VAEP originally assigns a single expected value per action based on empirical scoring outcomes, our extension separates completion and reward components, allowing for a more granular and interpretable attribution of value. Figure 1 provides an overview of the structure of the framework.

At its core, VAEP consists of two additive components: an offensive (ΔP_{scores}) and a defensive value ($\Delta P_{\text{concedes}}$). These are computed as the differences in scoring and conceding probabilities before and after an action, respectively. To disentangle completion risk from action value, we first isolate the influence of success and failure on the estimated outcome probabilities. To do this, we generate two manipulated versions of the test dataset: one in which all actions are treated as if they were successful, and one where all actions are assumed to have failed. For each action in both sets, we compute the forward-looking scoring and conceding probabilities—denoted $P(\text{scores} \mid \text{success})$ and $P(\text{concedes} \mid \text{fail})$, respectively. In practical terms, $P(\text{scores} \mid \text{success})$ translates to the probability of scoring within the next k actions, given that the action is successful and $P(\text{concedes} \mid \text{fail})$ translates to the probability of conceding within the next k actions, given that the action has failed. To incorporate completion uncertainty, we then weight these counterfactual probabilities with the completion probability. Specifically, $\text{xSuccess}(a_i)$ is used to weight the scoring potential in the success scenario, while its complement $1 - \text{xSuccess}(a_i)$ is used to weight the conceding risk in the failure scenario. This yields the following adjusted outcome probabilities for each action:

$$P(\text{scores} \mid \text{success})_{\text{adjusted}}(a_i) = \text{xSuccess}(a_i) \cdot P(\text{scores} \mid \text{success})(a_i) \qquad (8)$$

$$P(\text{concedes} \mid \text{fail})_{\text{adjusted}}(a_i) = (1 - \text{xSuccess}(a_i)) \cdot P(\text{concedes} \mid \text{fail})(a_i) \qquad (9)$$

These adjusted probabilities are then plugged into the original VAEP computation to derive refined values. By first calculating the difference in adjusted scoring and conceding probabilities before and after each action and then aggregating the adjusted VAEP score for action a_i, we obtain:

$$\Delta P(\text{scores} \mid \text{success})_{\text{adjusted}}(a_i) = P(\text{scores} \mid \text{success})_{\text{adjusted}}(S_i) - P(\text{scores} \mid \text{success})_{\text{adjusted}}(S_{i-1}) \qquad (10)$$

$$\Delta P(\text{concedes} \mid \text{fail})_{\text{adjusted}}(a_i) = P(\text{concedes} \mid \text{fail})_{\text{adjusted}}(S_i) - P(\text{concedes} \mid \text{fail})_{\text{adjusted}}(S_{i-1}) \qquad (11)$$

$$VAEP_{\text{adjusted}}(a_i) = \Delta P(\text{scores} \mid \text{success})_{\text{adjusted}}(a_i) - \Delta P(\text{concedes} \mid \text{fail})_{\text{adjusted}}(a_i) \qquad (12)$$

This adjusted score reflects both the strategic value of the action and the uncertainty of its completion, resulting in a more interpretable and decision-aware evaluation. By explicitly modeling risk as a contextual feature of completion, our framework provides a nuanced extension of VAEP that better captures the reality of player decision-making under uncertainty.

4 Application: Integrating xSuccess Into Performance Evaluation

In the following section, we present an initial empirical implementation of the proposed framework, demonstrating the feasibility of modeling completion success and integrating it into risk-aware evaluation.

4.1 Data and Experimental Setup

We used publicly available event data from StatsBomb [22], which is part of the StatsBomb Open Data initiative. The dataset covers the 2015/2016 season across Europe's top five leagues (England, Germany, Spain, Italy, France), including 1823 games and approximately 3.6 million on-ball actions, with full annotation of outcomes and contextual information. To ensure balanced representation and avoid team-level bias, we performed a stratified random split into training and test sets, assigning 50% of the matches to each partition [21]—sufficient even for less frequent action types such as shots or fouls [14].

The feature and label representation for VAEP is adopted directly from the existing framework, utilizing the standardized SPADL action encoding as described in Decroos et al. [8]. For xSuccess, a custom feature set was selected based on domain knowledge and assumptions about the key factors influencing action success (see Table 1). The label is binary, indicating whether the action was successful (1) or not (0).

For model training, we used XGBoost [6], which is known for its strong performance on structured and imbalanced data and has also been used in the original VAEP implementation [8]. Model performance was evaluated using standard

Table 1. xSuccess feature definitions.

Attribute	Description
`seconds`	the action's start time
`start_x`	the x location where the action started
`start_y`	the y location where the action started
`action_type`	the type of the action (e.g., pass, shot, dribble)
`bodypart`	the player's body part used for the action
`action_distance`	the length of the action in meters
`distance_to_goal`	the distance from the action's end point to the center of the goal
`shot_angle_centered`	the centered angle between ball location and goalposts

metrics commonly applied in probabilistic classification tasks [10]. The Brier Score was used to assess the calibration of predicted probabilities [5]. To evaluate the model's discriminative ability, we used the area under the Receiver Operating Characteristic curve (ROC-AUC) [11].

4.2 Results

The following section evaluates the model performance, compares original and adjusted VAEP values, and illustrates the practical application of the proposed framework using a real-world goal sequence.

Model Evaluation. The classifiers used to predict original VAEP components show strong performance: For P_{scores}, the Brier score is 0.009, indicating well-calibrated probability estimates, and ROC-AUC is 0.82, demonstrating solid discriminatory ability. For P_{concedes}, the Brier score is 0.002, with a ROC-AUC of 0.79, reflecting similarly good performance. These values are in line with, and consistently slightly better than, those reported in the original VAEP paper by Decroos et al. (e.g., Brier scores of 0.014 and 0.006; ROC-AUCs of 0.76 and 0.73 for scoring and conceding probabilities, respectively, using XGBoost) [8].

The xSuccess model obtains a Brier Score of 0.067, substantially improving over a baseline score of 0.094 (based on action type averages), thus reflecting reasonable calibration. It also achieves a ROC-AUC of 0.95, indicating robust classification performance. This high value is mainly driven by frequent and well-predictable actions such as passes or shots. Less frequent or more difficult action types (e.g. take on, interception or tackle) show lower individual ROC-AUC scores but have limited impact on the overall metric. However, some action types in the dataset (e.g., dribbles or clearances) are annotated in such a way that they consistently have only one outcome label. As these structurally one-sided distributions distort classification metrics, we re-evaluated the model after excluding all action types with only one unique result label. The overall ROC-AUC then drops to 0.87—a more conservative but still strong indicator of model quality. We decided to retain all action types for reasons of completeness and consistency, acknowledging that their outcome definitions depend on the data provider and may not always reflect true action difficulty. Notably, even in these cases, predicted xSuccess scores remain close to, but not exactly, 1.0, maintaining some degree of discriminative value. Supporting this, the aggregate sum of predicted completion probabilities (1,501,376.4) closely aligns with the actual number of successful actions (1,500,934), indicating a good calibration-in-the-large [23]. Additionally, we verified calibration across action types. For passes, which dominate the dataset, the model predicts an average success probability of 79.14%, closely matching the observed success rate of 79.08%. For less frequent actions such as shots, the predicted average (9.70%) also aligns well with the actual success rate (9.64%), supporting consistent model behavior across the action space. Calibration curves for both passes and shots further support this finding, showing well-aligned predicted and observed success rates across all probability bins.

For $\text{VAEP}_{\text{adjusted}}$, classical classifier metrics such as Brier Score or ROC-AUC are not directly applicable due to the compositional nature of the model. To assess the quality of the probability-weighted value estimates, we aggregate the xSuccess-weighted $P(\text{scores} \mid \text{success})_{\text{adjusted}}$ values (see Fig. 1) and divide it by 10 (reflecting the $k=10$ action horizon), obtaining a total of 2,279.6. This aligns remarkably well with the total xG (2,273.5) from the StatsBomb dataset, which is widely regarded as a benchmark for high-quality expected goal modeling. To further examine calibration beyond this aggregate alignment, we generated a calibration plot comparing predicted $P(\text{scores} \mid \text{success})_{\text{adjusted}}$ values against the actual frequency of goals (see Fig. 2). The plot confirms good calibration in the lower and mid-range bins, which account for the vast majority of actions, as can be seen from the included histograms. A slight overestimation is observed in the top prediction bin, which is consistent with the fact that both $P(\text{scores} \mid \text{success})_{\text{adjusted}}$ and xG slightly exceed the actual number of goals (2,076). This effect is more pronounced in the quantile-binned plot (Fig. 2A), where a wide range of prediction values (from about 0.05 to nearly 1) are grouped into a single top bin, and fewer samples in this range increase variance and apparent overestimation. The uniform binning plot (Fig. 2B), which distributes values evenly across bins, shows better alignment in the higher bins despite the small number of points, indicating that the apparent large deviation seen in the quantile-binned plot is largely due to the wide range of values aggregated there rather than a true calibration issue. Overall, the near equivalence and good calibration provides strong evidence that our framework produces coherent and interpretable probabilistic estimates that are consistent with established outcome-based models.

Comparison of VAEP and $\text{VAEP}_{\text{adjusted}}$. To assess the impact of outcome bias across the entire dataset, we compare ΔP_{scores} and $\Delta P_{\text{concedes}}$ from both the original VAEP and the adjusted VAEP formulation (Fig. 3).

A few key observations emerge: First, the presence of outcome bias is clearly visible in the original VAEP values—for both offensive and defensive contributions (A) & C)). Actions with successful outcomes are systematically assigned

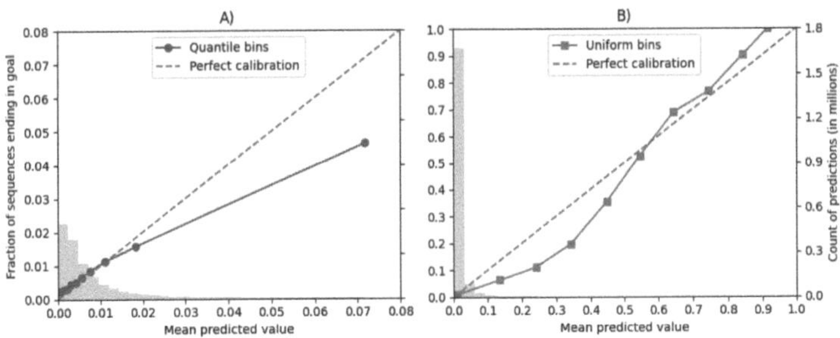

Fig. 2. Calibration plots of $P(\text{scores} \mid \text{success})_{\text{adjusted}}$ using (A) quantile binning and (B) uniform binning. The colored lines show the mean predicted value per bin against the observed goal frequency. The dashed diagonal represents perfect calibration. Histograms (gray) on the secondary axis display the distribution of predicted probabilities, with counts shown in millions.

higher offensive values and lower defensive values, even when contextual similarity is high. In contrast, the adjusted VAEP values exhibit no such clear separation, suggesting a more neutral and context-sensitive evaluation. A separate comparison excluding shots—where outcome bias is particularly strong—yields highly similar patterns, with only minor visual differences in the outlier distribution. This suggests that the observed effects of outcome-driven distortion are not limited to shot events, but reflect a broader structural bias in the original formulation.

In terms of completion probability (B) & D)), we observe a strong linear relationship for "likely" outcomes: high completion probability aligns well with offensive value, and low probability with stronger defensive penalties. However, for the inverse cases—unlikely successes or failures—the original VAEP values tend to show extreme variance. These outliers are more effectively regulated in the adjusted formulation due to xSuccess-based weighting. As a result, unrealistic value spikes driven by rare outcomes are suppressed, stabilizing long-term model behavior and improving robustness.

Applied Insights: Goal Sequence from Dortmund vs. Hoffenheim. To demonstrate the practical utility of our framework, we present an applied insight derived from real match data: a goal sequence from Borussia Dortmund's 3–1 home win over TSG Hoffenheim. The sequence visualization and corresponding action-level values are shown in Fig. 4.

This example illustrates several key insights. First, it highlights a limitation of xG, which assigns value exclusively to the shot-taker. In contrast, xSuccess and VAEP provide a more comprehensive view by evaluating every action in a sequence based on its completion probability and contribution to future outcomes.

xSuccess, in particular, reveals important nuances of completion risk: while Schmelzer's initial pass was classified as nearly certain to succeed, the subsequent actions were considerably riskier.

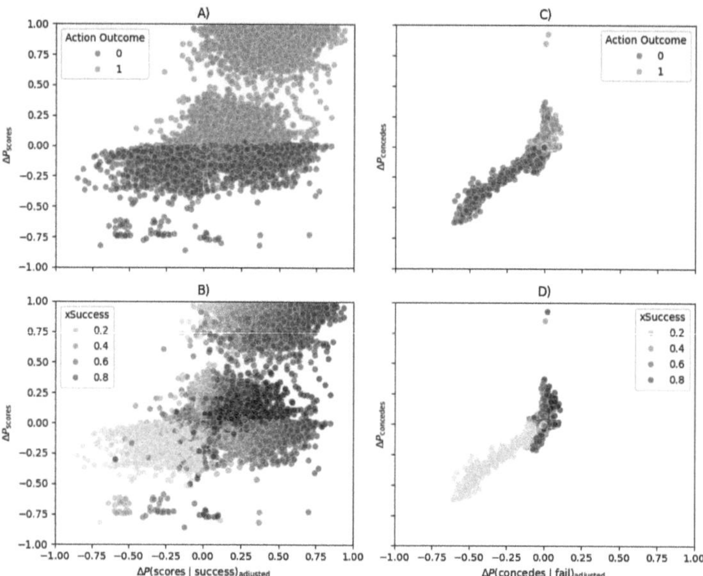

Fig. 3. Comparison of sub-values of the original VAEP and its adjusted formulation. A) Scatterplot displaying the offensive values with markers colored by the binary action outcome. B) Scatterplot displaying the offensive values with markers colored by the xSuccess values. C) Scatterplot displaying the defensive values with markers colored by the binary action outcome. D) Scatterplot displaying the defensive values with markers colored by the xSuccess values.

Comparing VAEP to $\text{VAEP}_{adjusted}$, multiple effects become apparent. Most notably, adjusted values are consistently lower than their counterparts, reflecting the removal of outcome bias. This correction is particularly visible in high-risk actions. For instance, Gündoğan's forward pass with a low completion probability receives a negative $\text{VAEP}_{adjusted}$ value, indicating that, on average, such a pass would more likely harm than help the team by leading to a turnover.

Similarly, Piszczek's difficult cross—executed with a sliding tackle just before the byline—is more realistically valued by $\text{VAEP}_{adjusted}$. The most striking example, however, is Ramos's header: while the standard VAEP model yields a high value of 0.822 (likely due to its proximity to the actual goal), $\text{VAEP}_{adjusted}$ provides a much more moderate score closely aligned with the action's xG of 0.115. This highlights one of the original model's shortcomings: namely, that SPADL-based VAEP tends to equate the value of a successful shot to its outcome minus its xG, thereby overstating the contribution in post-hoc evaluations.

While such values are not intended for single-action predictions, this example demonstrates that even on a per-action level, the adjusted framework yields values that more accurately reflect contextual difficulty and completion risk—offering a more realistic approximation of true performance.

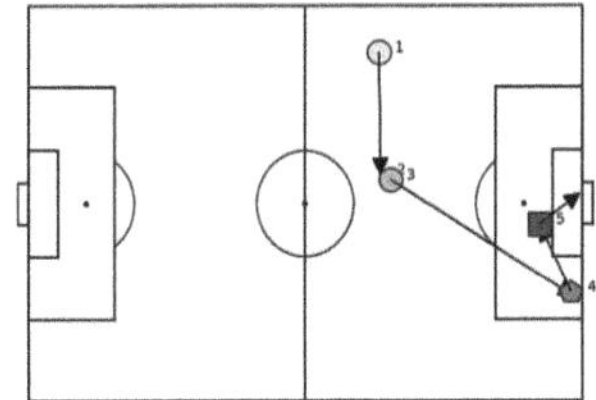

ID	Time	Type	Player	xSuccess	xG	VAEP	VAEP$_{adjusted}$
1	84:11	Pass	Schmelzer	0.948	0.000	0.005	0.001
2	84:13	Dribble	Gündoğan	1.000	0.000	0.004	0.003
3	84:14	Pass	Gündoğan	0.071	0.000	0.038	-0.008
4	84:17	Cross	Piszczek	0.353	0.000	0.113	0.035
5	84:18	Shot	Ramos	0.235	0.115	0.822	0.194

Fig. 4. Action sequence leading to Dortmund's third goal against Hoffenheim (85'), illustrating the spatial and temporal progression of the actions. The corresponding table provides a quantitative breakdown of each action, including xSuccess and value contributions based on the proposed frameworks.

Beyond post-hoc evaluation, our framework is particularly suited for evaluating contextual decision-making. Our approach primarily focuses on identifying players who optimally balance risk and reward by selecting actions with a favorable combination of expected value and success probability. While traditional scouts might seek players like Gündoğan who attempt bold, high-impact passes, players with differing passing styles and success rates may end up with similar VAEP$_{adjusted}$ values, since these reflect expected rather than actual outcomes. However, by isolating specific types of actions (e.g., line-breaking passes) and comparing a player's actual completion rate with the xSuccess-based baseline for those actions, it becomes possible to identify individuals who consistently outperform expectation. This allows practitioners to move beyond raw action success and toward deeper insight into player intent, decision quality, and reliability under varying game conditions.

5   Conclusion

We proposed a risk-aware extension to existing soccer action value models by introducing xSuccess, a model that estimates the probability of successful completion for each on-ball action. Unlike outcome-driven frameworks such as VAEP, our approach explicitly separates completion likelihood from strategic value, enabling a more nuanced and interpretable assessment of player decision-making. Empirical evaluations confirm that xSuccess is well-calibrated and aligns closely with real-world success rates, while $P(\text{scores} \mid \text{success})_{adjusted}$ is consistent with an expected goal benchmark. Moreover, our adjusted value formulation reduces outcome bias and mitigates extreme value distortions often seen in original models, particularly in low-probability but high-impact events. A case study and aggregated analysis demonstrate that our framework better reflects both tactical intent and completion risk. Future work could explore refinements for xSuccess such as incorporating tracking data, player-specific or archetype-based features, and training action-type-specific models with tailored feature engineering.

This paves the way for more context-sensitive player evaluation and highlights the importance of integrating probabilistic reasoning into modern soccer analytics.

Disclosure of Interests. The authors have no competing interests to declare that are relevant to the content of this article.

References

1. Anzer, G., Bauer, P.: Expected passes. Data Min. Knowl. Discov. **36**(1), 295–317 (2022). https://doi.org/10.1007/s10618-021-00810-3
2. Bernoulli, D.: Exposition of a new theory on the measurement of risk. Econometrica **22**(1), 23 (1954). https://doi.org/10.2307/1909829
3. Bransen, L., Robberechts, P., Van Haaren, J., Davis, J.: Choke or shine? Quantifying soccer players' abilities to perform under mental pressure. In: Proceedings of the 13th MIT Sloan Sports Analytics Conference, pp. 1–25 (2019). https://www.semanticscholar.org/paper/bc2c2545f4d25cda7b362e3e93069abc86306b38
4. Brechot, M., Flepp, R.: Dealing with randomness in match outcomes: how to rethink performance evaluation in European club football using expected goals. J. Sports Econ. **21**(4), 335–362 (2020). https://doi.org/10.1177/1527002519897962
5. Brier, G.W.: Verification of forecasts expressed in terms of probability. Monthly Weather Rev. **78**(1), 1–3 (1950). https://doi.org/10.1175/1520-0493(1950)078<0001:VOFEIT>2.0.CO;2
6. Chen, T., Guestrin, C.: XGBoost: a scalable tree boosting system. In: Proceedings of the 22nd ACM SIGKDD International Conference on Knowledge Discovery and Data Mining, pp. 785–794. KDD '16, ACM (2016). https://doi.org/10.1145/2939672.2939785
7. Davis, J., Decroos, T., Robberechts, P.: Introducing atomic SPADL: A new way to represent event stream data (2020). https://dtai.cs.kuleuven.be/sports/blog/introducing-atomic-spadl:-a-new-way-to-represent-event-stream-data/. Accessed 11 June 2025
8. Decroos, T., Bransen, L., Van Haaren, J., Davis, J.: Actions speak louder than goals: valuing player actions in soccer. In: Proceedings of the 25th ACM SIGKDD International Conference on Knowledge Discovery & Data Mining. KDD '19, ACM (2019). https://doi.org/10.1145/3292500.3330758
9. Feather, N.T.: Expectancy-Value Approaches: present Status and Future Directions, pp. 395–420. Routledge (2021). https://doi.org/10.4324/9781003150879-21
10. Ferri, C., Hernández-Orallo, J., Modroiu, R.: An experimental comparison of performance measures for classification. Pattern Recogn. Lett. **30**(1), 27–38 (2009). https://doi.org/10.1016/j.patrec.2008.08.010
11. Hanley, J.A., McNeil, B.J.: The meaning and use of the area under a receiver operating characteristic (ROC) curve. Radiology **143**(1), 29–36 (1982). https://doi.org/10.1148/radiology.143.1.7063747
12. Heckhausen, J., Heckhausen, H. (eds.): Motivation and Action. Springer eBook Collection, Springer, Cham, 3rd ed. 2018 edn. (2018)
13. Hellström, T., Dignum, V., Bensch, S.: Bias in machine learning – what is it good for? (2020). https://doi.org/10.48550/ARXIV.2004.00686
14. Koshute, P., Zook, J., McCulloh, I.: Recommending training set sizes for classification. arXiv preprint arXiv:2102.09382 (2021)

15. Lamas, L., Senatore, J.V., Fellingham, G.: Two steps for scoring a point: creating and converting opportunities in invasion team sports. PLOS ONE **15**(10), e0240419 (2020). https://doi.org/10.1371/journal.pone.0240419
16. Llana, S., Madrero, P., Fernández, J., Barcelona, F.: The right place at the right time: advanced off-ball metrics for exploiting an opponent's spatial weaknesses in soccer. In: Proceedings of the 14th MIT Sloan Sports Analytics Conference (2020). https://www.semanticscholar.org/paper/8fc0d83684301b6ba2aa459bbed548515e2462f2
17. von Neumann, J., Morgenstern, O.: Theory of Games and Economic Behavior. Princeton University Press, Princeton, NJ, 3 edn. (1953), third edition
18. Power, P., Ruiz, H., Wei, X., Lucey, P.: Not all passes are created equal. In: Proceedings of the 23rd ACM SIGKDD International Conference on Knowledge Discovery and Data Mining. ACM (2017). https://doi.org/10.1145/3097983.3098051
19. Robberechts, P., Van Roy, M., Davis, J.: un-xPass: measuring soccer player's creativity. In: Proceedings of the 29th ACM SIGKDD Conference on Knowledge Discovery and Data Mining, pp. 4768–4777. KDD '23, ACM (2023). https://doi.org/10.1145/3580305.3599924
20. Singh, K.: Introducing expected threat (xT) (2019). https://karun.in/blog/expected-threat.html. Accessed 13 May 2025
21. Singh, R., Mangat, N.S.: Stratified sampling. In: Elements of Survey Sampling, Kluwer Texts in the Mathematical Sciences, vol. 15, pp. 70–96. Springer, Dordrecht (1996). https://doi.org/10.1007/978-94-017-1404-4_5
22. StatsBomb: StatsBomb open data. https://github.com/statsbomb/open-data (2021). Accessed 19 May 2025
23. Van Calster, B., McLernon, D.J., van Smeden, M., Wynants, L., Steyerberg, E.W.: Calibration: the Achilles heel of predictive analytics. BMC Med. **17**(1) (2019). https://doi.org/10.1186/s12916-019-1466-7
24. Van Haaren, J.: "why would i trust your numbers?" On the explainability of expected values in soccer. arXiv preprint arXiv:2105.13778 (2021). https://www.semanticscholar.org/paper/09ff80f6990632e75ac6cd5f5f481a1c43f6d06b
25. Wunderlich, F., Seck, A., Memmert, D.: The influence of randomness on goals in football decreases over time. An empirical analysis of randomness involved in goal scoring in the English Premier League. J. Sports Sci. **39**, 2322-2337 (2021)

Next-Event Prediction in Soccer: Assessing the Impact of Team and Player Information

Raphaël Romero[1]($\boxtimes$)(iD), Yoosof Mashayekhi[1](iD), Fuyin Lai[1](iD), Maaike Van Roy[2]($\boxtimes$)(iD), Tijl De Bie[1](iD), and Jesse Davis[2](iD)

[1] IDLAB, Department of Engineering and Architecture, Ghent University, Ghent, Belgium
`raphael.romero@ugent.be`
[2] KU Leuven, Department of Computer Science, Leuven, Belgium
`maaike.vanroy@kuleuven.be`

Abstract. Next-event prediction in soccer is gaining attention as a core task, with applications in action value estimation, counterfactual simulation, and player style analysis. Prior work, such as the Large Event Model (LEM) framework, has focused on modeling sequences of events in an autoregressive manner. However, these models often overlook the influence of team and player identities. In this work, we extend the LEM framework to incorporate team-level and player-level information for predicting the next action type. Using the Wyscout dataset, we examine the impact of team identity, player identity, and player role on model performance. To this end, we conduct an experiment in which a variant of the LEM model based on a multi-layer perceptron (MLP) is trained, with player and team embeddings included as optional components. We compare the performance of the resulting model variants with heuristic baselines and an XGBoost classifier. Our findings show that, for soccer action type prediction, XGBoost and MLP-based models perform similarly and outperform baseline heuristics. We also confirm that incorporating a longer history of past events improves prediction performance compared to using only one past event. Finally, although including team or player embeddings does not substantially enhance predictive performance, our exploratory data analysis reveals that the learned player embeddings capture meaningful patterns related to player roles and team-specific playing style.

1 Introduction

A growing body of research in soccer analytics focuses on predicting the next event in a match based on previous actions. Applications include in-play forecasting [6], player style analysis [4,5], action value prediction [3], or more simply counterfactual soccer event simulation [8,10]. Machine learning has been widely applied to this task, with models like Seq2Event [13] and the more recent Large Event Model (LEM) [9,10], both of which model soccer events as following dynamic, language-like rules. However, the event-level features in these models

H. Rios-Neto et al. (Eds.): MLSA 2025, CCIS 2833, pp. 62–73, 2026.
https://doi.org/10.1007/978-3-032-15165-0_5

often focus only on the actions themselves, such as the type of action or its location on the field, and overlook player and team characteristics that could influence the next on-ball action. While this focus simplifies modeling, it ignores important signals such as a player's skills, role, or the team's playing style, all of which may influence the sequence of events. In this study, we overcome these limitations by extending the LEM framework [10] to incorporate team-level and player-level features into the next action type prediction task. Using the publicly available Wyscout dataset [11], we investigate how including the team identity, player identity, and role of the player performing an action affects model performance. We represent team and player identities using either one-hot encodings or learned embeddings, and categorize player roles based on standard positional types, and include them as one-hot encodings. Our evaluation spans a variety of modeling approaches, including neural networks, XGBoost classifiers, and heuristic baselines. Our main **contributions** can be summarized are follows.

1. We adapt the Large Event Model (LEM) model to train team and player embeddings from event data, in order to capture individual behavioral signatures.
2. We introduce `ConditionalMajority`, a purely memory-based baseline predictor, which predicts the next action type as the most frequent one observed following the current action type in the training data. We show that this approach achieves surprisingly strong performance and arguably should be used as a reference for faithful model evaluation.
3. We empirically evaluate the impact of including player-level and team-level information on next action type prediction.
4. We analyze the effect of including player role and team-level information on player embeddings learned in the next action type prediction task.

2   Related Work

Due to the global popularity of the sport and wide data availability, soccer analytics has attracted a growing body of research [2]. Therein, the most relevant work for this paper can be categorized into two main areas which we discuss below.

Event-based Modeling in Soccer Analytics. Earlier soccer analytics research primarily focused on game-level analysis and player performance prediction. More recently, however, attention has shifted toward event-based modeling, which aims to extract useful insights directly from in-game events. Examples of such insights include interpretable player representations [4], assessments of player style [12], and action value prediction [3]. These event-level insights can ultimately support tactical decision-making [1].

Soccer Event Prediction. Inspired by the success of sequential models in language modeling, recent research has increasingly focused on modeling sequences of soccer events. For example, Beal et al. [1] model a soccer match as a multi-stage stochastic game, predicting in-match state transitions and estimating the payoff of team actions, defined as the probability of transitioning to more favorable game states. Simpson et al. [13] propose Seq2Event, a model that predicts the next match event's action type and location by learning game state representations through RNN or Transformer architectures. More recently, Mendes-Neves et al. [10] introduce Large Event Models (LEMs) which sequentially predict the next event, including its type, precision, and other attributes, based on features derived from past events.

Our work lies at the intersection of soccer event prediction and player-level analysis, where we extend the LEM framework to learn player and team representations directly from event data.

3   Preliminaries

One of the most common and widely used types of data about soccer matches is called *event data*. Here, human annotators collect data about the important on-the-ball events that occur during a match, such as tackles, passes, and shots. Therefore a soccer match can be viewed as a sequence $\mathcal{H} = \{e(t_1), \ldots, e(t_N)\}$ where each event $e(t_i)$ includes its timestamp t_i and attributes such as action type, location, involved players, and success.

Definition 1 (Next Event Prediction). *Given a history of events $\mathcal{H}_{t_n}$ up to time t_n, the goal is to estimate the conditional probability of the next event $e(t_{n+1})$: $p(e(t_{n+1}) \mid \mathcal{H}_{t_n})$.*

Since encoding the full history is impractical, prior work [10,13] adopts an autoregressive approach, conditioning on the last k events: $\{e(t_{n-k+1}), \ldots, e(t_n)\}$. Each event can include multiple attributes (e.g., location, time, action type, player), but we focus on predicting the next **action type**, denoted $y(t_{n+1})$, using feature vectors $f(t_i)$ that may include spatial, outcome, and contextual (e.g., player, team) information.

4   Methodology

In this section, we first introduce the task, dataset, and features used in this study. We then describe the models investigated in this work.

4.1   Next Action Type Prediction Task

In this work we focus on predicting the next **action type** $y(t_{n+1})$ of the next event based on the features of the past k events, denoted $f(t_n), \ldots, f(t_{n-k+1})$. While our focus is on action type prediction, the same framework can be extended to other event attributes such as location, timing, or success. Prior work [9,13] primarily relies on features such as location, time, and past action types. However, in this paper we investigate the effect of incorporating team and player information, using techniques which we further describe below.

4.2   Data Format and Features

We use the Wyscout dataset made publicly available by Pappalardo et al. [11], which includes event, match, player, and team data from top European leagues and major tournaments (e.g., 2018 World Cup, Euro 2016). We preprocess the data using the LEM pipeline [10], which structures matches as sequences of time-stamped on-ball events. Each event is represented by a feature vector comprising action-level and player-level attributes, detailed in Table 1. Following [9], categorical features are one-hot encoded, and numerical features are normalized to the $[0, 1]$ range.

Table 1. Event features and their descriptions.

Feature	Description	Level	Feature Type	Encoding
`action_type`	Type of the event (e.g., pass, shot, duel).	Action	Categorical	One-hot
`period`	The period of the match, indicating first half or second half.	Action	Categorical	Binary
`minute`	The minute of the game when the event occurred, normalized.	Action	Numerical	–
`successful`	Indicates if the action was successful or not.	Action	Categorical	Binary
`goal`	Indicates if the action resulted in a goal.	Action	Categorical	Binary
`is_home_team`	Indicates if the action is performed by the home team.	Action	Categorical	Binary
`loc_x, loc_y`	The spatial coordinates where the event took place on the pitch, normalized.	Action	Numerical	–
`home_score, away_score`	Scores of the home and away teams, normalized.	Action	Numerical	–
`team_id`	Unique identifier for the player's team.	Player	Categorical	Embedding (MLP)/ Categorical (XGBoost)
`player_id`	Unique identifier for the player who performed the action.	Player	Categorical	Embedding (MLP)/ Categorical (XGBoost)
`player_role`	The role of the player who performed the action, one of Goalkeeper, Defender, Midfielder, Forward.	Player	Categorical	One-hot

4.3   Models

In this work, we study the effect of adding player-level and team-level features to the event prediction task. To do so, we adapt two models: one `XGboost` model which is known to perform well on mixed-type tabular data, and a neural network model which we describe below. Let's denote $x(t_n)$ the set of action-level features at time t_n, $\mathsf{p}(t_n)$ the id of the player who performed the action at time t_n, $\mathsf{t}(t_n)$ the id of the team of the player who performed the action at time t_n, and $\mathsf{r}(t_n)$ the role of the player who performed the action at time t_n.

LEM-MLP Model. LEM [10] uses a multi-layer perceptron (MLP) to classify the next action type. We extend it to incorporate team and player information through learned embeddings that capture latent contextual signals. Let g^{t} and g^{p} denote embedding functions for team and player, respectively. The model predicts the next action type $y(t_{n+1})$ based on the past k events and, optionally, contextual features from the most recent event:

$$p(y(t_{n+1}) \mid \mathcal{H}_{t_n}) = \text{MLP}\Big[g^{\text{t}}(\text{t}(t_n)) \mid g^{\text{p}}(\text{p}(t_n)) \mid \text{r}(t_n) \mid x(t_n) \mid \ldots \mid x(t_{n-k+1})\Big],$$

where $\mid$ denotes feature-wise concatenation. While the model above describes the general architecture, we experiment with several model variants to study the effect of different types of player-level information:

1. **Base**: Action-level features only.
2. $+$ **Team Embedding**: Adds embedded `team_id` via g^{t}.
3. $+$ **Team & Player Embedding**: Adds both `team_id` and `player_id` via g^{t} and g^{p}.
4. $+$ **Team Embedding & Player Role**: Adds team embedding and one-hot encoded `player_role`.
5. $+$ **Team & Player Embedding & Player Role**: Full variant combining all above predictors.

5   Experimental Settings

This section describes the dataset, the methods used for comparison, and the choice of hyperparameters for each method.

5.1   Dataset

The data consists of soccer events from different countries in season 2017/2018 [11]. In total, there are 33 different action types, such as simple pass, cross, shot, foul, etc. For more details regarding the competition statistics and the distribution of the action types, please see Appendix A. In this paper, we use the data only from the **Premier League**. We split the data into train, validation, and test sets, where we use the first 26 weeks of games for the train set, the next four games for the validation set, and the last eight games for the test set.

5.2   Evaluated Methods

We evaluate the following methods for next action type prediction:

- **Heuristics**: We include three baselines—`Random`, which selects uniformly at random; `Majority`, which always predicts the most frequent action; and `ConditionalMajority`, which predicts the most frequent next action conditioned on the current one.

- XGBoost: A widely used gradient boosting method trained with a multi-class classification loss.
- MLP: A multi-layer perceptron (MLP)-based model trained using a binary cross-entropy loss applied independently across action types, following the original LEM formulation [10].

Random and Majority are feature-agnostic, while ConditionalMajority uses only the previous action type. For XGBoost and MLP, we report results across different feature configurations (team_id, player_id, player_role) and history lengths $k \in \{1, 3\}$.

5.3 Hyperparameter Tuning

We performed hyperparameter tuning with Asynchronous Successive Halving [7] technique. We perform early stopping based on validation loss, and select the best results for each method based on validation F1-score. For MLP, we tune dropout from range 0.0 to 0.3, batch size from $\{256, 512\}$, learning rate from 0.001 to 0.1, and the hidden size from $\{[64], [256], [512], [64, 32], [128, 64]\}$. We also tune player embedding dimension from $\{2, 8, 32, 64\}$ and team embedding dimension from $\{2, 8, 32\}$. For XGBoost, we tune maximum depth from $\{2, 4, 6\}$ and learning rate from 0.001 to 0.1.

6 Results

This section presents experimental results, starting with a quantitative model comparison, followed by an exploratory analysis of the learned embeddings.

6.1 Quantitative Evaluation

We evaluate the methods in terms of accuracy and F1-score for the next action type prediction. Table 2 shows the result of this experiment. As expected, the Random baseline performs poorly due to the large number of classes. In contrast, Majority achieves higher accuracy by exploiting the skewed action distribution (see Appendix A), but fails on F1-score, reflecting its bias toward the dominant class. Meanwhile, ConditionalMajority, which conditions predictions on the previous action type, offers a substantial improvement in both metrics—highlighting the strong dependency between consecutive actions. The trained transition table it uses is provided in Appendix B.

Turning to the learned models, both XGBoost and MLP significantly outperform all heuristics. Notably, even the simplest variants ($k = 1$, no additional features) exceed the best baseline. Furthermore, performance improves consistently with longer histories ($k = 3$), confirming the importance of temporal context. Overall, the two methods are comparable: MLP achieves slightly better accuracy, while XGBoost performs better on F1-score.

We observe that additional inputs have the greatest impact when $k = 1$. Specifically, team identity (team_id) contributes little, while player_role and `player_id` yield more substantial gains, although the benefit of `player_id` diminishes when `player_role` is already included.

Table 2. Results for next action type prediction.

Method	k	team_id	player_id	player_role	accuracy	f1-score
Random	–	–	–	–	0.030	0.017
Majority	–	–	–	–	0.413	0.017
ConditionalMajority	1	–	–	–	0.541	0.134
XGBoost	1	no	no	no	0.554	0.259
XGBoost	1	yes	no	no	0.554	0.251
XGBoost	1	yes	no	yes	0.565	0.272
XGBoost	1	yes	yes	no	0.564	0.255
XGBoost	1	yes	yes	yes	0.562	0.268
XGBoost	3	no	no	no	0.593	0.312
XGBoost	3	yes	no	no	0.592	0.300
XGBoost	3	yes	no	yes	0.597	0.313
XGBoost	3	yes	yes	no	0.586	0.296
XGBoost	3	yes	yes	yes	0.598	0.307
MLP	1	no	no	no	0.560	0.259
MLP	1	yes	no	no	0.561	0.258
MLP	1	yes	no	yes	0.570	0.262
MLP	1	yes	yes	no	0.570	0.260
MLP	1	yes	yes	yes	0.571	0.262
MLP	3	no	no	no	0.603	0.272
MLP	3	yes	no	no	0.602	0.277
MLP	3	yes	no	yes	0.607	0.304
MLP	3	yes	yes	no	0.607	0.294
MLP	3	yes	yes	yes	0.604	0.276

6.2   Exploratory Data Analysis of Obtained Player Embeddings

In this section, we conduct an exploratory analysis of the player embeddings obtained using different configurations of the `MLP` model. Figure 1 illustrates how including team and role information in the input features affects the structure of the learned embeddings. Two main insights emerge from these visualizations:

Embeddings Encode Role Information. Figures 1a and 1b display player embeddings colored by player role. When the player role is *not* included in the input features (Fig. 1a), the embeddings tend to cluster by role, suggesting the embeddings implicitly encode role-related structure. In contrast, when the player role is included (Fig. 1b), the clustering disappears, as the model uses the

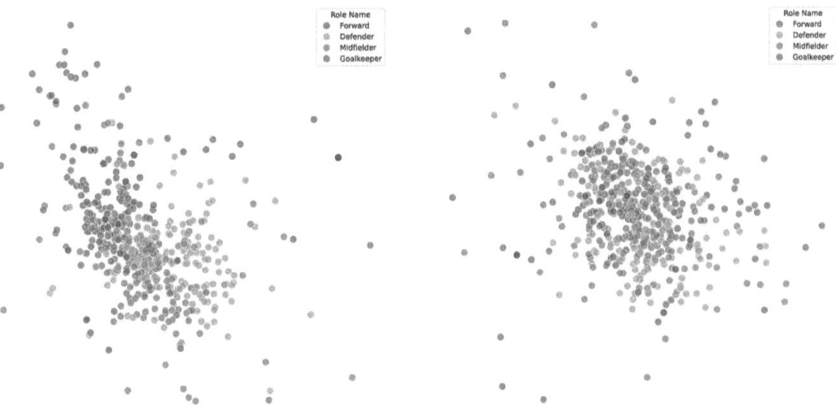

(a) Without player role in features. The learned player embeddings tend to cluster by role.

(b) With player role in features. The role information is provided, so the embeddings no longer cluster by role.

(c) Without team embedding. The model learns player embeddings that tend to cluster by team.

(d) With team embedding. Team-level information is provided separately, so player embeddings no longer cluster by team.

Fig. 1. Two-dimensional player embeddings trained jointly with MLP with $k = 3$ (i.e. features are from three past events). The first two subfigures show the embeddings of all players in the Premier League, colored by role, while the last two subfigures show the embeddings of players from selected teams in the Premier League, colored by team.

provided role input directly. This indicates that the embeddings tend to encode some other aspects of player characteristics. Such embeddings could directly be useful for player profiling as they encode event-based player characteristics complementary to known features such as player roles.

Embeddings Encode Team Information. Figures 1c and 1d show player embeddings colored by team. When the team embedding is *not* used (Fig. 1c), the embeddings cluster by team. However, when the team embedding is included (Fig. 1d), the clustering effect vanishes, suggesting that the model does not need capture team-specific patterns in the player embeddings, as the team information is provided separately. This difference indicates that the learn embeddings tend to encode some notion of team-specific playing style.

7   Conclusion

In this work, we conducted a comparative study of next-action prediction models in soccer, focusing on the influence of player- and team-level information. Our experiments reveal several key insights.

First, the `ConditionalMajority` baseline, which predicts the most frequent next action conditioned on the current one, performs surprisingly well. We recommend using it in next action type prediction benchmarks to ensure fair and meaningful evaluation. We also find that `MLP` and `XGBoost` achieve similar overall performance but offer complementary advantages. `XGBoost` yields a slightly higher F1-score, indicating better handling of class imbalance, while `MLP` enables end-to-end learning and allows player and team embeddings to be trained directly from data. Increasing the sequence length consistently improves performance across models, consistent with findings from the LEM framework [9]. Although player embeddings do not significantly improve predictive accuracy, our analysis shows they capture meaningful behavioral patterns, such as player roles and team styles. This suggests they may still be valuable for interpretability and player profiling. Interesting avenues for future work include enriching contextual features with representations (hand-crafted or learned) of other players on the pitch at event time, and exploring, depending on feature complexity, whether more sophisticated architectures improve performance.

Acknowledgments. The research leading to these results has received funding from the European Research Council under the European Union's Seventh Framework Programme (FP7/2007-2013) (ERC Grant Agreement no. 615517), and under the European Union's Horizon 2020 research and innovation programme (ERC Grant Agreement no. 963924); from the Special Research Fund (BOF) of Ghent University (BOF20/IBF/117); from the Flemish Government under the "Onderzoeksprogramma Artificiële Intelligentie (AI) Vlaanderen" programme; from the FWO (project no. G0F9816N, 3G042220); from the interuniversity BOF (iBOF) programme "Automating Data Science: the Next Frontiers" (BOF20/IBF/117); and from the KU Leuven Research Funds (C14/24/091).

Use of Large Language Models The authors declare that Large Language Models (LLMs) were used to assist in code generation for the experiments and to refine the writing of the manuscript.

A   Dataset

Table 3 shows the statistics of the national competitions present in the Wyscout dataset published by [11].

Table 3. Competition Statistics

Competition	#matches	#events	#players
Spanish first division	380	628,659	619
English first division	380	643,150	603
Italian first division	380	647,372	686
German first division	306	519,407	537
French first division	380	632,807	629
Total	1826	3,071,395	3,074

Figure 2 shows the distribution of the action types in session 2017/2018 session of several countries.

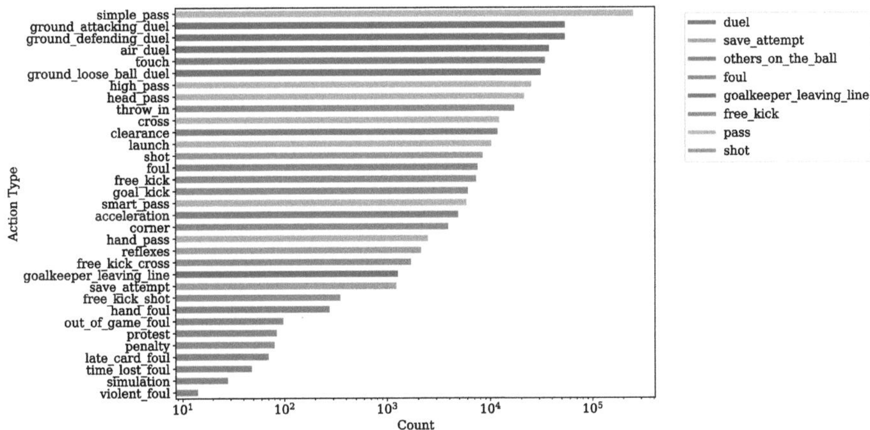

Fig. 2. Distribution of action types in the 2017/2018 Premier League season using the Wyscout format. Action types are grouped into broader categories, represented by color coding.

B   Conditional Majority Predictor

In Table 4 we show the computed transitions used by the `ConditionalMajority` predictor to predict the next action type.

Table 4. Most frequent transitions as stored by the `ConditionalMajority` predictor. The table shows the current action type and the next action type that is most frequently observed after it in the training dataset.

Current action type	Next action type
air_duel	air_duel
ground_attacking_duel	ground_defending_duel
ground_defending_duel	ground_attacking_duel
ground_loose_ball_duel	ground_loose_ball_duel
foul	free_kick
hand_foul	free_kick
late_card_foul	throw_in
out_of_game_foul	free_kick
protest	free_kick
simulation	free_kick
time_lost_foul	free_kick
violent_foul	free_kick_cross
corner	air_duel
free_kick	simple_pass
free_kick_cross	air_duel
goal_kick	air_duel
penalty	reflexes
throw_in	simple_pass
goalkeeper_leaving_line	air_duel
acceleration	simple_pass
clearance	throw_in
touch	simple_pass
cross	touch
hand_pass	simple_pass
head_pass	simple_pass
high_pass	simple_pass
launch	air_duel
simple_pass	simple_pass
smart_pass	simple_pass
reflexes	simple_pass
save_attempt	simple_pass
free_kick_shot	goal_kick
shot	goal_kick

References

1. Beal, R., Norman, T., Chalkiadakis, G., Ramchurn, S.: Optimising game tactics for football (2020)
2. Davis, J., et al.: Methodology and evaluation in sports analytics: challenges, approaches, and lessons learned. Mach. Learn. **113**(9), 6977–7010 (2024). https://doi.org/10.1007/s10994-024-06585-0
3. Decroos, T., Bransen, L., Van Haaren, J., Davis, J.: Actions speak louder than goals: valuing player actions in soccer. In: Proceedings of the 25th ACM SIGKDD International Conference on Knowledge Discovery & Data Mining, pp. 1851–1861 (2019). https://doi.org/10.1145/3292500.3330758
4. Decroos, T., Davis, J.: Player vectors: characterizing soccer players' playing style from match event streams. In: Machine Learning and Knowledge Discovery in Databases: European Conference, ECML PKDD 2019, Würzburg, Germany, September 16–20, 2019, Proceedings, Part III, pp. 569–584. Springer-Verlag, Berlin, Heidelberg (2019). https://doi.org/10.1007/978-3-030-46133-1_34
5. Decroos, T., Van Roy, M., Davis, J.: SoccerMix: representing soccer actions with mixture models. In: Dong, Y., Ifrim, G., Mladenić, D., Saunders, C., Van Hoecke, S. (eds.) Machine Learning and Knowledge Discovery in Databases. Applied Data Science and Demo Track, vol. 12461, pp. 459–474. Springer International Publishing, Cham (2021). https://doi.org/10.1007/978-3-030-67670-4_28
6. Klemp, M., Wunderlich, F., Memmert, D.: In-play forecasting in football using event and positional data. Sci. Rep. **11**(1), 24139 (2021). https://doi.org/10.1038/s41598-021-03157-3
7. Li, L., et al.: A System for Massively Parallel Hyperparameter Tuning (2020). https://doi.org/10.48550/arXiv.1810.05934
8. Mendes-Neves, T., Meireles, L., Mendes-Moreira, J.: Estimating Player Performance in Different Contexts Using Fine-tuned Large Events Models (2024). https://doi.org/10.48550/arXiv.2402.06815
9. Mendes-Neves, T., Meireles, L., Mendes-Moreira, J.: Forecasting Events in Soccer Matches Through Language (2024). https://doi.org/10.48550/arXiv.2402.06820
10. Mendes-Neves, T., Meireles, L., Mendes-Moreira, J.: Towards a foundation large events model for soccer. Mach. Learn. (2024). https://doi.org/10.1007/s10994-024-06606-y
11. Pappalardo, L., et al.: A public data set of spatio-temporal match events in soccer competitions. Sci. Data **6**(1), 236 (2019). https://doi.org/10.1038/s41597-019-0247-7
12. Robberechts, P., Van Roy, M., Davis, J.: Un-xPass: measuring soccer player's creativity. In: Proceedings of the 29th ACM SIGKDD Conference on Knowledge Discovery and Data Mining, pp. 4768–4777. ACM, Long Beach CA USA (2023). https://doi.org/10.1145/3580305.3599924
13. Simpson, I., Beal, R.J., Locke, D., Norman, T.J.: Seq2Event: learning the language of soccer using transformer-based match event prediction. In: Proceedings of the 28th ACM SIGKDD Conference on Knowledge Discovery and Data Mining, pp. 3898–3908. ACM, Washington DC USA (2022). https://doi.org/10.1145/3534678.3539138

A Unified Spatio-Temporal Graph Model to Predict Multi-Agent Movement

Ricardo Furbino[1,2]([✉]), João Lucas Lage Gonçalves[1,3],
Gabriel Valadão Meira[1,4], Wagner Meira Jr.[1], Thiago C. Porto[5],
and Adriano C. M. Pereira[1]

[1] Universidade Federal de Minas Gerais, Belo Horizonte, MG 31.270-901, Brazil
{ricardofurbino,joao.lucas,gabriel.valadao,meira,adrianoc}@dcc.ufmg.br
[2] src | ftbl, St. Louis, USA
ricardo@srcftbl.com
[3] Gemini Sports Analytics, Miami, USA
joao@geminisports.ai
[4] Clube Atlético Mineiro, Belo Horizonte, Brazil
gabriel.valadao@atletico.com.br
[5] Atalanta Bergamasca Calcio, Bergamo, Italy
thiago@atalanta.it

Abstract. Predicting movement in multi-agent continuous systems, such as football, presents significant challenges due to the dynamic and interactive nature of the environment. This work proposes a novel approach to movement prediction by leveraging a graph-unified representation, where football players are modeled as nodes and their interactions in time and space as edges. The proposed architecture, GuardiolAI, integrates Graph Neural Networks (GNNs) with Generative AI techniques, specifically Variational Autoencoders (VAEs), to capture both spatial and temporal dependencies in a unified manner. Unlike traditional methods that process spatial and temporal data separately, our approach models these aspects concurrently within a single graph structure. The methodology involves encoding tracking data from possession sequences into graph-based representations and employing GATv2 layers to learn adaptive attention weights across spatial and temporal dimensions. The model is evaluated using standard movement prediction metrics such as the average displacement error (ADE), mean squared error (MSE), and final displacement error (FDE), and is compared against a constant-velocity baseline. Experimental results demonstrate that the proposed approach achieves competitive performance and provides insight into player interactions and team dynamics.

Keywords: Multi-Agent Systems · Graph Neural Networks · Movement Prediction · Trajectory Forecasting · Generative AI · Football Analytics

1 Introduction

Recent advances in generative modeling introduce new ways to create and process information. Attention-based models [22] and other techniques to generate highly relevant and coherent outputs [9, 14] achieved impressive performance in tasks like text and image generation. Another area of interest is the modeling of **multi-agent continuous systems**, in which multiple entities interact within a shared, continuous environment over time. Advances in Graph Neural Networks (GNNs) have shown promise in capturing intricate relationships in such systems. Researchers are exploring how attention mechanisms within GNNs can improve the understanding of complex structured data [5, 23], leading to better predictive models in dynamic environments.

Football is a prime testbed: twenty-two players and a ball interacting in a shared space, with modern tracking systems recording their positions up to 30 Hz. In addition, the trajectory of each player depends both on personal intent and on the real-time movements of teammates and opponents, creating rich, interdependent patterns that drive game strategy. While attention-enhanced GNNs can capture such interdependencies in a graph structure, applying them to forecast future player positions remains underexplored, as far as we were able to verify. Therefore, we raise the question: *Can we build a model that accurately predicts player movements during a football match using generative AI and GNNs?*

This work aims to address this **Movement Prediction (MP)** problem by developing an architecture that predicts agent movements within the complex environment of a football match, using recent advances in deep learning. We cast a possession sequence, during which the team in possession of the ball remains the same, as a **unified graph**: each player in a frame is a node and every pair of players is linked by edges that encode both spatial proximity and temporal succession. The model draws on the generative capabilities of Variational Autoencoders (VAE) [14] and integrates them with the learning power of Graph Neural Networks (GNN) [5], using the unified graph as input and predicting the next seconds of the possession sequence. We benchmark against a constant-velocity baseline, report ADE/FDE/MSE, and inspect attention weights for interpretability, underscoring the promise of unified graph-generative approaches for movement prediction in sports analytics.

2 Related Work

Variational Autoencoders (**VAEs**) [11, 14] learn compact latent distributions and generate diverse, realistic samples across different domains. Although trajectory-forecasting literature often employs conditional VAEs (CVAEs), injecting both the observed past and future as explicit conditional to the decoder [16, 24], this is not strictly required. Recent work shows that a plain VAE—where the decoder receives only a sampled latent z that encodes the past—is sufficient for accurate future prediction: Syed & Morris [21] use a recurrent VAE that encodes pedestrian motion history (plus interaction/scene context) and decodes future trajectories from the latent code. We encode players' trajectories and decode the future movements for players. However, the VAE framework alone does not deal with inter-agent and temporal relationships.

Complex **multi-agent** problems have used Graph Neural Networks (**GNNs**), which extend the Deep Learning framework to handle data structures beyond traditional tabular formats, as an architecture due to its permutation invariance characteristic. GAT [23] stands out by utilizing **attention mechanisms** to prioritizes important nodes, enhancing the model's focus on critical relationships in graph data without relying on heavy computational operations. **GATv2** [5] further improves the flexibility of attention mechanisms, allowing dynamic computation of attention coefficients, particularly useful in complex and dynamic graph structures. Meanwhile, spatio-temporal hybrids (e.g. ASTGCN [10], T-GCN [27]) layer temporal filters on graph convolutions to forecast traffic. These approaches still process space and time separately.

In sports analytics, static GCNs evaluate individual frames for player impact [15,20], and set-piece models fuse CVAEs with GATv2 for corner prediction [25]. RNN+GCN hybrids map events to tracking data [7], and also use VAE to solve overlapping runs [3] and counterattack [8] detection in soccer. Transformer-only schemes [6] and imitation learning models [12] forecast positions from sequences, while diffusion denoising techniques [13] are being employed with transformers to improve tracking data quality, modeling player movements to enhance data provision. *Yet none embed continuous, multi-frame space–time dependencies in a single graph enhanced with attention.* Our work fills this gap by unifying spatial and temporal modeling for prediction of continuous football movement.

3   Methodology

In this section, we explain the data used to train the model, how we use it to construct a graph representing a possession sequence, the model that encodes and decodes the possession, the experiments made, and the evaluation of the model.

3.1   Spatio-Temporal Possession Sequences Using Tracking Data

We use PFF FC's 30 Hz broadcast tracking data[1] (190 English Premier League 22/23 matches) obtained with computer vision algorithms, fetched via GraphQL/JSON using 'gandula' python package[2] and preprocessed into pandas[3] DataFrames with position, velocity, and acceleration features. We extract continuous **possession sequences**—periods of uninterrupted ball control by a team—and downsample the frames to 5 Hz. Also, we removed possession sequences that included players with abnormal velocities, an issue that can happen in collection.

In sports analytics research, prior work typically separates temporal (RNN or transformer) and spatial (GNN or transformer) modules, or prioritize creating time embeddings before processing spatial relationships, others follow the reverse order, and some fuse them via custom attention schemes [1–3,6–8,13,26].

---

[1] https://fc.pff.com.
[2] https://pypi.org/project/gandula/.
[3] https://pandas.pydata.org/docs/.

We propose a novel approach to model the game as a unified graph structure, that integrates both spatial and temporal dimensions, allowing for simultaneous processing. Formally, the input graph is defined as $\mathcal{G} = (\mathcal{V}, \mathcal{E})$, where $\mathcal{V}$ is the set of nodes representing the players, and $\mathcal{E} \subseteq \mathcal{V} \times \mathcal{V}$ denotes the set of edges encoding spatial and temporal relationships.

In our formulation, a node $v \in \mathcal{V}$ corresponds to a player p_i in a given frame f_{in_j}. Within the same frame, each player p_i is connected to every other player $p_{k \neq i}$ via a **spatial edge** e_s, forming the set $\mathcal{P}_j = p_1, p_2, \ldots, p_\mathcal{N}$. This spatial connectivity captures player interactions within each frame.

To incorporate temporal continuity, we construct **temporal edges** e_t that link each player to its previous-frame ($f_{in_{j-1}}$) self, effectively capturing motion dynamics over time. This unified representation enables the simultaneous processing of spatial and temporal relations.

The decoder predicts the frames $j = \mathcal{M} + 1 \ldots \mathcal{M} + \mathcal{T}$, reusing the frame $\mathcal{M}$ as the first output. Sequences shorter than $\mathcal{M} + \mathcal{T}$ are zero-padded with "ghost" nodes to match node counts.

Each node and edge contains multiple features to enrich the learning process. Specifically, we define:

- Node features: (x,y) position, velocity decomposed into x and y axes, acceleration in x and y, angle to the ball, distance to the ball, and a boolean indicating team possession. Position is normalized from 0 to 1 according to pitch length (105 m x 68 m), and the other features are normalized from 0 to 1 according to max-min in the possession.
- Edge features: booleans indicating same-team relationships, within-frame connectivity (all players in the same frame are connected), and cross-frame temporal links.

We implement all graphs with PyTorch Geometric[4] and focus exclusively on open-play sequences (set-pieces excluded) [17]. For experimentation, we define $\mathcal{M} = 15$ input frames and $\mathcal{T} = 14$ output frames, which correspond to 3 and 2.8 s, respectively. For sequences >30 frames, we slide a fixed 30-frame window ($\mathcal{M} + \mathcal{T}$) and backtrack at the end to fit exactly 30 frames.

3.2 GuardiolAI: A Graph-Unified Encoder–Decoder

GuardiolAI (short for **G**raph-**U**nified **A**rchitecture for **D**ynamic **I**nference and **O**ptimization in **L**earning with **A**rtificial **I**ntelligence), is a VAE–based [14] graph encoder–decoder for player-trajectory prediction (Fig. 1). We cast each possession sequence as a unified graph—nodes are player–frames, edges capture both spatial proximity and temporal succession—and train GuardiolAI to compress the observed M input frames into a latent representation before reconstructing the next T frames.

In our design, the encoder processes only the past M frames' node and edge features through stacked GATv2 layers, producing per-node parameters μ and σ.

---

[4] https://pytorch-geometric.readthedocs.io/en/latest/.

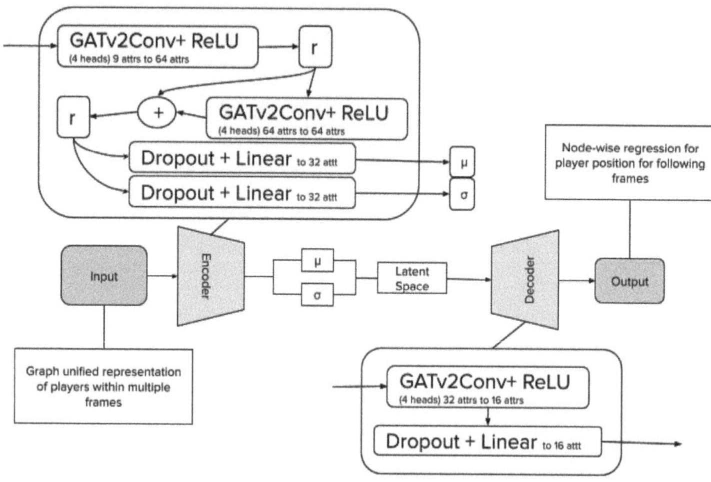

Fig. 1. Representation of the proposed architecture.

A latent sample z drawn from $\mathcal{N}(\mu, \sigma^2)$ then drives the decoder, which mirrors the encoder's GATv2 stack to predict the future positions. Crucially, the decoder is driven solely by z (and its own previous outputs when rolling forward), so all temporal and spatial context is captured within z and no past frames are re-introduced at decoding time.

GATv2 is particularly well-suited for this task due to its ability to capture node dependencies flexibly while incorporating edge features, which allows us to take advantage of our data design by assessing the model to balance weights across both spatial and temporal dimensions. Specifically, each GATv2 layer aggregates: *(i)* current-frame neighbors (spatial context); *(ii)* self-links from prior frames (temporal continuity); and *(iii)* indirect cross-frame context via stacked layers.

This layered propagation mechanism ensures that a player's representation in the latent space is informed not only by their immediate spatial surroundings but also by the influence of prior movements, leading to more coherent and temporally smooth predictions when decoding as well.

Reconstruction and Regularization. The loss function employed in this work is designed to balance the trade-off between reconstruction accuracy and latent space regularization in a variational autoencoder framework. The total loss, denoted as $\mathcal{T}$ consists of two primary components: the reconstruction loss and the regularization loss.

The reconstruction loss, $\mathcal{T}_{\text{rec}}$, quantifies the discrepancy between the predicted output $\hat{y}$ and the original output y, ensuring that the model generates accurate predictions. Specifically, the reconstruction loss is computed using the Average Displacement Error (ADE) metric, which measures the Euclidean distance between predicted and ground-truth trajectories across all time steps. Given a set of predicted positions $\hat{y}_t$ and ground-truth positions y_t for a sequence of length $1 + \mathcal{T}$, where $\mathcal{T}$ denotes the number of output frames plus the last frame of the input, for $\mathcal{N}$ players, ADE is defined as $\text{ADE} = \frac{1}{\mathcal{N}} \frac{1}{\mathcal{T}+1} \sum_{p=1}^{\mathcal{N}} \sum_{t=1}^{\mathcal{T}+1} \|\hat{x}_t^p - x_t^p\|_2$.

This metric provides a comprehensive evaluation of the model's prediction accuracy by averaging displacement errors across the entire trajectory, thereby penalizing deviations from the expected trajectory over time. To ensure stable optimization together with the regularizations, the reconstruction loss is normalized using a dynamic scaling factor γ, which is adaptively updated during training to reflect the minimum observed reconstruction error, leading to the formulation $\mathcal{L}\text{rec}\prime = \frac{\mathcal{L}\text{rec}}{\gamma} + \log(\gamma)$, in which γ is updated iteratively as $\gamma = \min(\gamma, \mathcal{L}_{\text{rec}})$ [4].

The regularization loss, $\mathcal{L}\text{reg} = D\text{KL}\big(q(z|x) \parallel p(z)\big)$, is based on the Kullback-Leibler (KL) divergence, which penalizes deviations of the latent variable distribution $q(z|x)$ from a predefined prior $p(z)$. This regularization enforces a structure latent space by encouraging the approximate posterior $q(z|x)$ to align with a known prior distribution, in our work, a standard Gaussian $\mathcal{N}(0,1)$. By doing so, the model learns to map similar inputs to nearby points in latent space, ensuring smoothness and continuity in the learned representations. Therefore, during inference, when sampling from the prior $p(z)$, the model is more likely to generate diverse and realistic samples that align with the data distribution seen in the training phase. Without proper regularization, the latent space may become too sparse, leading to unreal sample generation.

The final loss, referred to as the Dynamic Generative Loss (DGL) [4], is then formulated by combining scaled reconstruction and regularization:

$$\mathcal{L} = \frac{\mathcal{L}\text{rec}}{\gamma} + \log(\gamma) + \beta \cdot \mathcal{L}\text{reg} \tag{1}$$

3.3   Experiments

The dataset used was divided into train, test and validation, in a rate of 0.8, 0.1, 0.1, respectively. We used train and validation in the experiments and the test set to evaluate the model. We find the best parameters using optuna[5] framework, which led to the architecture having 2 layers with 4 heads of size 64 each in the encoder, that outputs embeddings of size 32, and having 1 layer with 4 heads of size 32 each in the decoder. Both encoder and decoder have a dropout of 0.1.

We perform a Learning Rate Range Test by exponentially increasing the learning rate from 0.000001 to 1 over a single epoch and selected the rate at which the training loss reached its minimum before diverging (0.01) [18]. Then, using that value as max_lr, we applied a OneCycleLR schedule with dividing factor = 25, final dividing factor = 0.0001, and cosine annealing to ramp up and down smoothly over the 20 training epochs. AdamW optimizer was employed as the learning rate optimization algorithm, with initial learning rate being 0.0004 1e-2/25 and having weight decay = 0.0001.

---

[5] https://optuna.org.

3.4 Forecasting Schemes and Evaluation Metrics

Metrics. We report *Average Displacement Error* (ADE), *Mean Squared Error* (MSE) and *Final Displacement Error* (FDE), all in meters. A naïve **constant velocity** extrapolator—each player's last observed velocity projected forward—serves as our primary baseline.

Why Re-anchoring? The raw GuardiolAI decoder predicts future frames in absolute pitch coordinates. Because the last observed frame f_M is fed back into the decoder, small sensor noise at f_M becomes amplified, producing a visible error spike in the first two predicted frames (see Fig. 3). To suppress this artefact we apply a re-anchoring transformation: for each possession we translate every predicted trajectory by an offset vector Δ computed as follows:

1. Select anchor frame:
   - f_{M+1} for `hybrid_first_frame`;
   - f_{M+2} for `hybrid_second_frame`.
2. Reference point: extrapolate the baseline from f_M to the anchor time, yielding $\hat{\mathbf{x}}_p^{\text{constant-velocity}}$.
3. Offset: $\Delta = \hat{\mathbf{x}}_p^{\text{constant-velocity}} - \hat{\mathbf{x}}_p^{\text{raw}}$.
4. Shift: add Δ to every future-frame prediction for every player.

Forecasting Schemes. We therefore evaluate four variants that differ only in how they handle the first two predicted frames and the re-anchoring step:

- **raw**: keep the repeated frame (f_M appears twice) exactly as decoded.
- **exclude_repeated**: drop the repeated frame; no re-anchoring.
- **hybrid_first_frame**: drop the repeat, then re-anchor using the constant velocity estimate at f_{M+1}.
- **hybrid_second_frame**: use the constant velocity path for the first two unseen frames and re-anchor the rest at f_{M+2}.

This suite isolates the benefit of the rigid shift while keeping the core model unchanged.

4 Experimental Results

The GuardiolAI variants show clear strengths and weaknesses relative to the constant velocity baseline (Table 1). While the baseline still achieves the lowest ADE (2.01 m) and MSE (12.58 m^2), all GuardiolAI modes improve on final-step accuracy: both the raw and exclude_first_frame predictions cut FDE from 4.38 m to 4.10 m (a 6.4 % reduction). Re-anchoring further closes the gap in full-trajectory metrics. The hybrid_first_frame scheme lowers ADE to 3.23 m and MSE to 18.39 m^2, and the hybrid_second_frame setting reduces ADE to 2.66 m (35 % lower than 4.09 m and 0.65 m away from baseline) and MSE to 15.20 m^2 (36 % lower than 23.57 m^2). Although these still trail the baseline, they demonstrate

Table 1. ADE, MSE, and FDE (in meters) for the constant velocity baseline and GuardiolAI under four prediction modes. Note: 'raw' an extra frame.

Model	ADE	MSE	FDE
Constant Velocity	**2.02**	**12.58**	4.38
GuardiolAI (raw)	4.12	23.88	**4.10**
GuardiolAI (exclude_first_frame)	4.09	23.57	**4.10**
GuardiolAI (hybrid_first_frame)	3.23	18.39	5.55
GuardiolAI (hybrid_second_frame)	2.67	15.20	4.51

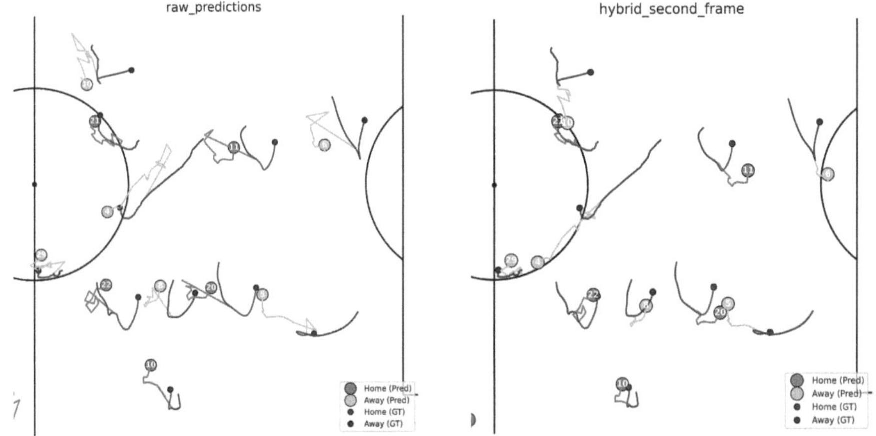

Fig. 2. Sample of prediction made with GuardiolAI in raw (left) and hybrid_second_frame (right) modes.

that simple frame-anchoring strategies can substantially improve both average and squared-error metrics.

Figure 3 shows per-frame error with respect to the actual player position in that frame. The raw predictions spike on the first two frames – reflecting high jitter—then level off. When we reanchor (either first or second frame), the error at the whole trajectory drops significantly and it starts to have the same constant behavior as the constant velocity error. Considering the error difference between frames 17 and 28, it is remarkable that the error associated with Constant Velocity grows faster than the error associated with GuardiolAI configurations. In particular, velocity_baseline error increased 460%, while hybrid_second_frame increased 369%. Figure 2 shows a prediction sample for the hybrid_second_frame strategy.

Figure 4 shows how attention is distributed between spatial and temporal edges across the network. Given that each node's hidden state is updated by

$$h_u^{(t)} = \phi\Big(h_u^{(t-1)}, \bigoplus_{v \in N_u} a\big(h_u^{(t-1)}, h_v^{(t-1)}, e_{vu}, g\big)\, \psi\big(h_v^{(t-1)}\big) \Big).$$

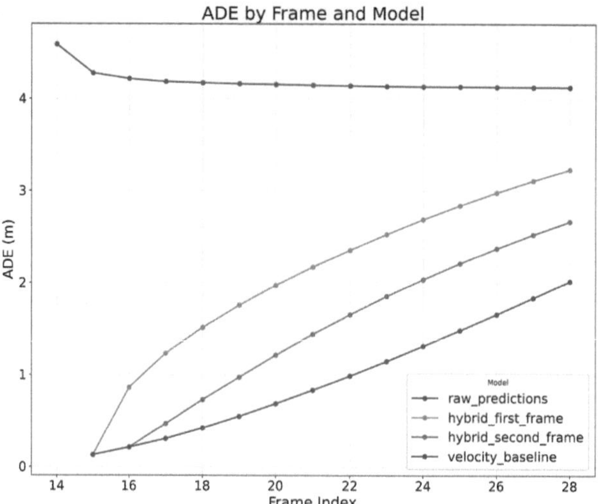

Fig. 3. Per-frame cumulative ADE for raw, reanchored predictions and constant veloc-ity.

where $a(\cdot)$ computes the attention weight between node u and its neighbor v based on their previous hidden states $h_u^{(t-1)}, h_v^{(t-1)}$, the edge features e_{vu}, and global context g, while $\psi(\cdot)$ transforms the neighbor's features and $\phi(\cdot)$ fuses the aggregated message with the node's prior state [5]. The values in the figure are the attention score per head per layer, indicating how much each neighbor type contributes to the node update. In the encoder, spatial edges carry more weight in the first layer, but in a low magnitude. Temporal edges become dominant by

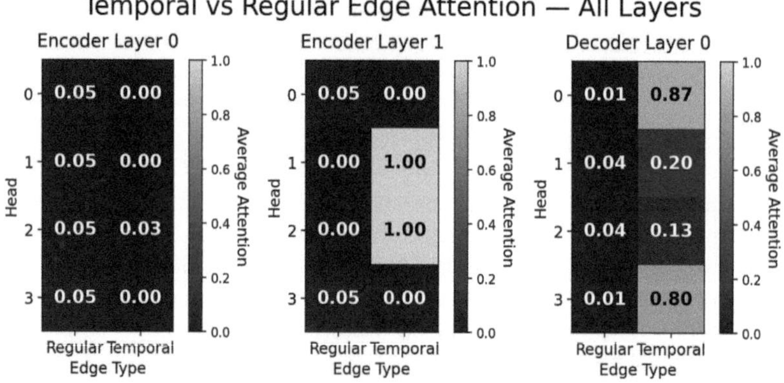

Fig. 4. Attention score per head per layer, indicating how much each neighbor type contributes to the node update and revealing the shift in focus from spatial relationships in early layers to temporal edges, with higher values, in later layers.

the second layer and remain overwhelmingly dominant throughout the decoder. This pattern confirms that, while inter-player relationships are encoded, the model still relies primarily on each player's own prior position to predict their next move.

5 Conclusion and Future Work

In this work, we explore how to represent a possession sequence in football using graphs that unify spatial and temporal dimensions simultaneously. A basic set of node features was defined, which can be extended to incorporate additional attributes. We propose two types of edges, which are, in practice, represented by two sets of edge features: *spatial* edge features that capture player relationships within the same timestamp; and *temporal* edge features that model relationships between the same player across different timestamps.

Using this representation, we designed and trained a state-of-the-art architecture, GuardiolAI, to predict player movements on the field, a task referred to as Movement Prediction (MP). The attention mechanisms introduced by GATv2 [5] empower the model with the capability to predict agent trajectories using dynamically assigned weights to nodes, while also giving some interpretability to results. Future work will explore alternative model architectures – such as integrating graph neural networks with temporal learning, employing transformer-based representations, and latent diffusion models – to benchmark different approaches for movement prediction. The goal is to find solutions to the absence of temporal edges in the first frame, which affected the predictions, as the experimental results demonstrated.

The VAE-based encoder-decoder architecture facilitates the exploration of latent space representations, an area we intend to investigate further in future studies. Additionally, we aim to extend the movement prediction framework to a Conditional Movement Prediction (CMP) approach by adapting the VAE structure into a CVAE [19], which would allow the model to condition predictions based on prior information.

Acknowledgements. This work was partially supported by CNPq, CAPES, FAPEMIG and by project IAIA - INCT on AI.

References

1. Alcorn, M.A., Nguyen, A.: baller2vec++: A look-ahead multi-entity transformer for modeling coordinated agents. Pre-print (2021)
2. Alcorn, M.A., Nguyen, A.: baller2vec: A multi-entity transformer for multi-agent spatiotemporal modeling. Pre-print (2021)
3. Anzer1, G., Bauer, P., Brefeld, U., Fassmeyer, D.: Detection of tactical patterns using semi-supervised graph neural networks. MIT Sloan (2022)

4. Asperti, A., Trentin, M.: Balancing reconstruction error and kullback-leibler divergence in variational autoencoders. IEEE Access **8**, 199440–199448 (2020). https://doi.org/10.1109/ACCESS.2020.3034828
5. Brody, S., Alon, U., Yahav, E.: How attentive are graph attention networks? (2021). https://arxiv.org/abs/2105.14491
6. Capellera, G., Ferraz, L., Antonio Rubio, A.A., Moreno-Noguer, F.: Footbots: A transformer-based architecture for motion prediction in soccer. IEEE ICIP (2024). https://arxiv.org/abs/2406.19852
7. Everett, G., Beal, R.J., Matthews, T., Early, J., Norman, T.J., Ramchurn, S.D.: Inferring player location in sports matches: Multi-agent spatial imputation from limited observations (2023). https://arxiv.org/abs/2302.06569
8. Fassmeyer1, D., Anzer, G., Bauer, P., Brefeld, U.: Toward automatically labeling situations in soccer. Front. Sports Act. Living (2021). https://www.frontiersin.org/journals/sports-and-active-living/articles/10.3389/fspor.2021.725431/full
9. Goodfellow, I.J., et al.: Generative adversarial networks (2014). https://arxiv.org/abs/1406.2661
10. Guo, S., Lin, Y., Feng, N., Song, C., Wan, H.: Attention based spatial-temporal graph convolutional networks for traffic flow forecasting. In: The Thirty-Third AAAI Conference on Artificial Intelligence (AAAI-19) (2019). https://ojs.aaai.org/index.php/AAAI/article/view/3881
11. Higgins, I., et al.: beta-VAE: Learning basic visual concepts with a constrained variational framework. ICLR (2017). https://openreview.net/forum?id=Sy2fzU9gl
12. Hoang, L., Carr, P., Yue, Y., Lucey, P.: Data-driven ghosting using deep imitation learning. MIT Sloan Conference 2016 (2016). www.sloansportsconference.com/research-papers/data-driven-ghosting-using-deep-imitation-learning
13. Hughes, H., et al.: Approaching in-venue quality tracking from broadcast video using generative ai (2024)
14. Kingma, D.P., Welling, M.: Auto-encoding variational bayes (2013). https://arxiv.org/abs/1312.6114
15. Sahasrabudhe, A., Bekkers, J.: A graph neural network deep-dive into successful counterattacks. MIT Sloan (2023)
16. Salzmann, T., Ivanovic, B., Chakravarty, P., Pavone, M.: Trajectron++: Dynamically-feasible trajectory forecasting with heterogeneous data. ECCV (2020). https://link.springer.com/chapter/10.1007/978-3-030-58523-5_40
17. Shirozu, Y.: What is the transition between set pieces and open play? (2022). https://footballbunsekicom.com/set-piece/what-is-the-transition-between-set-pieces-and-open-play
18. Smith, L.N., Topin, N.: Super-convergence: Very fast training of neural networks using large learning rates. arXiv (2017). https://arxiv.org/pdf/1708.07120
19. Sohn, K., Yan, X., Lee, H.: Learning structured output representation using deep conditional generative models. Advances in Neural Information Processing Systems (2015). https://dl.acm.org/doi/10.5555/2969442.2969628
20. Stöckl, M., Seidl, T., Marley, D., Power, P.: Making offensive play predictable - using a graph convolutional network to understand defensive performance in soccer. MIT Sloan Conference 2021 https://www.statsperform.com/wp-content/uploads/2021/04/Making-Offensive-Play-Predictable.pdf
21. Syed1, A., Morris, B.T.: Semantic scene upgrades for trajectory prediction. Machine Vision and Applications (2023). https://doi.org/10.1007/s00138-022-01357-z
22. Vaswani, A., et al.: Attention is all you need (2017). https://arxiv.org/abs/1706.03762

23. Veličković, P., Cucurull, G., Casanova, A., Romero, A., Liò, P., Bengio, Y.: Graph attention networks (2017). https://arxiv.org/abs/1710.10903
24. Walker, J., Marino, K., Gupta, A., Hebert, M.: The pose knows: video forecasting by generating pose futures. In: Proceedings of the IEEE International Conference on Computer Vision (2017). https://arxiv.org/pdf/1705.00053
25. Wang, Z., et al.: TacticAI: an AI assistant for football tactics. Nat. Commun. **15**(1), 1–13 (2024)
26. Yeh, R.A., Schwing, A.G., Huang, J., Murphy, K.: Diverse generation for multi-agent sports games. IEEE/CVF (2019)
27. Zhao, L., et al.: T-GCN: a temporal graph convolutional network for traffic prediction. IEEE Transactions on Intelligent Transportation Systems-2019 (2018). https://arxiv.org/pdf/1811.05320

Through the Gaps: Uncovering Tactical Line-Breaking Passes with Clustering

Oktay Karakuş[1,2(✉)] (iD) and Hasan Arkadaş[2]

[1] School of Computer Science and Informatics, Cardiff University, Cardiff, UK
karakuso@cardiff.ac.uk
[2] Dead Ball Analytics Limited, Barry CF63 2QQ, UK
hasan@deadball-analytics.com

Abstract. Line-breaking passes (LBPs) are crucial tactical actions in football, allowing teams to penetrate defensive lines and access high-value spaces. In this study, we present an unsupervised, clustering-based framework for detecting and analysing LBPs using synchronised event and tracking data from elite matches. Our approach models opponent team shape through vertical spatial segmentation and identifies passes that disrupt defensive lines within open play. Beyond detection, we introduce several tactical metrics, including the space build-up ratio (SBR) and two chain-based variants, LBPCh^1 and LBPCh^2, which quantify the effectiveness of LBPs in generating immediate or sustained attacking threats. We evaluate these metrics across teams and players in the 2022 FIFA World Cup, revealing stylistic differences in vertical progression and structural disruption. The proposed methodology is explainable, scalable, and directly applicable to modern performance analysis and scouting workflows.

1 Introduction

Over the past decade, football analytics has been transformed by the rise of data science and the availability of high-resolution spatiotemporal data. This evolution has enabled analysts and researchers to move beyond basic statistics toward deeper tactical insights. Seminal contributions like Expected Goals (xG) [9,13,15,20] and pass valuation frameworks [5,6,12] have highlighted the importance of space, movement, and context in shaping match outcomes.

Within this landscape, line-breaking passes (LBPs) have emerged as a key tactical mechanism, enabling teams to penetrate opponent defensive or midfield lines and access advanced attacking zones. These passes often lead to goal-scoring opportunities by disrupting spatial structure and eliminating multiple defenders through mostly vertical play [12,25]. Despite their importance, identifying LBPs from raw data remains a nontrivial task. Definitions vary across commercial platforms and academic literature, often relying on proprietary labels or manual annotations [2,6,22]. Moreover, many existing methods lack interpretability and do not explicitly account for the opponent's team structure.

H. Rios-Neto et al. (Eds.): MLSA 2025, CCIS 2833, pp. 86–96, 2026.
https://doi.org/10.1007/978-3-032-15165-0_7

In this paper, we introduce an unsupervised, data-driven framework to detect and quantify LBPs using a clustering-based model of defensive structure. Leveraging synchronised event and tracking data from the 2022 FIFA World Cup, our method segments opponent team shape into vertical defensive bands and identifies passes that disrupt these formations. Unlike approaches reliant on predefined formations or proprietary labels, our model infers spatial disruption directly from positional configurations at the time of the pass.

Beyond detection, we propose novel tactical metrics to evaluate the quality and intent of LBPs, including the Space Build-up Ratio (SBR), LBPCh[1] (a single LBP leading to a shot), and LBPCh[2] (linked LBPs culminating in a goal attempt). These measures enable rich team and player profiling of verticality and offensive structure. Our framework is interpretable, reproducible, and scalable, making it suitable for both tactical analysis and scouting applications, and laying the groundwork for future learning-based extensions.

2   Related Work

In football analytics, a key distinction exists between *progressive passes*, which advance the ball significantly toward the opponent's goal (typically by 10–30 m [1]), and *line-breaking passes* (LBPs), which explicitly penetrate structured lines of opposing players [27]. While progressive passes capture directional intent, they do not account for defensive positioning. LBPs, by contrast, reflect a team's ability to disrupt shape and bypass opponents vertically. Their tactical value has been widely acknowledged across both academic and applied domains. Foundational work such as [12] introduced pass value frameworks based on ball movement and team contribution, while follow-up studies incorporated spatial awareness and defensive structure [4,24]. Michalczyk [17] further showed that LBPs double the likelihood of leading to a goal compared to other passes.

Identifying LBPs from data is challenging due to the need to model the opponent's shape. Some rule-based methods rely on tracking data to identify defensive lines and geometrically evaluate whether a pass intersects them [17]. StatsBomb's 360 approach [27] uses a combination of positional data and heuristics such as forward movement and relative position of defenders to classify LBPs. Recent efforts have focused specifically on identifying and characterising LBPs via learning-based methods, for example, Michalczyk [17] proposed geometric heuristics based on line intersection to classify passes, while [10] experimented with supervised learning models trained on annotated examples. Industry systems such as StatsBomb 360° [27] and Driblab's Arrigo [8] offer proprietary methods for detecting line-breaking actions using freeze-frame contextual data. However, these systems often rely on predefined formations or third-party annotations, limiting interpretability and reproducibility.

The accurate representation of a defensive organisation is central to identifying LBPs. Early approaches used spatiotemporal clustering to infer team formations [3]. More recent work captures dynamic shape: Narizuka and Yamazaki [19] applied hierarchical clustering to connectivity graphs built from Delaunay triangulations of player positions. Others model team compactness using geometric descriptors like convex hulls [16], or spatial dispersion measures such as interline distances. Zardiny and Bahramian [28] proposed a clustering framework that extracts possession-specific shape patterns based on spatial and geometric features.

Several metrics aim to quantify the impact of actions on team shape. The "packing" metric [14] remains a popular benchmark for assessing how many defenders are bypassed by a pass. Others have explored changes in convex hull size or shape symmetry to capture disruption. Possession-value models such as Expected Threat (xT) [21], Valuing Actions by Estimating Probabilities (VAEP) [7,26] or On-Ball Value (OBV) [23] implicitly reward LBPs by assigning higher value to passes entering dangerous zones.

Relation to Our Approach. While prior work has addressed LBP detection, team shape modelling, and structural metrics independently, our approach combines these strands in a unified, unsupervised framework by clustering opponent positions and detecting penetrations. We quantify vertical disruption directly from spatiotemporal data without supervision, and this interpretability allows for deeper tactical insights into player-team level vertical progression.

3   Datasets

We use the publicly available 2022 FIFA World Cup dataset released by PFF FC[1], which provides synchronised event and tracking data for all 64 matches. This enables detailed spatiotemporal analysis of player behaviour, team structure, and ball progression. Each match includes structured JSON files containing: *event data* (timestamped on-ball actions with spatial and contextual tags), *tracking data* (29.97 Hz player and ball positions), *metadata* (pitch dimensions, orientation, frame rate), and *roster data* (linking jersey numbers to player IDs and roles). We use smoothed tracking positions to reduce jitter. For example, the Senegal vs Netherlands match contains 1,800+ events and 160,000 tracking frames. This rich context forms the foundation for our unsupervised line-breaking pass detection framework.

4   Methodology

Our methodology aims to detect and quantify LBPs using a clustering-based model of opponent team structure. We also introduce tactical metrics such as SBR and LBP chains to evaluate their spatial and strategic impact.

4.1   Line-Breaking Pass Detection via Clustering

We model the opponent team shape using vertical segmentation. At the time of each pass, opponent player positions are grouped into k clusters based on their x-axis coordinates using agglomerative clustering [18]. This approach groups players into vertical bands approximating tactical lines (e.g., a back four or midfield

---

[1] https://www.blog.fc.pff.com/blog/pff-fc-release-2022-world-cup-data.

block). In order to represent the opponent team structure, we apply dynamic vertical clustering at the moment each pass is made. Rather than fixing the number of clusters k a priori, our method adapts to the spatial configuration of the defending team, allowing for tactical fluidity. A minimum of two players is required to form a cluster, ensuring that each group meaningfully reflects collective defensive organisation. This dynamic clustering approach accommodates a wide range of formations and pressing schemes, from compact mid-blocks to expansive high lines, enabling more accurate detection of passes that dissect these structures. As a result, each pass is evaluated against a context-aware segmentation of the defensive line, rather than rigid tactical templates.

Let a pass p_i occur at time t_i, with passer position $s_i = (x_s, y_s)$ and receiver position $r_i = (x_r, y_r)$ where axes x and y refer to the axes along the sideline and along the goal line, respectively. Let $\{C_j\}_{j=1}^{k}$ denote the set of vertical opponent clusters at t_i, where each cluster C_j is represented by a vertical segment defined by a horizontal centroid x_j, and a vertical span $[y_{\min}^{(j)}, y_{\max}^{(j)}]$, based on the minimum and maximum y-coordinates of players in C_j. We define a pass as line-breaking under the clustering model if it crosses the x-centroid of any cluster and intersects the vertical segment defined by that cluster's lateral span. Formally:

$$\text{LBP}_{\text{cluster}}(p_i) = \mathbb{I}\left(\exists C_j : x_j \in (x_s, x_r) \land \text{SegmentIntersects}(p_i, C_j)\right) \qquad (1)$$

where $\text{SegmentIntersects}(p_i, C_j)$ is true if the path from s_i to r_i intersects the vertical segment at $x = x_j$, bounded by $[y_{\min}^{(j)}, y_{\max}^{(j)}]$. In addition to structural intersection, we apply two supporting filters: (1) the pass must bypass at least two opponents, based on their lateral proximity to the pass vector, and (2) the pass must be forward, relative to team orientation.

(LBP Volume) The total number of LBPs per team or player serves as a baseline measure of verticality and structural aggression. Frequent LBPs suggest proactive build-up play, tactical sharpness, or positional superiority. At the player level, they highlight individuals who consistently attempt to break lines, often midfielders or wide players inverting centrally.

(Direct Vertical Threat, LBPCh^1) To measure the immediate impact of LBPs, we define *LBPCh*^{1} as the subset of LBPs that directly lead to a shot or an assist within the same possession. These actions indicate a direct vertical threat, with little delay or buildup between structural disruption and goal creating chances. High LBPCh^1 values reflect players/teams capable of fast, incisive play after breaking lines.

(Sustained Vertical Progression, LBPCh^2) In contrast to immediate threat, *LBPCh*^{2} measures sustained tactical progression, and identifies cases where one LBP is immediately followed by another within the same team possession. This sequence then concludes with a shot/assist. It captures structurally coherent attacks that maintain vertical momentum across multiple passes, often revealing more collective and layered approaches to play.

4.2 Space Build-Up Ratio (SBR)

To complement structural disruption, we define the *SBR* as a spatial metric that quantifies whether a pass moves the ball into a less congested area. Let $A_p = \pi d_p^2$ and $A_r = \pi d_r^2$ be circular estimates of space around the passer and receiver based on the distance to their nearest opponent. Hence, SBR is:

$$\mathrm{SBR}(p_i) = \frac{A_r - A_p}{A_p} = \frac{d_r^2}{d_p^2} - 1. \tag{2}$$

A positive SBR indicates that the receiver is under less pressure than the passer, interpreted as *space opened up*. A negative value reflects an increase in defensive pressure. This metric is used to compare the spatial gain of different LBPs and can be related to downstream outcomes such as assists or shots. Figure 1 illustrates a detected LBP with an annotated SBR. Opponent players form three visually structured defensive layers, suggesting a 3-4-3 formation. The pass breaks both the forward and midfield vertical lines, reaching a receiver (green star) positioned in a higher-space region, with an SBR of 16.52. Semi-transparent circles represent the local area around each player.

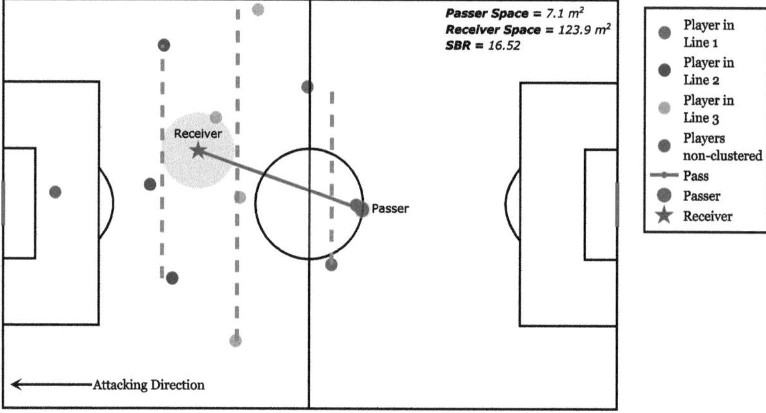

Fig. 1. Illustration of an LBP and an SBR.

5 Experimental Evaluation

We begin our analysis by examining which teams and players most frequently attempt to break opponent structures through LBPs. Unlike simple pass counts, LBP volume highlights how often a team or player chooses to disrupt vertical opponent lines, a critical marker of tactical intent and progressive play. Across all 64 matches and 21,349 passes in the dataset, the proposed model identified 7,477 LBPs, averaging around 117 per match. Figure 2 presents teams and players ranked by total number of LBPs over the tournament.

From a team perspective, a high volume of LBPs reflects a deliberate tactical commitment to progressing through structured defensive lines rather than bypassing them via wide areas. Possession-oriented sides such as Croatia, Argentina, France, and Spain dominate the rankings, with Serbia also notable for frequent line-breaking despite a lower overall volume. These teams consistently seek central occupation and third-man combinations, principles aligned with modern positional play. Notably, three of the four semi-finalists rank among the top teams in total LBP count, underscoring the strategic value of vertical penetration in elite tournament success.

At the player level, midfielders and fullbacks emerge as primary line-breakers often responsible for initiating build-up, operating between lines, and delivering progression into advanced zones. Standout contributors such as Gvardiol, Rodri, and Otamendi exemplify these roles, functioning as deep facilitators who not only disrupt opposition shape but also help maintain compact defensive structure during transitions. Their involvement in LBPs highlights the blend of technical precision and tactical intelligence required to consistently play through pressure.

5.1 Spatial Impact: The Role of SBR

To assess the spatial effectiveness of LBPs, we plot cumulative SBR against the percentage of LBPs yielding positive SBR values, focusing on the top 50 players by LBP count. In Fig. 3, bubble size indicates average pass distance, while colour denotes pass verticality. This visualisation reveals distinct tactical profiles: players like Tchouaméni and Gvardiol, in the upper/mid right region, consistently generate space and accumulate high total gains. In contrast, Amrabat shows a high success rate but modest cumulative values despite topping the verticality scale, reflecting shorter controlled disruptions.

The framework also exposes cases where volume alone is misleading. Despite his high LBP count shown in Fig. 2, Andersen registers low cumulative SBR and few space-generating passes, showing that frequent LBPs does not guarantee tactical value. In general, SBR offers a more nuanced and unsupervised measure of progression. Unlike pass distance, which can misrepresent impact, SBR captures the receiver's spatial advantage, helping distinguish between merely long passes and truly effective ones. It is important to note that all top 50 players in this analysis exhibit verticality values above 0.6, underscoring the strong association between LBPs and vertical tactical build-up.

5.2 From Break to Threat: Direct Line-Break to Chance (LBPCh^1)

While LBPs inherently reflect verticality and structural disruption, not all such passes culminate in tangible offensive rewards. To assess the immediate impact of LBP, we define LBPCh^1 as the subset of LBP that directly precedes a shot/assist within the same possession phase.

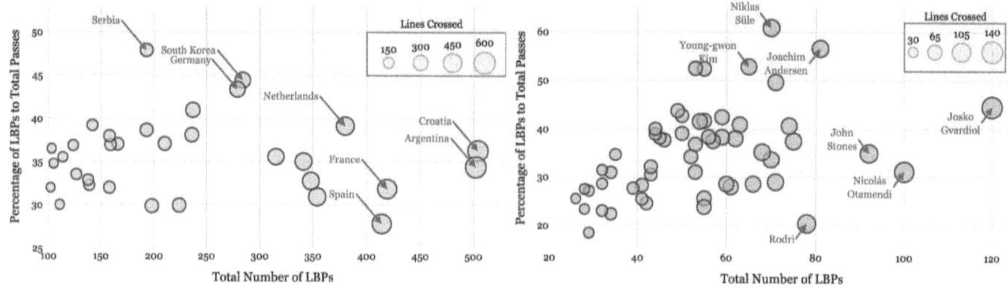

Fig. 2. Most frequent line-breakers as detected by our clustering-based model. **Left**: Team-level; **Right**: Player-level. Each bubble represents an entity about LBPs where the *bubble size* reflects the total number of defensive lines broken.

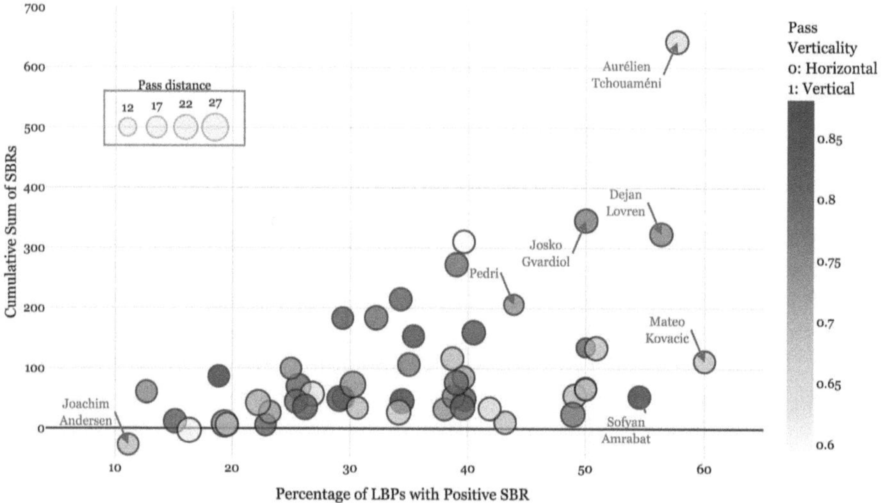

Fig. 3. Space progression effectiveness of the top 50 players. The x-axis shows the percentage of LBPs with positive SBR, whilst the y-axis represents the cumulative SBR. Bubble size indicates average pass distance, and colour encodes pass verticality.

Figure 4 presents team/player-level summaries of LBPCh[1] instances. At the team level (Fig. 4b), traditional possession-heavy sides such as Spain, France, Croatia and Portugal lead the total LBPCh[1] events, combining high structural disruption with immediate offensive conversion. Interestingly, Morocco and South Korea also appear in the top ranks, highlighting their efficient use of direct vertical sequences, often built through transitional attacks rather than prolonged build-up. From a player perspective (Fig. 4a), Theo Hernández stands out as the only player in the dataset with four LBPCh[1] events. His performance underlines the value of progressive fullbacks in modern systems, able to carry or pass through pressure and deliver directly threatening balls into the final third. A cluster of players, including Pedri, Amrabat, and Fred, follow closely with two instances each. These midfielders are known for their positional awareness and capacity to operate between lines, often acting as the link between phases of possession and final-third penetrations.

The plots incorporate both cumulative SBR and pass verticality to provide deeper tactical context. Higher cumulative SBR values suggest that not only were these passes progressive, but they also opened up significant space for receivers. For example, Jordi Alba and Juranovic deliver $LBPCh^1$ passes with relatively lower verticality but high SBR, indicating subtle through balls into expanding pockets rather than long direct deliveries. In contrast, Amrabat, Pedri and Kovacic exhibit high verticality with shorter build-ups, likely reflecting more abrupt, transitional progressions from deeper areas.

5.3 Sustained Threat: LBP Chains Leading to Chances ($LBPCh^2$)

While $LBPCh^1$ reflect individual tactical sharpness or isolated exploitation of space, longer chains of connected LBPs culminating in shots offer deeper insight into coordinated vertical build-up. To evaluate this sustained threat, we introduce $LBPCh^2$, defined as two consecutive LBPs within the same possession phase that result in a shot, goal, or assist.

Figure 5 summarises the 13 such sequences detected in the entire tournament. These multi-pass sequences, though rare, signal the capacity to construct coherent progression through compact opponent formations. From a team-level perspective, Argentina emerges as a notable case. Despite two of their three $LBPCh^2$ sequences being ruled offside by VAR, they reveal clear tactical coordination. In both cases, Papu Gómez acted as the connector, receiving the first LBP and immediately delivering a second. This repetition not only indicates structured build-up but also points to Argentina's midfield balance, where wide creators like Gómez operate between lines. France, Germany, and Spain also feature, demonstrating that top sides are capable of stringing vertical actions in phases. Only one chain in the data set resulted in a goal: the Morocco sequence involving Aguerd-Hakimi-En-Nesyri, which illustrates how $LBPCh^2$ can serve as a direct scoring route even for defensively focused teams.

On the player level, the figure highlights key roles within the chain: *Initiators* like Enzo Fernández, Josip Juranović, and Adrien Rabiot consistently make the first vertical incision. *Connectors* such as Cheikhou Kouyaté and Achraf Hakimi provide continuity, either through turns or quick layoffs. *Finishers* include elite attackers like Ousmane Dembele, Lionel Messi and Kylian Mbappé. Interestingly, xG values across these sequences remain mostly below 0.10. This supports the notion that $LBPCh^2$ sequences often occur under spatial pressure, requiring multiple actions to unlock central zones. High cumulative SBRs and verticality are common, reflecting the nature of these chain-progressions as strategic rather than opportunistic.

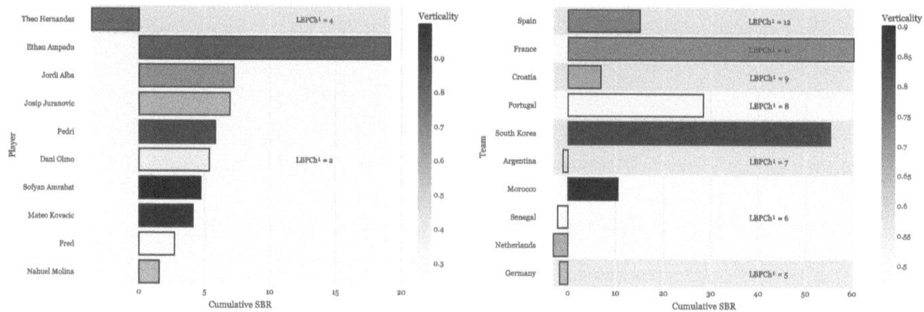

Fig. 4. Direct Line-Breaks to Chances (LBPCh[1]). Team (Left) and Player (Right) Level. Bars (i) represent the cumulative SBR for LBPs that directly led to a shot, (ii) are coloured by average pass verticality, and (iii) are ordered by total LBPCh[1].

Team	Opponent		Stage	Initiator	Connector	Final Destination	Outcome	xG	Cum. SBR
Senegal	Netherlands		Group	Idrissa Gueye	Cheikhou Kouyaté	Ismaïla Sarr	Shot	0.04	-0.32
Senegal	Netherlands		Group	Cheikhou Kouyaté	Nampalys Mendy	Krépin Diatta	Shot	0.02	-0.80
Argentina	Saudi Arabia		Group	Nicolás Otamendi	Papu Gómez	Lionel Messi	Disallowed goal	0.00	-1.51
Argentina	Saudi Arabia		Group	Nahuel Molina	Papu Gómez	Lautaro Martinez	Disallowed goal	0.00	-0.56
South Korea	Uruguay		Group	Moon-hwan Kim	Kang-in Lee	Gue-sung Cho	Shot	0.03	-1.22
France	Denmark		Group	Adrien Rabiot	Kylian Mbappé	Ousmane Dembele	Shot	0.03	29.46
Australia	Denmark		Group	Aziz Behich	Jackson Irvine	Mitchell Duke	Shot	0.03	10.15
Argentina	Poland		Group	Enzo Fernandez	Lionel Messi	Marcos Acuña	Shot	0.04	-0.97
Morocco	Canada		Group	Nayef Aguerd	Achraf Hakimi	Youssef En-Nesyri	Goal	0.28	8.97
Germany	Costa Rica		Group	Antonio Rüdiger	Joshua Kimmich	Jamal Musiala	Shot	0.04	-1.14
Spain	Morocco		R16	Aymeric Laporte	Jordi Alba	Marco Asensio	Shot	0.23	0.28
Croatia	Brazil		QF	Josip Juranovic	Marcelo Brozovic	Andrej Kramaric	Shot	0.03	-0.20
France	Morocco		SF	Raphael Varane	Antoine Griezmann	Kylian Mbappé	Shot	0.08	3.48

Fig. 5. Summary of all detected LBPCh[2] sequences. Each row represents an LBPCh[2]. The table includes the initiating, connecting, and finishing players, match details, final outcomes (with xG) and chain cumulative SBR values.

6   Conclusion

In this study, we introduced an unsupervised, clustering-based framework to detect and analyse line-breaking passes (LBPs) using synchronised event and tracking data. By modelling defensive structure through dynamically segmented vertical clusters, our method evaluated each pass in terms of structural disruption and spatial progression. To capture the impact of these passes more effectively, we proposed the Space Buildup Ratio (SBR) as a novel metric to distinguish between merely vertical and genuinely progressive passes.

Applied to all 64 matches of the 2022 FIFA World Cup, our framework uncovered meaningful tactical signals. LBPs were frequently associated with teams advancing deep into the tournament, while fullbacks and deep midfielders emerged as pivotal contributors. Through SBR, we revealed significant player-level variation in spatial impact–insights not evident from LBP volume alone.

To further link structural disruption to attacking threat, we introduced two derived metrics: LBPCh[1], which captures direct chances following a single LBP, and LBPCh[2], which reflects sustained build-up through chained LBPs. These metrics offer interpretable tools for scouting, performance evaluation, and tactical profiling.

While advanced valuation models like xT [21], VAEP [7], and EPV [11] have reshaped how we quantify on-ball actions, our LBPCh metrics are not intended to rival these systems. Instead, they provide tactical context specific to line-breaking intent, capturing whether an attacking sequence originates from actions that penetrate defensive structures. These perspectives are complementary: x-value models operate agnostically to how value is generated, whereas LBPCh shines a light on why certain progressions matter structurally.

Looking ahead, future work may integrate LBPCh-style metrics with outcome-driven models to bridge structure with value. We also aim to extend our clustering-based framework as either a pretext task or an interpretable module within learning-based pipelines. To support ongoing research and transparency in football analytics, we will release code and curated metrics via the GitHub page (https://github.com/CoDIS-Lab/Breaklines) following the conference presentation.

References

1. Progressive pass. https://dataglossary.wyscout.com/progressive_pass/ (2021). Accessed 30 May 2025
2. Andrienko, G., et al.: Visual analysis of pressure in football. Data Min. Knowl. Disc. **31**(6), 1793–1839 (2017). https://doi.org/10.1007/s10618-017-0513-2
3. Bialkowski, A., Lucey, P., Carr, P., Yue, Y., Sridharan, S., Matthews, I.: Large-scale analysis of soccer matches using spatiotemporal tracking data. In: Proceedings of the 2014 IEEE International Conference on Data Mining, pp. 725–730. IEEE (2014)
4. Bransen, L.: Valuing passes in football using ball event data. Master Thesis, Erasmus University Rotterdam (2017). https://thesis.eur.nl/pub/41346/Bransen.pdf
5. Bransen, L., Van Haaren, J., van de Velden, M.: Measuring soccer players' contributions to chance creation by valuing their passes. J. Quant. Anal. Sports **15**(2), 97–116 (2019)
6. Decroos, T., Bransen, L., Van Haaren, J., Davis, J.: Actions speak louder than goals: valuing player actions in soccer. In: KDD (2019)
7. Decroos, T., Bransen, L., Van Haaren, J., Davis, J.: VAEP: an objective approach to valuing on-the-ball actions in soccer. In: Proceedings of the Twenty-Ninth International Conference on International Joint Conferences on Artificial Intelligence, pp. 4696–4700 (2021)
8. DribLab: Arrigo: line-breaking actions and ball into space. https://www.driblab.com/blog/arrigo-line-breaking-actions-and-ball-into-space (2025). Accessed30 May 2025
9. Eggels, H., Van Elk, R., Pechenizkiy, M.: Explaining soccer match outcomes with goal scoring opportunities predictive analytics. In: 3rd Workshop on Machine Learning and Data Mining for Sports Analytics (MLSA 2016). CEUR-WS. org (2016)

10. El Kadi, T.: Machine learning models for detecting line-breaking passes in football matches. https://www.cs.vu.nl/~wanf/theses/el_kadi-bscthesis.pdf (2024). Accessed30 May 2025
11. Fernández, J., Bornn, L., Cervone, D.: A framework for the fine-grained evaluation of the instantaneous expected value of soccer possessions. Mach. Learn. **110**(6), 1389–1427 (2021). https://doi.org/10.1007/s10994-021-05989-6
12. Gyarmati, L., Kwak, H., Rodriguez, P.: QPASS: a merit-based evaluation of soccer passes. In: KDD Workshop on Large-Scale Sports Analytics (2014)
13. Hewitt, J.H., Karakuş, O.: A machine learning approach for player and position adjusted expected goals in football (soccer). Franklin Open **4**, 100034 (2023)
14. Ireland, J.: What the heck are packing points in soccer? Only the best statistic ever. https://expandyourgame.com/using-packing-points-soccer-game-statistic/ (2021). Accessed30 May 2025
15. Lucey, P., Bialkowski, A., Monfort, M., Carr, P., Matthews, I.: Quality vs Quantity: Improved shot prediction in soccer using strategic features from spatiotemporal data (2015)
16. Memmert, D., Lemmink, K., Sampaio, J.: Current approaches to tactical performance analyses in soccer using position data. Sports Med. **47**(1), 1–10 (2017)
17. Michalczyk, K.: How impactful are line-breaking passes? https://www.statsperform.com/resource/how-impactful-are-line-breaking-passes/ (2020). Accessed 30 May 2025
18. Müllner, D.: Modern hierarchical, agglomerative clustering algorithms. arXiv preprint arXiv:1109.2378 (2011)
19. Narizuka, T., Yamazaki, Y.: Clustering algorithm for formations in football games. Sci. Rep. **9**(1), 13172 (2019)
20. Scholtes, A., Karakuş, O.: Bayes-xG: player and position correction on expected goals (xG) using Bayesian hierarchical approach. Front. Sports Active Living **6**, 1348983 (2024)
21. Singh, K.: Introducing expected threat (XT). https://karun.in/blog/expected-threat.html (2018). Accessed July 2023
22. Stats perform: generative AI powered football insights: at scale. https://www.statsperform.com/opta-vision/ (2023). Accessed30 May 2025
23. StatsBomb: OBV: On-Ball Value model documentation. https://statsbomb.com/articles/soccer/statsbomb-obv-model/ (2023). Accessed30 May 2025
24. Szczepański, L., McHale, I.: Beyond completion rate: evaluating the passing ability of footballers. J. R. Stat. Soc. A. Stat. Soc. **179**(2), 513–533 (2016)
25. Tayyab: Space creation – using tracking data to quantify line breaking passes & space creation. Medium blog post (2024). https://half-space.medium.com/space-creation-4e928f989f84
26. Van Roy, M., Robberechts, P., Decroos, T., Davis, J.: Valuing on-the-ball actions in soccer: a critical comparison of XT and VAEP. In: Proceedings of the AAAI-20 Workshop on Artificial Intelligence in Team Sports. AI in Team Sports Organising Committee (2020)
27. Yorke, J.: Statsbomb 360: exploring line-breaking passes. https://statsbomb.com/articles/soccer/statsbomb-360-exploring-line-breaking-passes/ (2022). Accessed 30 May 2025
28. Zare Zardiny, A., Bahramian, Z.: A two-stage spatio-geometrical clustering of football team shape for post-match review. Acad. J. Clin. Res. Rep. **1**(1), 1–14 (2025)

Pitch-Wide Space Evaluation for Soccer Transitions

Yohei Ogawa[1], Rikuhei Umemoto[1], and Keisuke Fujii[1,2]($\boxtimes$) (iD)

[1] Graduate School of Informatics, Nagoya University, Nagoya, Japan
`fujii@i.nagoya-u.ac.jp`
[2] Center for Advanced Intelligence Project, RIKEN, Osaka, Japan

Abstract. Soccer is a sport played on a pitch where effective use of space is crucial. Decision-making during transitions, when possession switches between teams, has been increasingly important, but research on space evaluation in these moments has been limited. Recent space evaluation methods such as OBSO (Off-Ball Scoring Opportunity) use scoring probability, so it is not well-suited for assessing areas far from the goal, where transitions typically occur. In this paper, we propose OBPV (Off-Ball Positioning Value) to evaluate space across the pitch. OBPV extends OBSO by introducing the field value model, which evaluates the entire pitch, and by employing the transition kernel model, which reflects positional specificity through kernel density estimation of pass distributions. Experiments using La Liga 2023/24 season tracking and event data show that OBPV highlights effective space utilization during counter-attacks and reveals team-specific characteristics in how the teams utilize space after positive and negative transitions.

Keywords: soccer · space evaluation · mathematical model · transition

1 Introduction

Advances in soccer science and technology have sharpened player performance and raised the overall pace of play [29]. Transition phases, contested at especially high speed to regain or keep possession, are viewed as a prime expression of team style. Studies from the German Bundesliga and English Premier League indicate that transition quality strongly influences both attacking and defensive outcomes; better decision-making in these moments therefore increases the likelihood of winning [40, 72].

This study aims to identify the requirements for successful counter-attacks that arise during transitions and to characterize a transition-oriented team style. In coaching, knowing which factors enable effective counter-attacks is essential, while scouting benefits from understanding an opponent's transition profile. Earlier work has shown that transitions shape match outcomes [4, 54] and pinpointed key components of counter-attacking play [28]. Other studies have examined

H. Rios-Neto et al. (Eds.): MLSA 2025, CCIS 2833, pp. 97–119, 2026.
https://doi.org/10.1007/978-3-032-15165-0_8

shifts from attack to defence [2,5]. However, these investigations seldom considered pitch-wide spatial configurations (e.g., $105 \times 68\,\mathrm{m}$ in soccer), and transition analyses that emphasize space remain scarce (for details, see Appendix A).

Here, we present a pitch-wide space evaluation method. It can be adopted to various scenarios, including transitions. Early research visualized pitch control with Voronoi maps [65], followed by motion-based models for player movement [8,26]. OBSO (Off-Ball Scoring Opportunity) later provided a mathematical framework that assigns each location a likelihood of producing a goal on first touch [62,63]; the model has since been transferred to other sports [32,34]. However, OBSO's goal-oriented model design undervalues zones distant from the goal where direct scoring is unlikely (e.g., transition phase between teams would be challenging).

In this paper, we propose the OBPV (Off-Ball Positioning Value) model, which modify OBSO to evaluate the entire pitch. Using this model, we can evaluate spaces such as starting points of counter-attacks based on a mathematical model that is easy to interpret. In addition, it is possible to evaluate the space during transitions, which has not been focused on in previous research [34,62,63].

The contributions of this study are as follows. (1) The proposal of a mathematical model that evaluates space with the starting point of transitions and counter-attacks. (2) Among the modules in previous OBSO model [62], the field value model was used instead of the score model to enable pitch-wide evaluation in the attack process, and the transition kernel model was used instead of the transition model to reflect the positional specificity of the pitch by estimating the kernel density from the pass distribution in each area. (3) The experiment revealed the importance of effective use of space in counter-attacks and the transition characteristics of each team in the 2023/24 La Liga season.

2   Preliminary for Space Evaluation

We first outline the evaluation baseline called OBSO [62]. OBSO evaluates an off-ball player by considering the joint probability

$$P_{OBSO}(G|D) = \Sigma_{r \in R \times R} P(S_r \cap C_r \cap T_r | D) \tag{1}$$

$$= \Sigma_r P(S_r | C_r, T_r, D) P(C_r | T_r, D) P(T_r | D), \tag{2}$$

where G denotes a goal and D represents a single frame of game data such as player positions and velocities. The details in OBSO are given in Appendix B. $P(S_r)$ is the probability of scoring from an arbitrary point $r \in R \times R$ on the pitch, assuming the next on-ball event occurs there. $P(C_r)$ is the probability that the passing team will control a ball at point r. $P(T_r)$ is the probability that the next on-ball event occurs at point r. For simplicity, $P(S_r|D), P(T_r|D), P(C_r|D)$ are assumed to be independent if the parameter $\alpha = 0$ in the original work implementation [62]. Then, the joint probability can be decomposed into a series of conditional probabilities as follows:

$$P_{OBSO}(G|D) = \Sigma_{r \in R \times R} P(S_r | D) P(C_r | D) P(T_r | D). \tag{3}$$

$P(C_r|D)$ is the probability that the attacking team will control the ball at point r assuming the next on-ball event occurs there, which is called the potential pitch control field (PPCF). $P(T_r|D)$ is defined as a fixed two-dimensional Gaussian distribution with the current ball coordinates as the mean. $P(S_r|D)$ is simply calculated as a value that decreases with the distance from the goal. We used the grid data and computed $P(C_r|D)$ and $P(T_r|D)$ according to Appendix B.

The overview of the OBSO [62] is illustrated in Fig. 1 top. In OBSO, the scoring probability was calculated as the output $P(S_r|D)$ of the score model as a function of the distance from the goal. However, a limitation of this model is that it is designed to predict scoring opportunities, which results in generally low evaluations for positions far from the goal. To address this issue, we propose a new model in the next section.

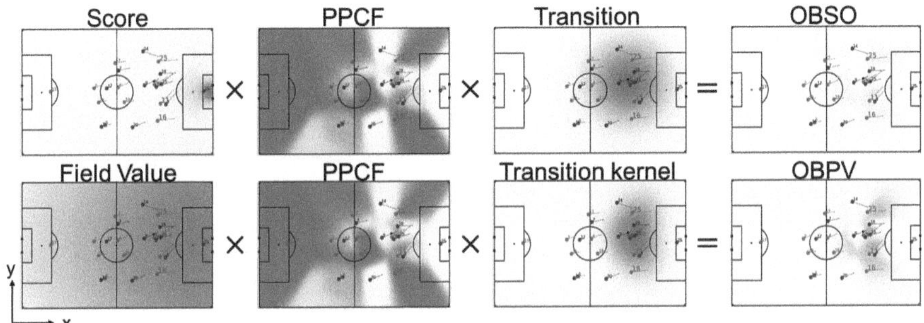

Fig. 1. Overview OBSO and OBPV. In this figure, attacking players are red, defensive players are blue, and the ball is black. The center of the field is set as the origin (0, 0). An attacking player, holding the ball near the center, initiates an attack from left to right along the x-axis. These models consist of three components. OBSO: the Score model, PPCF, and the Transition model. OBPV: the Field value model, PPCF, and the Transition kernel model. Notably, OBSO yields low evaluations in this pitch scenario, whereas OBPV provides a more comprehensive, pitch-wide assessment.

3   Proposed Method

In this section, we describe the proposed spatial evaluation model and the dataset used to construct it. Since OBSO is a score-prediction-based metric, locations farther from the goal generally receive lower evaluations (Fig. 1 top). To address this issue, we propose a pitch-wide space evaluation model called OBPV (Fig. 1 bottom). OBPV is composed of the field value model, which represents the importance of each location during the attacking phase; the PPCF, which is the same as that used in OBSO; and the transition kernel model, which estimates the next on-ball event location based on actual pass distributions using kernel density estimation. Through these modifications, OBPV enables spatial evaluation during attacking phases that is not limited to scoring opportunities.

In the OBPV, the model represents the likelihood that the attacking team can complete a pass to each point on the pitch, as well as how important that location is within the context of the attack. Unlike OBSO, OBPV uses the importance of each location on the pitch as a weighted factor expressed by the following equation for a point r:

$$OBPV_r = w_{field} \times P(C_r|D)P(TK_r|D),\tag{4}$$

where w_{field} is represented by the field value model and $P(TK_r|D)$ is represented by the transition kernel model. By modeling more realistic pass destinations, the framework effectively suppresses the evaluation of players positioned behind the ball, leading to more contextually appropriate assessments.

3.1 Dataset

Here we describe the dataset used for constructing the transition kernel model in Sect. 3.3. We used event data provided by Statsbomb and tracking data provided by SkillCorner in Spain's top-tier division, La Liga, from the 2023/24 season. The event data records information on individual events such as passes and shots. It includes details such as the location of the player performing the event, the body part used to touch the ball, and information about the receiving player for passes. The tracking data captures the positions of all players and the ball on a frame-by-frame basis, with a frame rate of 10 fps. Both datasets include inherent uncertainty in the player and ball positions. Additionally, there are temporal discrepancies between the two datasets, which were resolved using a rule-based synchronization algorithm [70] that utilizes player and ball positions. Events for which synchronization failed were excluded from the evaluation in Sect. 4, under the assumption that either the player or ball positions were sometimes unreliable in one of the datasets (10% excluded).

3.2 Field Value Model

In the previous score model [62], locations closer to the goal are given relatively high evaluations, while areas farther from the goal are generally rated lower. As a result, it becomes unsuitable for evaluating space in situations where scoring is not the primary focus. To address this issue, we propose the field value model in our OBPV (Off-Ball Positioning Value) framework as a replacement for the Score model. The field value model considers the weight across the entire pitch, enabling spatial evaluation without solely focusing on scoring opportunities. The following parameters were set based on the pitch geometry of the FIFA standard.

We represent spatial importance at position (x, y) by

$$w_{field}(x, y) = \exp\left(-\frac{y^2}{2\sigma(x)^2}\right) \times weight(x),\tag{5}$$

We utilized this Field Valuation approach to enable the evaluation of areas that are typically difficult to assess with the Score model, such as the regions adjacent to the penalty area, thereby recognizing their importance. The details

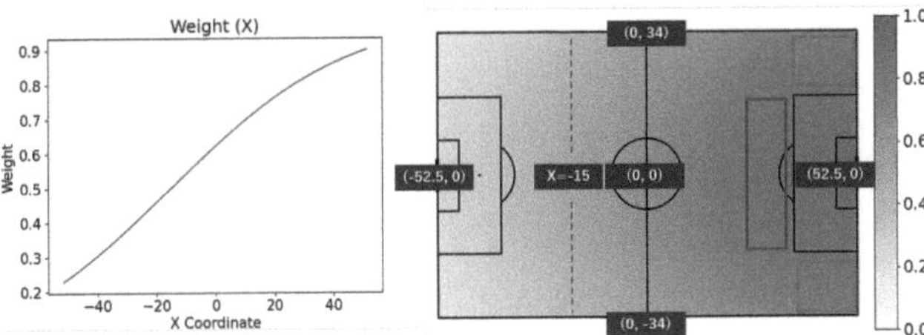

Fig. 2. Sigmoid function and field value model. (Left) The sigmoid function is applied along the X-axis of the pitch. (Right) Field value model when attacking from left to right. Darker red indicates higher importance, while areas closer to white represent lower importance. The weight decreases as the position moves away from the goal along the length of the pitch, and also as it moves toward the sidelines. The area adjacent to the penalty box, marked in green, and the vital area, marked in blue, are assigned higher values.

are also given in Appendix C and the coordinates and visualization are given in Fig. 2. In short, the longitudinal component $weight(x) = \left(1 + \exp(-(x + 15)/30)\right)^{-1}$ is a sigmoid with the midpoint $(weight = 0.5)$ at $x = -15$ m. This shape mirrors the gradual increase in attacking importance while preserving high values in the final third.

Lateral decay is modeled by a Gaussian whose spread narrows as play moves away from the goal: $\sigma(x) = 34 \times (1 + weight(x))$. Near the penalty area, the large $\sigma(x)$ keeps flanks almost as valuable as central lanes, whereas in deeper zones, the reduced $\sigma(x)$ concentrates value around the center. Consequently, the field value model highlights the corridors beside the penalty box and the "vital" central zone, providing an interpretable, pitch-wide baseline for transition analysis.

The differences between OBSO and OBPV, which arise from the use of the field value model, are illustrated in Fig. 1 (more precisely, see Appendix Fig. 6 using the same transition models). In OBSO, which uses the Score model, the overall evaluation tends to be low. In contrast, OBPV, which incorporates the field value model, evaluates a wider variety of spaces. While it may be difficult to attempt a direct shot from the evaluated spaces, areas around player #25 and #16 in red suggest potential opportunities for crosses, and the space in front of player #11 offers multiple effective options for the next play. These observations indicate that OBPV is capable of appropriately evaluating space during the attacking phase.

3.3   Transition Kernel Model

Here we describe the transition kernel model, one of the components of OBPV. The tendency of pass destinations varies depending on the location on the pitch. For example, passes from wide areas are more likely to be directed inward. Therefore, in this study, the transition kernel model was constructed using Kernel Density Estimation (KDE) based on actual pass distributions.

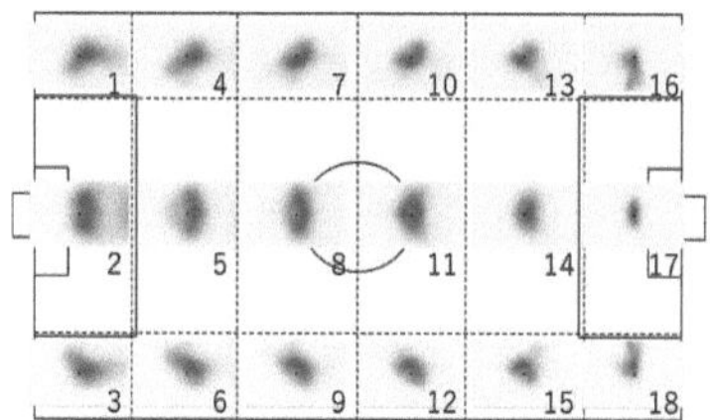

Area number	Number of passes	Area number	Number of passes
1, 3	11415	2	52662
4, 6	35417	5	55000
7, 9	55446	8	77886
10, 12	57379	11	62392
13, 15	41454	14	28158
16, 18	20400	17	6462

Fig. 3. The distribution of transition model and the number of passes used for kernel density estimation. (Left) The distribution of the transition kernel model is shown in each area. The direction of attack is to the right. (Right) The number of passes used for kernel density estimation is displayed. The dataset includes mirrored data, so the number of passes used is twice the number of passes made [22]. In Area 17, the number is lower because players tend to opt for shooting rather than passing.

KDE is one of the non-parametric methods for estimating probability density functions. In KDE, it is assumed that input variable $x_1, x_2, ..., x_n$ are independent and identically distributed, and the approximation of the probability density function is given by:

$$\hat{f}_h(x) = \frac{1}{nh} \sum_{i=1}^{n} K\left(\frac{x - x_i}{h}\right), \tag{6}$$

where h represents the bandwidth, and K represents the kernel function. Although various functions can be used as kernel functions, we used Gaussian distribution according to the previous work [62]. A prior study [8] estimated a soccer player model by KDE, considering the player's speed and direction. This study demonstrated that the coverage area differs for each player position, which means that the assumption of fixed transition model of OBSO method [62] has a problem in particular on a whole pitch.

In our transition kernel model, we estimate the distribution of passes. Due to the variability in the dataset, considering ball speed and direction was deemed inappropriate and we did not use them. We used the start and end positions of passes as the input variable. Previous study [8] fixed the kernel bandwidth h to 0.7, thus smoothing could not adapt to sample dispersion or sample size. Here we employ Silverman's data-driven method [59], which selects the bandwidth by minimizing the asymptotic mean integrated squared error (AMISE). Assuming a Gaussian kernel and approximating the true density by a Gaussian, analytic minimization of the AMISE gives:

$$h_{Silverman} = \left(\frac{3}{4}n\right)^{-\frac{1}{5}} \times \sqrt{\hat{\sigma}} \times 2, \tag{7}$$

where $\hat{\sigma}$ denotes the unbiased variance of the data, and n is the number of data points. Thus $h_{Silverman}$ becomes narrower as n increases and wider as the data variance grows, reducing the risk of under- or over-smoothing relative to a fixed bandwidth. The spatial distribution of pass start-end points contains sparse regions interspersed with dense clusters; our aim is to reveal overall trends rather than fine local peaks. In addition, we adopt a smoother estimate by doubling Silverman's bandwidth after the visual evaluations. Finally, we obtain the transition kernel model $P(TK_r) = \hat{f}_{h_{Silverman}}(x)$.

In this study, due to the data limitation, instead of modeling distributions for each player, we considered the distribution for each area of the pitch. The pitch division used in this study is shown in Fig. 3 left. This pitch division method has been adopted in several studies [6, 47]. It is a simple division approach and is advantageous due to its clear delineation of the vital area. The number of passes used is shown in Fig. 3 right.

The estimated transition distributions for each area are shown in Fig. 3 left. This model successfully captures the distinctive characteristics of each area. In side areas, the distributions exhibit higher values toward the center, allowing for a more natural evaluation of player positioning. Additionally, values for backward transition are generally suppressed, resulting in relatively higher evaluations for forward spaces across the pitch. The example difference between the use of the transition kernel and previous transition models (Gaussian distributions independent from areas) [62] is illustrated in Appendix Fig. 7.

4   Experiments

Here we validate the effectiveness of our OBPV model via the experiments. The dataset we used is the same as the one described in Sect. 3.1. This section first examines whether OBPV discriminates between successful and failed counter-attacks, then characterizes La Liga teams' transition profiles, and finally discusses how OBPV differs from the conventional OBSO metric. In Sect. 4.1 and 4.2, OBPV was calculated for three events from the starting point based on the previous research [32].

4.1   Can OBPV Discriminate Successful Counter-Attacks at Starting Point?

First, we describe the results of the space evaluation focusing on the starting point of counter-attacks by discriminating successful and failed counter-attacks. In this study, counter-attacks that ended with a shot were defined as successful, while those that did not were defined as failed, and their use of space was compared accordingly. We used events labeled "From Counter" in the play pattern data provided by Statsbomb. Among these, only sequences in which the same team maintained possession for three consecutive events were included in the analysis. According to the definition of From Counter, three conditions must be met: (1) The possession started with an open play turnover outside the counter-attacking team's final third. (2) The possession was at least 75% direct towards the goal. (3) The counterattack travelled at least 18 yd towards the goal. We computed OBPV over the three events in each counter-attack and used the maximum OBPV within each sequence for comparison. Among the evaluated counter-attacks, 191 were classified as successful and 164 as failed.

The mean values for successful and failed counter-attacks were 0.478 and 0.426, respectively. Since normality of the two distributions was not confirmed in the results shown in Appendix Fig. 8, we used the Mann-Whitney U test, a non-parametric test for the comparison of the medians between two independent groups. The test yielded $p = 2.44 \times 10^{-6}$, confirming that successful counter-attacks had significantly higher OBPV than failed counter-attacks. The effect size was $d = 0.243$, indicating a small to moderate effect. These findings suggest that effective space utilization might be a contributing factor to the success of counter-attacks. The previous OBSO [62] takes near zero values at the starting point of counter-attacks as shown later in Sect. 4.3, thus the comparison between successful and failed counter-attacks would be difficult.

4.2   La Liga Team Transition Characteristics Using OBPV

Next, we show the results of the space evaluation, focusing on the starting point of transition events to explain the La Liga teams. The frequencies of transition events are higher than counter-attacks. Firstly, we describe the results of OBPV calculations at the starting point of positive transitions, which refer to transitions from defense to attack. Secondly, we describe those of negative transitions (from attack to defense). This study identified transition events as sequences in which possession changed between the two teams for three consecutive events. Set pieces such as throw-ins, goal kicks, free kicks, and kick-offs after goals were excluded from the analysis. The average numbers of positive and negative transitions with their standard deviations for all teams are 595.85 ± 75.70 and 595.85 ± 50.25, respectively.

OBPV at the Starting Point of Positive Transitions. In positive transitions, we focused on transitions occurring farther from the opponent's goal, as these are considered more indicative of each team's tendencies. Therefore, transitions that occurred within 35 m of the team's own goal were selected for evaluation. Based on the results presented in this study, the space evaluation captures how each team plays after regaining possession in deep areas. Moreover, since transitions in deeper areas are more likely to create wide open space ahead, this range is considered suitable for space evaluation.

Fig. 4 Left presents a scatter plot where the vertical axis represents the increase in OBPV from the first to the third event of a transition, and the horizontal axis shows the average number of passes per sequence [1]. The teams with greater OBPV increases are considered to have adopted aggressive positioning in fewer events, indicating a tendency for quick and aggressive attacks. A moderate negative correlation was observed between the two variables, excluding Real Madrid and Barcelona, which show exceptional performances, with a Spearman's correlation coefficient of $r = -0.71$. This suggests that teams aiming for fast and aggressive attacks tend to lose possession more quickly. Despite having a higher

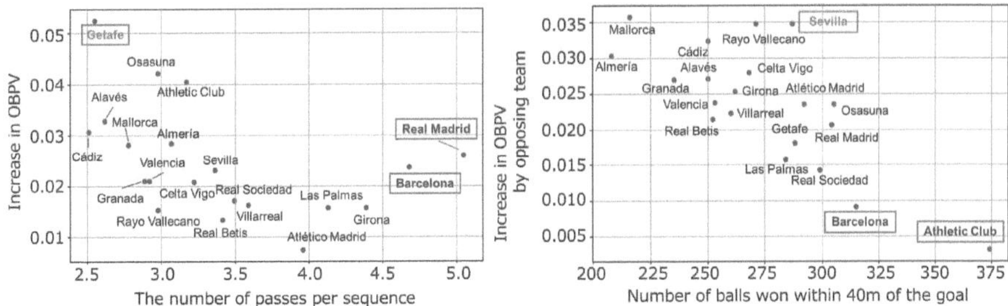

Fig. 4. The correlations of OBPV increase during positive and negative transitions and other statistics. (Left) The relationship between OBPV increase during positive transitions and the number of passes per sequence [1] is shown. (Right) The relationship between the increase in OBPV during negative transitions and the number of balls won within 40 m of the goal [1] is shown.

number of passes, Real Madrid and Barcelona showed relatively large increases in OBPV, indicating that they are strong teams capable of maintaining possession even in aggressive situations. This aligns with the final standings of the 2023/24 season, where Real Madrid ranked first and Barcelona second, showing exceptional performance, justifying their exclusion from this analysis. Furthermore, Getafe showed a notably higher increase in OBPV than other teams, confirming that they are a particularly aggressive side when launching attacks, even after regaining possession in deeper pitch areas.

OBPV at the Starting Point of Negative Transitions. In negative transitions, the behavior following ball loss in advanced areas was considered to capture team tendencies better. Therefore, transitions occurring within 35 m of the opponent's goal were selected for evaluation. Additionally, since losing possession in higher areas often creates large open spaces ahead from the opponent's perspective, this range is deemed suitable for conducting space evaluation.

Figure 4 Right shows a scatter plot with the vertical axis representing the increase in OBPV from the first to the third event of a transition, and the horizontal axis representing the number of balls won within 40 m of the goal [1]. Here, the OBPV reflects how much OBPV the opposing team generated against the target team. In this scatter plot, teams with a smaller increase in OBPV are considered to have executed a high-quality press that effectively prevented the opponent from exploiting space after losing the ball. A moderate negative correlation was confirmed between these variables, with a Spearman correlation coefficient of $r = -0.67$. This suggests that high-quality pressing that prevents space exploitation leads to more frequent balls won in advanced areas. Furthermore, both Barcelona and Athletic Club exhibited particularly low increases in OBPV, indicating that they performed excellent pressing among the 20 teams. Notably, Athletic Club also showed high OBPV increases on the left side of Fig. 4, suggesting they play an aggressive style of soccer both offensively and defensively. On the other hand, Sevilla had a relatively large increase in OBPV despite a moderate number of balls won. This may be attributed to individual performance, as Sevilla has a forward who recorded the highest number of successful tackles among forwards [17], suggesting that individual ability had a significant impact. The player won many balls despite the team was not able to shut down space effectively.

4.3   The Difference Between OBPV and OBSO

Finally, we compared the differences between OBPV and OBSO [62]. The scatter plot shown in Fig. 5 Left visualizes OBPV and OBSO values calculated for the events evaluated in Sect. 4.2. It was confirmed that the proposed OBPV enabled a broader range of evaluations for events with similar scores under OBSO. This was particularly evident in situations farther from the goal, which were previously given low evaluations, but where players potentially had a significant positive impact.

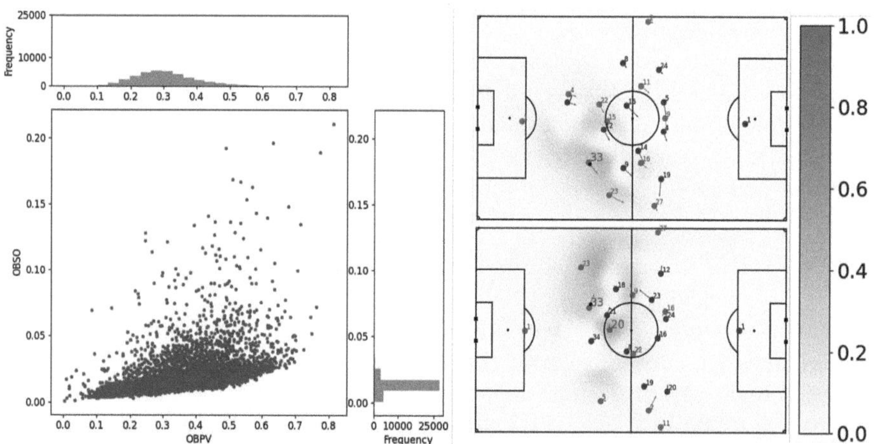

Fig. 5. The comparison of OBPV and OBSO, and two similar situations but different OBPVs. (Left) OBPV and OBSO value histograms for the events evaluated in Sect. 4.2. (Right) Two similar example situations but different OBPVs are shown. In both examples, the red team attacks from left to right, with the blue team defending. The black circle represents the ball. In these two scenes, OBSO scores were very similar: 0.01816 and 0.01817 (both red #33). However, OBPV evaluations differed greatly: 0.29968 (upper: red #33) and 0.50267 (lower: red #20).

Examples of such positive impacts identified by OBPV are shown in Fig. 5 right. The positioning of red #20 in the lower example is an instance of what is called a penetrative pass target [52,61]—a pass directed to a teammate surrounded by defenders, enabling bypassing the defensive line. As such, the positioning of red #20 in the lower example is likely to serve as a crucial attacking point. This demonstrates that OBPV successfully identified the critical difference between the two examples that OBSO failed to reveal.

5   Conclusion

In this paper, we proposed OBPV to evaluate space across the pitch, including the starting points of transitions. Experiments using La Liga season data showed that OBPV highlights effective space utilization during counter-attacks and reveals team-specific characteristics in how the teams utilize space after positive and negative transitions. Future work includes the application to the different league datasets, incorporating factors such as interceptions during ball movement [34], as well as incorporating players' posture and body orientation, which are not available in the current dataset.

Acknowledgments. This study was financially supported by JSPS KAKENHI 23H03282 and NEDO Intensive Support Program for Young Promising Researchers 24021654.

Appendix

A   Related Work

A.1   Predictive Analysis of Team Sports Using Tracking Data

In many team sports, including soccer, predictive analysis using tracking data (positional information of players and ball) is widely used [23,75]. Cervonet et al. expressed how much scoring is expected at the end of a basketball possession as EPV (Expected Possession Value) [10,11]. This method is also used in Soccer [20] and Handball [33,46]. There have also been many predictive analyses focusing on goals, for example, Chang et al. evaluated the difficulty of shots and the ability to shoot successfully separately [12], Lucey et al. estimated the probability of the occurrence of chances [38], and Fujii et al. used the Koopman Spectral Kernels to predict the probability of successful shots [24]. Furthermore, many studies evaluated players based on their scoring opportunities. McHale et al. evaluated players based on a single score without considering position and style of play [41,42]. In contrast, Pappalardo et al. evaluated player performance in a multidimensional and role-specific way [49], and Decroos and Davis used player vectors to identify players' playing styles [14]. Decroos et al. proposed VAEP (Valuing Actions by Estimating Probabilities), which evaluates player actions based on their impact on the result of the game while taking into account the previous context [13]. However, in soccer, scoring chances are rare situations, so predictive analysis based on scoring chances is not reliable. Therefore, some researchers have focused on defense by learning ball recovery probability and probability of being attacked [67,69], and Umemoto and Fujii evaluated player positioning in defense using counterfactuals [68].

Many predictive analyses that focused on each type of action have also been conducted. Power et al. evaluated passes by estimating both the risk and reward of a pass [50]. Goes et al. evaluated passes based on whether they disrupt the opponent's defensive construction [27], and Bransen et al. evaluated passes based on how much they contributed to the xG based on similar past passing data [7]. Rahimian et al. predict and quantify Penetrative passes [51], and they built a predictive model of the intended recipient of the pass and the player who actually receives it [52], and Robberechts et al. quantify players' creativity [57]. Some researchers have also evaluated the receiver as well as the passer [15,25, 37]. Robberechts quantified the pressure decisions as VPEP (Valuing Pressure decisions by Estimating Probabilities), based on the VAEP [56], and Merckx et al. automated the press analysis [45]. VanRoy et al. analyzed buildup tactics using Markov decision processes and described the defensive construction against buildup [71]. Furthermore, as a method for action prediction, a study based on Transformer, which is used to construct a language model, has been conducted [43,44,60,76]. In this study, the following space assessment approach is useful for evaluating player positioning for events that have no clear label and are difficult to predict, such as counter-attacks and counter-presses that occur from transitions.

A.2   Space Evaluation for Team Sports

When evaluations are based on on-ball events, they often fail to assess off-ball players since only a subset of players is targeted. Moreover, off-ball time is longer than on-ball time, making it crucial to evaluate off-ball movement. Consequently, many studies have focused on evaluating off-ball movement. This evaluation has enabled the discovery of the value of players who were previously overlooked in event-based assessments. As a rule-based off-ball evaluation, Supola et al. evaluated off-ball cutting in basketball [64]. Lamas et al. showed that off-ball movement affects the probability of getting an open shot in basketball [35]. Wu et al. quantitatively evaluated off-ball offensive contributions by considering player position and team cooperation [73]. Link et al. evaluated dangerousness of space as the probability of a player scoring a goal at each moment of ball possession [36], and Fernandez evaluated moves that create space for teammates [18].

Off-ball evaluations using mathematical models are also being developed. In studies considering players' dominance areas, Voronoi partitioning has been performed by treating players as generating points. Taki et al. conducted a Voronoi partitioning that calculates the minimum arrival time while considering players' speed and acceleration, evaluating space based on dominance areas [65]. Additionally, regarding player motion models, Fujimura and Sugihara used a one-dimensional motion model [26], and Brefeld et al. proposed a method utilizing a model based on kernel density estimation [8]. Furthermore, Martens et al. used a data-driven motion model [39], and Narizuka et al. used players' arrival time to weight the field [48].

The model proposed in this study is an extension based on OBSO (Off-Ball Scoring Opportunity) proposed by Spearman [62,63]. OBSO is a model that quantifies where a player should receive a pass to maximize scoring opportunities, using the positions of players and the ball. For more details, see Sect. B. Rios-Neto et al. extended OBSO to tracking data and provided a new perspective [55]. Additionally, the studies by Teranishi et al. [66], Yeung et al. [74], and Umemoto and Fujii [68] each proposed models that extend OBSO. The idea of OBSO also applies to other sports, with Kono and Fujii extending it to basketball [34] and Iwashita et al. extending it to ultimate [32].

The USO (Ultimate Scoring Opportunity) model [32] uses pitch-wide weighting for spatial evaluation. USO calculates spatial value based on a combination of PPCF (as used in OBSO), positional weight (w_{area}), and distance weight ($w_{distance}$). In the w_{area} component, spatial importance is assessed based on ease of scoring or passing, with the end zone—analogous to the goal in soccer—assigned a weight of 1. The weights for other locations are determined by the normalized angle subtended by the end zone. In contrast, the field value model proposed in this study uses distance in both the longitudinal and lateral directions rather than angles with respect to the goal. This difference stems from the structural disparity between ultimate and soccer. In soccer, using angular weighting results in extremely low values in the corners of the pitch, which is inappropriate for evaluating spatial value. Therefore, angular information was excluded from the weighting scheme, and instead, distance to the goal along each axis was used.

Moreover, several models are considered potential replacements for OBSO components [19,21]. These models employ deep learning to generate pitch surfaces for scoring and transition analysis. However, despite their advanced capabilities, their implementation requires substantial data volumes and considerable computational resources for training, which can be prohibitive in academic and practical scenarios.

A.3   Research on Transitions in Soccer

In soccer, the decision-making during transitions, the moments of switching between attack and defense, has been considered important. Reep and Benjamin showed that transitions in the opponent's half have a high probability of leading to goals and significantly impact the overall performance of the team [54]. On the other hand, recent studies showed the importance of counter-attacks following ball recoveries in the defensive half. Barreira et al. showed that the effectiveness of an attack increases when a team connects passes after defensive actions such as tackles in their own half [4]. Liu et al. found that shots resulting from counter-attacks following ball recoveries in the defensive half have a significant impact on match outcomes [31]. These findings suggest that tactical changes and improvements in player skills have influenced the growing importance of ball recoveries in the defensive half, where more space is available. Wright et al. analyzed goals scored in the English Premier League and revealed that 65% of them resulted from transitions [72]. Furthermore, studies have been conducted on detecting transitions and evaluating counter-attacks that originate from transitions. Fassmeyer et al. utilized semi-supervised learning to detect counter-attacks and set-piece situations such as corner kicks [16]. Additionally, Hobbs et al. applied hierarchical clustering for transition detection and further assessed counter-attacks by calculating the defensive disorganization and the attacking threat level [30]. Moreover, Biermann et al. introduced the concept of Expected Counter, which predicts the success rate of counter-attacks and the defensive risk level [6]. Raudonius and Allmendinger evaluated individual players' contributions to counter-attacks using four metrics: the distance covered, the threat level of actions against opponents, the number of defenders bypassed, and the ability to control space on the field [53]. Gonzalez-Rodenas et al. found that vertical action within the first three seconds of winning the ball increased the probability of creating scoring opportunities and was effective in creating scoring opportunities on the counter only when the opposing defense was unbalanced [28].

On the defensive side, Peters et al. defined Rest Defence on a rule basis, and found that when Rest Defence works, it reduces the risk of shots by opposing teams or losing possession on a counter [2]. Additionally, in modern soccer, the concept of counter-pressing has become an essential factor that cannot be overlooked. Jürgen Klopp, who managed Liverpool FC until 2024 and achieved great success, popularized the tactical approach known as Gegenpressing [9], and Pep Guardiola, the manager of Manchester City, introduced the five-second rule in counter-pressing [3]. These managers have demonstrated success in the English Premier League, highlighting the importance of counter-pressing. Bauer and Anzer conducted a data-driven analysis of counter-pressing and revealed that successful counter-pressing significantly increases the goal-scoring rate, whereas failure leads to a substantial rise in conceding goals [5]. Vogelbein et al. analyzed the Bundesliga by dividing teams into three groups based on their rankings and comparing them. Their study demonstrated that the ability to quickly regain possession is a crucial factor in successful defensive performance [40]. In this study, we focused on space, which has not been widely considered in transition evaluation, and evaluated the space at the starting point of transitions.

B   OBSO Framework

As described in Sect. 2, $P(S_r|D)$, $P(T_r|D)$ and $P(C_r|D)$ are represented by the Score model, PPCF (the Potential Pitch Control Field), and the Transition model, respectively. The score model is explained in Sect. B.1, PPCF in Sect. B.2, and the Transition model in Sect. B.3. The overview of this model is illustrated in the upper section of Fig. 1. The implementation is based on the code at [58]. This framework is constructed by combining the Score model, PPCF, and the Transition model, enabling goal probability estimation at different points on the pitch. However, a limitation of this model is that it is designed to predict scoring opportunities, which results in generally low evaluations for positions far from the goal. To address this issue, we propose an improved model in Sect. 3.

B.1   Score Model

Here we describe the Score model, which is one of the models that constitute OBSO. This model represents the importance of the pitch based on score prediction. In OBSO, it is represented as follows:

$$S(\vec{r}|\beta) = [S_d(|\vec{r} - \vec{r_g}|)]^{\beta}. \tag{8}$$

Here, $\vec{r_g}$ denotes the position of the goal, and $S_d(x)$ refers to a monotonically decreasing function concerning distance. By setting the parameter β, it expresses the idea that even at the same distance, scoring becomes easier if there is no defensive pressure. In this study, we used the grid data included in the code that implemented OBSO independently of the original authors [58] as the Score model.

In the Score model, locations closer to the goal are given relatively high evaluations, while areas farther from the goal are generally rated lower. As a result, it becomes unsuitable for evaluating space in situations where scoring is not the primary focus. To address this issue, we propose the field value model in our OBPV (Off-Ball Positioning Value) framework as a replacement for the Score model. The field value model considers the weight across the entire pitch, enabling spatial evaluation without solely focusing on scoring opportunities.

B.2   PPCF

Here we describe PPCF, one of the models that constitute OBSO and OBPV. This model represents the players' occupancy on the pitch—specifically, it can be interpreted as the probability that a player from the same team will be able to control the ball if it is passed to a given location. The control probability of player j at a specific location $\vec{r}$ at time t is expressed as follows:

$$\frac{dPPCF_j}{dT}(t,\vec{r},T|s,\lambda_j) = \left(1 - \sum_k PPCF_k(t,\vec{r},T|s,\lambda_j)\right) f_j(t,\vec{r},T|s)\lambda_j. \tag{9}$$

Here, $f_j(t,\vec{r},T|s)$ represents the probability that player j reaches location $\vec{r}$ within time T. To model this, we compute the expected arrival time $\tau_{exp}(t,\vec{r})$, which represents the time required to reach a certain location $/vecr$, assuming the player accelerates with a constant acceleration a from the initial velocity $\vec{v_j}(t)$ up to the maximum speed v. In a previous study, the values $v = 5m/s$ and $a = 7m/s^2$ have been used. In practice, the actual arrival time may vary due to various factors such as uncertainty in tracking data, the players' direction, awareness, and tactical decisions. To avoid modeling all these factors directly, we use the cumulative distribution function (CDF) of the logistic distribution to compute the probability that player j at time t can reach location $\vec{r}$ within time T, as shown in the following equation:

$$f_i(t,\vec{r},T|s) = \frac{1}{1 + \exp\left(-\frac{T - \tau_{exp}(t,\vec{r})}{\sqrt{3}s/\pi}\right)}. \tag{10}$$

Here, $\sqrt{3}s/\pi$ represents the uncertainty in a player's arrival time. In this study, we set $s = 0.45$. λ_j denotes the control rate. A higher value of λ_j corresponds to a shorter time required to control the ball. This control rate is assumed to differ between the attacking and defending teams. The attacking team needs to control the ball accurately in order to shoot or make the next pass. In contrast, the defending team does not necessarily need to control the ball with high precision. To represent this distinction, we introduce the parameter κ. Using this parameter, the control rate is expressed by the following equation:

$$\lambda_i = \begin{cases} \lambda & (i \in A) \\ \kappa\lambda & (i \in B) \end{cases}. \tag{11}$$

Here, A denotes the set of attacking players, and B denotes the set of defending players. In a previous research, the values $\kappa = 1$ and $\lambda = 4.3$ were used, assuming that defending players also attempt to gain control of the ball before transitioning to attack. Based on this assumption, the same control rate was used for both attacking and defending teams in the calculations.

Then, by integrating Eq. 9 over T from 0 to ∞, the PPCF for each player can be computed. Additionally, in cases where a player from one team arrives significantly earlier than any player from the opposing team and and has sufficient time to control the ball, the PPCF for that team is set to 1, and that of the opposing team is set to 0.

B.3   Transition Model

Here we describe the Transition model, one of the components of OBSO. This model represents where the next on-ball event is likely to occur. In OBSO, it is assumed that the ball behaves similarly to a two-dimensional Brownian motion. This assumption is based on the idea that the ball's movement changes due to interactions such as passes, headers, blocks, and interceptions by players. Accordingly, OBSO considers a two-dimensional normal distribution. Furthermore, it is assumed that the player making the pass aims to send the ball to a location less likely to be intercepted. To reflect this, the Transition model incorporates the PPCF modeled in Sect. B.2, and is represented by the following equation:

$$T(t, \vec{r} \,|\, \sigma, \alpha) = N(\vec{r}, \vec{r_b}(t), \sigma) \cdot \left[\sum_{k \in A} PPCF_k(t, \vec{r}) \right]^\alpha. \tag{12}$$

In the implementation of OBSO used in this study, we set $\alpha = 0$ for simplification and directly used the two-dimensional normal distribution. However, in actual football games, the tendency of pass destinations varies depending on the location on the pitch—for example, passes from the side areas are often directed inward. To account for this, the transition kernel model proposed in this study divides the pitch into 18 regions and uses kernel density estimation based on the actual pass distributions within each area.

C Field Value Model

The field value model was constructed based on the following procedure. First, the following sigmoid function (Fig. 2 Left) is defined along the longitudinal direction of the pitch (X-axis).

$$weight(x) = \frac{1}{1 + \exp(-\frac{x+15}{30})}. \tag{13}$$

This function reflects the gradual change in importance across the pitch during an attacking phase, while maintaining high values near the goal area. At $X = -15$, which approximately marks the boundary between the defensive third (the third closest to the team's own goal) and the middle third of the pitch, the weight becomes $weight = 0.5$. The function is designed so that the weights are approximately 0.2 at one end of the pitch and 0.9 at the other. The slightly higher value than 0.2 at the lower end is due to the additional decrease in weight as the position moves closer to the sidelines.

In addition, a normal distribution is applied in the width direction of the pitch (Y-axis). The maximum value of this normal distribution is given by Eq. 13, and the standard deviation is defined by Eq. 14, where the variance decreases as the position moves farther from the goal along the X-axis. This function reflects the assumption that near the goal, the importance does not significantly change even if the position shifts toward the sidelines. In the equation, the constant 34 represents the distance from the center of the pitch to the sideline.

$$\sigma(x) = 34 \times \{1 + weight(x)\}. \tag{14}$$

Based on the above, the Field value at the position (x, y) is defined as follows:

$$w_{field}(x, y) = \exp\left(-\frac{y^2}{2\sigma(x)^2}\right) \times weight(x). \tag{15}$$

The field value model computed in this rule is illustrated on the right side of Fig. 2. In the field value model, the areas adjacent to the penalty area (outlined in green) and the vital area (outlined in blue) are highly valued. These areas are considered highly important in soccer; thus, the model can be regarded as appropriately capturing their significance.

D   Other Supplementary Figures

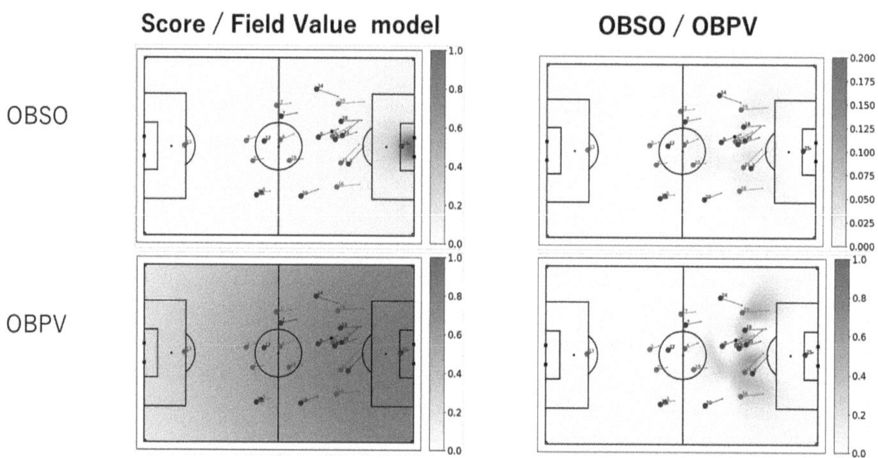

Fig. 6. Score model vs. Field value model. The upper row corresponds to OBSO (which uses the Score model, PPCF, and the Transition Kernel model), while the lower row corresponds to OBPV (which uses the field value model, PPCF, and the Transition Kernel model). In OBSO, the values tend to be smaller overall due to the influence of the Score model; therefore, the maximum value of the heatmap was set to 0.2. This value is considered appropriate for scenes near the goal.

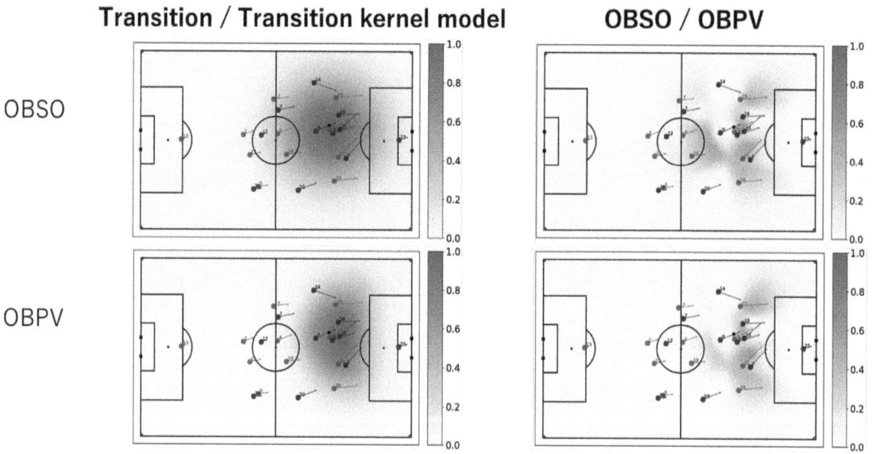

Fig. 7. Transition model vs. Transition kernel model. The upper row corresponds to OBSO (which uses the field value model, PPCF, and the Transition model), while the lower row corresponds to OBPV (which uses the field value model, PPCF, and the Transition kernel model).

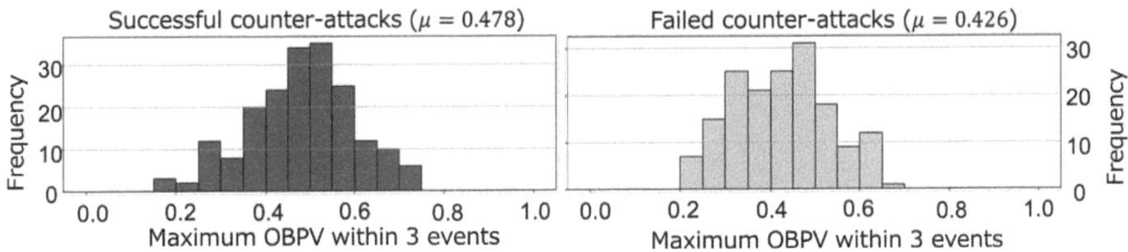

Fig. 8. OBPV of successful and failed counter-attacks. Successful counter-attacks showed higher OBPV values, with a statistically significant difference observed ($p < 1.0 \times 10^{-5}$).

References

1. Analyst, O.: Spanish la LIGA stats: 2023-24 season (2024). https://theanalyst. com/2023/08/spanish-la-liga-stats-2023-24. Accessed 14 Jan 2025
2. Peters, A., Parmar, N., Davies, M., James, N.: A rule-based approach to classify counterpressing – analysis of its risks and relationship with rest defence. Int. J. Perform. Anal. Sport, 1–17 (2025). https://doi.org/10.1080/24748668.2025.2473799
3. AS: Pep's five-second rule, the key to city's success (2018). https://en.as.com/en/ 2018/07/26/soccer/1532614241_079674.html. Accessed 13 Mar 2025
4. Barreira, D., Garganta, J., Guimarães, P., Machado, J., Anguera, M.T.: Ball recovery patterns as a performance indicator in elite soccer. Proc. Inst. Mech. Eng. Part P: J. Sports Eng. Technol. **228**(1), 61–72 (2014). https://doi.org/10.1177/ 1754337113493083
5. Bauer, P., Anzer, G.: Data-driven detection of CounterPressing in professional football. Data Min. Knowl. Discov. **35**(5), 2009–2049 (2021). https://doi.org/10. 1007/s10618-021-00763-7
6. Biermann, H., Yang, W., Wieland, F.G., Timmer, J., Memmert, D.: Quantification of turnover danger with xcounter. In: Brefeld, U., Davis, J., Van Haaren, J., Zimmermann, A. (eds.) Machine Learning and Data Mining for Sports Analytics, pp. 36–51. Springer Nature Switzerland, Cham (2024). https://doi.org/10.1007/ 978-3-031-02044-5
7. Bransen, L., Van Haaren, J., van de Velden, M.: Measuring soccer players' contributions to chance creation by valuing their passes. J. Quant. Anal. Sports **15**(2), 97–116 (2019)
8. Brefeld, U., Lasek, J., Mair, S.: Probabilistic movement models and zones of control. Mach. Learn. **108**(1), 127–147 (2018). https://doi.org/10.1007/s10994-018- 5725-1
9. Cataldo, V.F.: wie kann es sein, dass klopp noch keinen hattrick erzielt hat? (2015). https://www.sueddeutsche.de/sport/premier-league-bei-klopps- liverpoolern-klemmt-das-gaspedal-1.2695408. Accessed 13 Mar 2025
10. Cervone, D., D'Amour, A., Bornn, L., Goldsberry, K.: Pointwise: predicting points and valuing decisions in real time with nba optical tracking data. In: Proceedings of the 8th MIT Sloan Sports Analytics Conference, Boston, MA, USA, vol. 28, p. 3 (2014)
11. Cervone, D., D'Amour, A., Bornn, L., Goldsberry, K.: A multiresolution stochastic process model for predicting basketball possession outcomes. J. Am. Stat. Assoc. **111**(514), 585–599 (2016)

12. Chang, Y.H., Maheswaran, R.T., Kwok, S.J.J., Levy, T., Wexler, A.D., Squire, K.: Quantifying shot quality in the NBA. In: Proceedings of the 8th MIT Sloan Sports Analytics Conference (2014). https://api.semanticscholar.org/CorpusID: 221170672

13. Decroos, T., Bransen, L., Van Haaren, J., Davis, J.: Actions speak louder than goals: Valuing player actions in soccer. In: Proceedings of the 25th ACM SIGKDD Conference on Knowledge Discovery and Data Mining, pp. 1851–1861 (2019)

14. Decroos, T., Davis, J.: Player vectors: characterizing soccer players' playing style from match event streams. In: Brefeld, U., Fromont, E., Hotho, A., Knobbe, A., Maathuis, M., Robardet, C. (eds.) ECML PKDD 2019. LNCS (LNAI), vol. 11908, pp. 569–584. Springer, Cham (2020). https://doi.org/10.1007/978-3-030-46133-1_34

15. Dick, U., Link, D., Brefeld, U.: Who can receive the pass? A computational model for quantifying availability in soccer. Data Min. Knowl. Disc. **36**(3), 987–1014 (2022)

16. Fassmeyer, D., Anzer, G., Bauer, P., Brefeld, U.: Toward automatically labeling situations in soccer. Front. Sports Active Living **3** (2021). https://doi.org/10.3389/fspor.2021.725431, https://www.frontiersin.org/journals/sports-and-active-living/articles/10.3389/fspor.2021.725431

17. FBref: 2023-2024 la LIGA stats (2024). https://fbref.com/en/comps/12/2023-2024/2023-2024-La-Liga-Stats. Accessed 14 Jan 2025

18. Fernández, J., Bornn, L.: Wide open spaces: a statistical technique for measuring space creation in professional soccer. In: 12th MIT Sloan Sports Analytics Conference (2018)

19. Fernández, J., Bornn, L.: SoccerMap: a deep learning architecture for visually-interpretable analysis in soccer. In: Dong, Y., Ifrim, G., Mladenić, D., Saunders, C., Van Hoecke, S. (eds.) ECML PKDD 2020. LNCS (LNAI), vol. 12461, pp. 491–506. Springer, Cham (2021). https://doi.org/10.1007/978-3-030-67670-4_30

20. Fernández, J., Bornn, L., Cervone, D.: Decomposing the immeasurable sport: a deep learning expected possession value framework for soccer. In: 13th MIT Sloan Sports Analytics Conference (2019)

21. Fernández, J., Bornn, L., Cervone, D.: A framework for the fine-grained evaluation of the instantaneous expected value of soccer possessions. Mach. Learn. **110**(6), 1389–1427 (2021). https://doi.org/10.1007/s10994-021-05989-6

22. Feuerhake, U.: Recognition of repetitive movement patterns–the case of football analysis. ISPRS Int. J. Geo Inf. **5**(11), 208 (2016)

23. Fujii, K.: Machine learning in sports: Open approach for next play analytics (2025)

24. Fujii, K., Inaba, Y., Kawahara, Y.: Koopman spectral kernels for comparing complex dynamics: application to multiagent sport plays. In: Altun, Y., et al. (eds.) ECML PKDD 2017. LNCS (LNAI), vol. 10536, pp. 127–139. Springer, Cham (2017). https://doi.org/10.1007/978-3-319-71273-4_11

25. Fujii, K., et al.: Cognition and interpersonal coordination of patients with schizophrenia who have sports habits. PLoS ONE **15**(11), e0241863 (2020)

26. Fujimura, A., Sugihara, K.: Geometric analysis and quantitative evaluation of sport teamwork. Syst. Comput. Japan **36**(6), 49–58 (2005)

27. Goes, F.R., Kempe, M., Meerhoff, L.A., Lemmink, K.A.: Not every pass can be an assist: a data-driven model to measure pass effectiveness in professional soccer matches. Big Data **7**(1), 57–70 (2019)

28. Gonzalez-Rodenas, J., Lopez-Bondia, I., Calabuig, F., Pérez-Turpin, J.A., Aranda, R.: The effects of playing tactics on creating scoring opportunities in random

matches from us major league soccer. Int. J. Perform. Anal. Sport **15**(3), 851–872 (2015). https://doi.org/10.1080/24748668.2015.11868836

29. Gualtieri, A., Rampinini, E., Dello Iacono, A., Beato, M.: High-speed running and sprinting in professional adult soccer: Current thresholds definition, match demands and training strategies. a systematic review. Front. Sports Active Living **5** (2023). https://doi.org/10.3389/fspor.2023.1116293, https://www.frontiersin.org/journals/sports-and-active-living/articles/10.3389/fspor.2023.1116293

30. Hobbs, J., Power, P., Sha, L., Ruiz, H., Lucey, P.: Quantifying the value of transitions in soccer via spatiotemporal trajectory clustering. In: 12th MIT Sloan Sports Analytics Conference (2018). https://api.semanticscholar.org/CorpusID:221471459

31. Hongyou Liu, Miguel-Ángel Gomez, C.L.P., Sampaio, J.: Match statistics related to winning in the group stage of 2014 brazil fifa world cup. J. Sports Sci. **33**(12), 1205–1213 (2015). https://doi.org/10.1080/02640414.2015.1022578

32. Iwashita, S., Scott, A., Umemoto, R., Ding, N., Fujii, K.: Space evaluation based on pitch control using drone video in ultimate (2024). https://arxiv.org/abs/2409.14588

33. Kobayashi, R., Umemoto, R., Takeda, K., Fujii, K.: Score prediction using multiple object tracking for analyzing movements in 2-VS-2 handball. In: 2023 IEEE 12th Global Conference on Consumer Electronics (GCCE), pp. 946–947. IEEE (2023)

34. Kono, R., Fujii, K.: Mathematical models for off-ball scoring prediction in basketball. In: ECML-PKDD Workshop (2024)

35. Lamas, L., Santana, F., Heiner, M., Ugrinowitsch, C., Fellingham, G.: Modeling the offensive-defensive interaction and resulting outcomes in basketball. PLoS One **10**(12), 1–14 (2015). https://doi.org/10.1371/journal.pone.0144435

36. Link, D., Lang, S., Seidenschwarz, P.: Real time quantification of dangerousity in football using spatiotemporal tracking data. PLoS ONE **11**(12), e0168768 (2016)

37. Llana, S., Madrero, P., Fernández, J., Barcelona, F.: The right place at the right time: advanced off-ball metrics for exploiting an opponent's spatial weaknesses in soccer. In: Proceedings of the MIT Sloan Sports Analytics Conference (2020)

38. Lucey, P., Bialkowski, A., Monfort, M., Carr, P., Matthews, I.: quality vs quantity: improved shot prediction in soccer using strategic features from spatiotemporal data. In: Proceedings of MIT Sloan Sports Analytics Conference, pp. 1–9 (2014)

39. Martens, F., Dick, U., Brefeld, U.: Space and control in soccer. Front. Sports Active Living **3**, 676179 (2021)

40. Martin Vogelbein, S.N., Hökelmann, A.: Defensive transition in soccer – are prompt possession regains a measure of success? A quantitative analysis of German fußball-bundesliga 2010/2011. J. Sports Sci. **32**(11), 1076–1083 (2014). https://doi.org/10.1080/02640414.2013.879671, pMID: 24506111

41. McHale, I., Scarf, P.: Modelling soccer matches using bivariate discrete distributions with general dependence structure. Stat. Neerl. **61**(4), 432–445 (2007)

42. McHale, I.G., Scarf, P.A., Folker, D.E.: On the development of a soccer player performance rating system for the English premier league. Interfaces **42**(4), 339–351 (2012)

43. Mendes-Neves, T., Meireles, L., Mendes-Moreira, J.: Estimating player performance in different contexts using fine-tuned large events models. arXiv preprint arXiv:2402.06815 (2024)

44. Mendes-Neves, T., Meireles, L., Mendes-Moreira, J.: Forecasting events in soccer matches through language. arXiv preprint arXiv:2402.06820 (2024)

45. Merckx, S., Robberechts, P., Euvrard, Y., Davis, J.: Measuring the effectiveness of pressing in soccer. In: Workshop on Machine Learning and Data Mining for Sports Analytics (2021)
46. Müller, O., Caron, M., Döring, M., Heuwinkel, T., Baumeister, J.: Pivot: a parsimonious end-to-end learning framework for valuing player actions in handball using tracking data. In: International Workshop on Machine Learning and Data Mining for Sports Analytics, pp. 116–128. Springer (2021). https://doi.org/10.1007/978-3-031-02044-5_10
47. Narizuka, T., Yamamoto, K., Yamazaki, Y.: Statistical properties of position-dependent ball-passing networks in football games. Physica A: Stat. Mech. Appl. **412**, 157–168 (2014). https://doi.org/10.1016/j.physa.2014.06.037, https://www.sciencedirect.com/science/article/pii/S0378437114005123
48. Narizuka, T., Yamazaki, Y., Takizawa, K.: Space evaluation in football games via field weighting based on tracking data. Sci. Rep. **11**(1), 5509 (2021)
49. Pappalardo, L., et al.: PlayeRank: data-driven performance evaluation and player ranking in soccer via a machine learning approach. ACM Trans. Intell. Syst. Technol. (TIST) **10**(5), 1–27 (2019)
50. Power, P., Ruiz, H., Wei, X., Lucey, P.: Not all passes are created equal: objectively measuring the risk and reward of passes in soccer from tracking data. In: Proceedings of the 23rd ACM SIGKDD International Conference on Knowledge Discovery and Data Mining, pp. 1605–1613 (2017)
51. Rahimian, P., Kim, H., Schmid, M., Toka, L.: Pass receiver and outcome prediction in soccer using temporal graph networks. In: International Workshop on Machine Learning and Data Mining for Sports Analytics, pp. 52–63. Springer (2023). https://doi.org/10.1007/978-3-031-53833-9_5
52. Rahimian, P., da Silva Guerra Gomes, D.G., Berkovics, F., Toka, L.: Let's penetrate the defense: a machine learning model for prediction and valuation of penetrative passes. In: International Workshop on Machine Learning and Data Mining for Sports Analytics, pp. 41–52. Springer (2022). https://doi.org/10.1007/978-3-031-27527-2_4
53. Raudonius, L., Allmendinger, R.: Evaluating football player actions during counterattacks. In: Yin, H., et al. (eds.) IDEAL 2021. LNCS, vol. 13113, pp. 367–377. Springer, Cham (2021). https://doi.org/10.1007/978-3-030-91608-4_36
54. Reep, C., Benjamin, B.: Skill and chance in association football. J. Royal Stat. Soc. Ser. A (General) **131**(4), 581–585 (1968). http://www.jstor.org/stable/2343726
55. Rios-Neto, H., Jr., W.M., Vaz-de Melo, P.O.S.: A new look into off-ball scoring opportunity: taking into account the continuous nature of the game. In: FC Barcelona Analytics in Sports Tomorrow Congress (2020)
56. Robberechts, P.: Valuing the art of pressing. In: StatsBomb Innovation in Football Conference (2019)
57. Robberechts, P., Van Roy, M., Davis, J.: UN-XPass: measuring soccer player's creativity. In: Proceedings of the 29th ACM SIGKDD Conference on Knowledge Discovery and Data Mining, pp. 4768–4777 (2023)
58. Shaw, L.. LaurieontrackIng (2020). https://github.com/Friends-of-Tracking-Data-FoTD/LaurieOnTracking. Accessed 19 Nov 2024
59. Silverman, B.W.: Density Estimation for Statistics and Data Analysis, Monographs on Statistics and Applied Probability, vol. 26. Chapman and Hall, London (1986)
60. Simpson, I., Beal, R.J., Locke, D., Norman, T.J.: Seq2Event: learning the language of soccer using transformer-based match event prediction. In: Proceedings of the 28th ACM SIGKDD Conference on Knowledge Discovery and Data Mining, pp. 3898–3908 (2022)

61. Sotudeh, H.: Potential penetrative pass (P3). arXiv preprint arXiv:2302.10760 (2023)
62. Spearman, W.: Beyond expected goals. In: Proceedings of the 12th MIT Sloan Sports Analytics Conference, pp. 1–17 (2018)
63. Spearman, W., Basye, A., Dick, G., Hotovy, R., Pop, P.: Physics-based modeling of pass probabilities in soccer. In: Proceeding of the 11th MIT Sloan Sports Analytics Conference (2017)
64. Supola, B., Hoch, T., Baca, A.: Modeling the formation of defensive gaps in basketball: cutting on a teammate's drive. PLOS ONE **18**(2), 1–20 (2023). https://doi.org/10.1371/journal.pone.0281467
65. Taki, T., Hasegawa, J., Fukumura, T.: Development of motion analysis system for quantitative evaluation of teamwork in soccer games. In: Proceedings of 3rd IEEE International Conference on Image Processing, vol. 3, pp. 815–818. IEEE (1996)
66. Teranishi, M., Tsutsui, K., Takeda, K., Fujii, K.: Evaluation of creating scoring opportunities for teammates in soccer via trajectory prediction. In: International Workshop on Machine Learning and Data Mining for Sports Analytics, pp. 53–73. Springer (2022). https://doi.org/10.1007/978-3-031-27527-2_5
67. Toda, K., Teranishi, M., Kushiro, K., Fujii, K.: Evaluation of soccer team defense based on prediction models of ball recovery and being attacked: a pilot study. PLoS ONE **17**(1), e0263051 (2022)
68. Umemoto, R., Fujii, K.: Evaluation of team defense positioning by computing counterfactuals using StatsBomb 360 data. In: StatsBomb Conference (2023)
69. Umemoto, R., Tsutsui, K., Fujii, K.: Location analysis of players in UEFA euro 2020 and 2022 using generalized valuation of defense by estimating probabilities. arXiv preprint arXiv:2212.00021 (2022)
70. Van Roy, M., Cascioli, L., Davis, J.: ETSY: a rule-based approach to event and tracking data synchronization. In: ECML-PKDD Workshop, pp. 11–23 (2023)
71. Van Roy, M., Robberechts, P., Davis, J.: Optimally disrupting opponent build-ups. In: Proceedings of the 2021 StatsBomb Conference, pp. 1–16. London, UK (2021)
72. Wright, C., Atkins, S., Polman, R., Jones, B., Sargeson, L.: Factors associated with goals and goal scoring opportunities in professional soccer. Int. J. Perform. Anal. Sport **11**(3), 438–449 (2011). https://doi.org/10.1080/24748668.2011.11868563
73. Wu, Y., et al.: Obtracker: visual analytics of off-ball movements in basketball. IEEE Trans. Visual Comput. Graph. **29**(1), 929–939 (2023). https://doi.org/10.1109/TVCG.2022.3209373
74. Yeung, C., Fujii, K.: A strategic framework for optimal decisions in football 1-vs-1 shot-taking situations: an integrated approach of machine learning, theory-based modeling, and game theory. Complex Intell. Syst., 1–20 (2024)
75. Yeung, C., Ide, K., Someya, T., Fujii, K.: OpenStarLab: open approach for spatiotemporal agent data analysis in soccer. arXiv preprint arXiv:2502.02785 (2025)
76. Yeung, C.C., Sit, T., Fujii, K.: Transformer-based neural marked spatio temporal point process model for football match events analysis. arXiv preprint arXiv:2302.09276 (2023)

What Makes a Dribble Successful?
Insights From 3D Pose Tracking Data

Michiel Schepers[1], Pieter Robberechts[1,2(✉)] [ID], Jan Van Haaren[1,3] [ID],
and Jesse Davis[1,2] [ID]

[1] Department of Computer Science, KU Leuven, Leuven 3000, Belgium
`michiel.schepers@student.kuleuven.be,`
`{pieter.robberechts,jesse.davis}@kuleuven.be`
[2] Leuven.AI - KU Leuven Institute for AI, KU Leuven, Leuven 3000, Belgium
[3] Club Brugge KV, Knokke-Heist 8300, Belgium
`jan.vanhaaren@clubbrugge.be`

Abstract. Data analysis plays an increasingly important role in soccer, offering new ways to evaluate individual and team performance. One specific application is the evaluation of dribbles: one-on-one situations where an attacker attempts to bypass a defender with the ball. While previous research has primarily relied on 2D positional tracking data, this fails to capture aspects like balance, orientation, and ball control, limiting the depth of current insights. This study explores how *pose tracking data*—capturing players' posture and movement in three dimensions— can improve our understanding of dribbling skills. We extract novel pose-based features from 1,736 dribbles in the 2022/23 Champions League season and evaluate their impact on dribble success. Our results show that pose-based features (specifically, the lean angle of the attacker's torso and the relative alignment between the posture of the attacker and defender) are informative for predicting dribble success. Incorporating these pose-based features on top of features derived from traditional 2D positional data leads to a measurable improvement in the model's prediction performance.

1 Introduction

Although soccer is a team sport, matches are often decided by individual actions, such as one-on-one dribbles between an attacker and a defender [11]. Therefore, there is a continuous search for new ways to analyze, evaluate, and improve the technical skills involved in these direct confrontations.

Currently, analytical models that assess individual actions like one-on-one dribbles rely predominantly on 2D tracking data [4, 12], recording player and ball positions on the pitch's horizontal XY plane over time. While these models have yielded valuable insights, they fail to capture essential factors, such as balance, posture, and ball control, all of which influence the success of a dribble. Moreover, existing models often overlook the subtleties of the interaction between attacker and defender, limiting their predictive accuracy and interpretability.

H. Rios-Neto et al. (Eds.): MLSA 2025, CCIS 2833, pp. 120–135, 2026.
https://doi.org/10.1007/978-3-032-15165-0_9

For instance, an attacker may attempt to pass a defender on the side opposite their supporting leg to exploit a momentary imbalance.

With the continuous evolution of tracking technology, clubs increasingly have access to 3D pose tracking data, which captures the coordinates of key anatomical landmarks on players' bodies in real time [16]. While currently the main use of this data is in officiating, particularly for accurately determining offside decisions [9], its potential extends far beyond this.

In this paper, we propose a novel approach to analyzing dribbling success by extracting meaningful 3D features from pose tracking data. These features capture the player's ball control, balance, posture, and spatial interactions with the defender. We evaluate their relevance in explaining dribble success and examine whether incorporating these 3D biomechanical features into a logistic regression model improves predictive accuracy compared to models based solely on traditional 2D data.

Using a comprehensive dataset of 1,736 one-on-one dribbles from the 2022/23 UEFA Champions League season, our results demonstrate that integrating 3D features leads to a clear improvement in predictive performance. SHAP value analysis reveals that certain 3D biomechanical features play an important role in predicting dribble outcomes. Notably, the defender's posture relative to the attacker and the lean angle of the attacker's torso stand out as useful features. These findings suggest that 3D pose tracking data can significantly enhance the analysis of individual player actions, offering new perspectives for performance evaluation, scouting, and player development.

2 Background and Related Work

Pose Tracking Data. Until recently, soccer data primarily consisted of 2D information [15], tracking only the XY positions of players and the ball on the field, which limited analysis to a flat perspective. However, recent technological advances have transformed this approach with the introduction of 3D pose (or, skeleton) tracking data. This technology captures not only players' positions but also their body posture and movements in three dimensions, using a network of ultra-high-speed cameras. These recordings are analyzed with AI algorithms to reconstruct the 3D pose of each player [2]. This is done by calculating the coordinates of a number of anatomical landmarks on the player's body, such as the shoulders, hips, ankles, and knees. Figure 1 provides a visual representation of what is tracked by such a system.

Analysis and Modeling of Dribbles. Various studies have aimed to model dribbling dynamics and quantify player skills based on 2D data. A notable contribution is the VAEP model introduced by Decroos et al. [6], which estimates the value of individual player actions, including dribbles. The model predicts the probability that a team will score or concede a goal within a few subsequent actions, defining the value of a dribble as the change in expected scoring chances before and after the action. While this approach provides an objective measure of a dribble's impact, it offers limited insight into the underlying technical skills.

Fig. 1. The 29 anatomical points whose positions are tracked by the SkeleTRACK system (from [16]).

Complementing this, Brink et al. [4] focus specifically on the dynamics of one-on-one dribbles, introducing a behaviorally inspired model that simulates attacker-defender interactions by assigning physical parameters (such as speed and acceleration) and behavioral traits (such as attacker aggressiveness and defender hesitation) to players. Though valuable for exploring the conditions under which dribbles succeed or fail, this approach remains limited by 2D data, which lacks biomechanical information such as posture and balance.

Beyond data-driven approaches, sports science research has long investigated determinants of dribbling success through controlled experiments. For instance, Zago et al. [20] conducted tests with youth players measuring biomechanical variables like center of mass and step length, capturing physical dynamics not accessible via positional tracking data.

This paper aims to bridge these two research domains by extracting biomechanically-informed features from 3D pose tracking data and integrating them into quantitative models.

3   Data, Preprocessing and Feature Engineering

In this section, we first describe our data set and how we selected the dribbles that will be analyzed.

3.1   Data Set

For this study, we have used a dataset of 125 games from the 2022/23 UEFA Champions League season, provided by Club Brugge KV. For each game, the data consists of 2D positional tracking data, 3D pose tracking data, and event data. The positional and pose tracking data were collected by Hawk-Eye using the SkeleTRACK system and record the location of the ball, the centroid of each player and 29 anatomical landmarks for each player (Fig. 1), sampled at 25 Hz. The event data was collected by Stats Perform and contains a log of all on-the-ball actions that occurred during the game. Before analysis, the raw data must be prepared through synchronization and filtering to isolate relevant one-on-one dribbles. The pre-processing steps are detailed below, resulting in a dataset of 1,736 dribbles.

3.2   Data Preprocessing

First, we integrate the event data with the 2D and 3D tracking data by extracting a window from the tracking data for each dribble event. This window begins at the end of the event immediately preceding the dribble and ends at the start of the following event. This approach ensures that the tracking data captures the full context of the dribble, including both its lead-in and outcome.

To validate the synchronization, we analyze the trajectories of the player and the ball during successful dribbles. Intuitively, while dribbling, the ball should closely follow the player's movement. Therefore, we compute the cosine similarity between the velocity vectors of the attacker and the ball throughout the dribble window. We find that in 85% of successful dribbles, the trajectories are indeed aligned (average cosine similarity > 0.9). For the remaining 15%, discrepancies arise due to brief ball loss during complex skill moves, temporary occlusions, or tracking noise in the ball coordinates.

Second, missing pose data (typically caused by player occlusion or brief exits from the camera frame) is addressed using cubic spline interpolation [5] with natural boundary conditions. We experience that the interpolation method yields smooth motion trajectories that align with the player motion in the video data to a high degree.

3.3   Dribble Filtering

The construction of a one-on-one dribble dataset starts from all `TAKE_ON` events in the event data, which indicate *"an attempt by one player to dribble past an opponent"* [17]. Because not all such events represent meaningful one-on-one dribbles, we apply additional filtering criteria:

1. The player must cover at least 2 m and the dribbles must last at least 2 s. This requirement ensures sufficient movement to extract informative features.
2. The average ball speed must exceed 1.5 m/s during the dribble. This threshold filters out slow actions or duels lacking real progression, focusing only on genuine one-on-one dribbles where the attacker actively attempts to advance.
3. The maximum ball speed must remain below 11 m/s, as dribbling requires the ball to stay close to the player's feet and under control. Since players cannot realistically exceed this speed [3], higher ball velocities typically indicate an incorrectly labeled event such as a pass or shot rather than a dribble.
4. The endpoint must be closer to the opponent's goal than the start, ensuring attacking intent. Backward dribbles typically serve different purposes (e.g., ball retention or repositioning) and are therefore less relevant in the context of one-on-one offensive analyses.

These rules were developed through an iterative process involving manual video inspection to validate coverage and quality. Applying them yields a dataset of 1,736 dribbles: 690 successful and 1,046 unsuccessful, with success defined as the attacker retaining possession after beating the defender [17]. Each dribble is also linked to its primary defender, defined as the nearest opponent at the moment the dribble ends.[1]

3.4   Feature Engineering for Dribble Analysis

To characterize each dribble, we extracted eight features from the 2D positional tracking data and six features from the 3D pose data (Table 1). These features are computed over the entire tracking window aligned with the duration of the dribble (see Sect. 3.2).

The 2D features are based on methods proposed in previous studies [4,13]. They capture the dribble's location, the movement of the players, and their interactions, but in a relatively limited way. To describe the dribbles's position on the field, we included the distance to the nearest sideline and to the opponent's goal. Attacker and defender movement is captured by maximum speed, acceleration, and directional changes [10]. Interaction is quantified through relative speed (attacker minus defender) and a pressure score based on whether the attacker entered the defender's pressure zone, defined following Andrienko et al. [1].

Our novel 3D features capture the player's ball control, balance, and more detailed player interactions. To characterize ball control, we computed the average distance between the ball and the attacker's nearest foot, normalized by defensive pressure. By normalizing ball control in this way, the context of the dribble is taken into account, providing a more realistic measure of the player's skill depending on the situation in which they find themselves. We also calculated the frequency of ball touches, defined as local minima in the foot–ball distance trajectory. A higher frequency of ball contact generally indicates a more technical dribbling style, while a lower frequency suggests players who rely more on speed to get past their opponent. To assess the attacker's balance, we first estimated the player's center of mass (CoM) using an anthropometric model [18]. Based on the CoM, we then describe the player's balance with two features: imbalance (computed as the horizontal offset between the CoM and the midpoint between their feet) and torso lean angle (computed as the angle between the torso vector from hip to neck and the vertical axis). Finally, to capture the interaction between the attacker and defender, we consider whether the attacker attempts to pass on the side opposite the defender's weighted leg, as well as the alignment of each player's body direction relative to the vector connecting them.

Additional features and aggregations were considered but were not retained to avoid multicollinearity. For example, maximum speed and acceleration of attacker and defender were preferred over their averages because dribbles are

---

[1] Closeness is measured using Euclidean distance in the 2D tracking data. The end of the dribble is defined by the start timestamp of the next event.

explosive actions best characterized by peak values. Similarly, average pressure from nearby opponents was kept as it provides a more representative overall context than peak pressure. Appendix A provides a detailed description of all considered features.

Table 1. Extracted features, categories, and descriptions.

Feature	Category	Description
Dist. to sideline (Atk.)	2D Spatial	Distance from attacker's start position to nearest sideline (m)
Dist. to goal (Atk.)	2D Spatial	Distance from attacker's start position to opponent's goal (m)
Max speed (Atk.)	2D Kinematics	Peak speed reached by the attacker (m/s)
Max speed (Def.)	2D Kinematics	Peak speed reached by the defender (m/s)
Max acceleration (Atk.)	2D Kinematics	Highest acceleration of the attacker (m/s^2)
Max direction change (Atk.)	2D Kinematics	Maximum angular change in attacker's movement direction (°)
Max relative speed	2D Interaction	Maximum difference in speed between attacker and defender (m/s)
Avg. pressure score	2D Interaction	Average pressure exerted by nearby defenders on attacker (unitless)
Avg. norm. ball-foot dist.	3D Ball Control	Average distance between ball and attacker's nearest foot, normalized by defensive pressure (unitless)
Ball touch frequency	3D Ball Control	Number of ball touches per second, detected as local minima in foot-ball distance (touches/s)
Avg. imbalance	3D Pose	Average distance in the XY plane between the attacker's center of mass and the midpoint between the two feet (m)
P90 torso lean angle	3D Pose	90th percentile of attacker's lean angle relative to vertical, based on a vector from the neck to the hip midpoint. (°)
Pass side vs. weighted leg	3D Interaction	Whether the attacker attempts to pass the defender on the side opposite the defender's weighted leg, determined by comparing center of mass distance to each heel (binary)
Defender stance angle	3D Interaction	Alignment of each player's body direction relative to the vector connecting them (°)

4 Empirical Analysis of Dribble Success

Our empirical analysis of the features presented in Sect. 3.4 aims to answer the following two research questions:

Q1: **Can the addition of 3D pose-based features improve the prediction accuracy of existing 2D dribble outcome models?**

Q2: **Which features extracted from 3D pose tracking data are relevant for describing dribbles, and how do they impact the success rate of those dribbles?**

The first question focuses on examining the practical value of pose-based descriptors of dribbles in improving predictive models, while the second aims to understand how these features affect the success of dribbles. The next sections discuss the methodology and present the results.

4.1   Methodology

We compare a simple location-based baseline with a logistic regression model trained on both 2D tracking and 3D pose-derived features.

Baseline Model. To capture the influence of a dribble's location,[2] the pitch is divided into an 8×5 grid. For each cell, we compute the success rate as the proportion of successful dribbles starting in that zone. Predictions are made by assigning a new dribble the success rate of its corresponding cell. This naive model ignores contextual or biomechanical factors.

Predictive Model. The main model uses logistic regression [14] to predict dribble outcomes based on both 2D and 3D features. Logistic regression was chosen for its interpretability and its ability to reveal the individual contribution of each feature. All features were standardized by removing the mean and scaling to unit variance to ensure equal treatment. The model was trained with L2 regularization using the SAGA [7] solver, with a maximum of 1000 iterations. To address class imbalance, sample weights were set inversely proportional to class frequencies.

Evaluation. We assess model performance using five-fold cross-validation in terms of precision, recall, F1-score, and Brier score.

4.2   Q1: Impact of 3D Features on Model Performance

To assess the contribution of different feature sets to model performance, we conduct an ablation study across three configurations: a baseline model using only the dribble location, a 2D model incorporating spatiotemporal tracking features, and a full model combining both 2D and 3D pose-based features. Table 2 reports the results as average scores across folds, together with the standard deviations.

The baseline model achieves the highest precision but suffers from low recall, reflecting its limited ability to detect successful dribbles in an imbalanced

---

[2] It is generally more difficult to successfully complete a dribble compared to areas further from goal.

dataset. Introducing 2D features significantly improves recall and F1 score, highlighting the added value of basic kinematic features and features that capture the level of defensive pressure. Adding 3D pose features yields further gains across all metrics. Although the performance increase is modest, it indicates that pose-based information captures additional aspects of dribbling skill that are not represented in 2D tracking data alone.

Table 2. Model performance on dribble outcome prediction, demonstrating that adding 3D pose features improves predictive performance.

Model	Precision ↑	Recall ↑	F1 Score ↑	Brier score ↓
Baseline	**0.55 ± 0.08**	0.26 ± 0.04	0.35 ± 0.04	**0.2356 ± 0.0078**
2D Features Only	0.46 ± 0.02	0.53 ± 0.02	0.49 ± 0.02	0.2444 ± 0.0055
2D + 3D Features	0.47 ± 0.02	**0.57 ± 0.04**	**0.52 ± 0.03**	0.2429 ± 0.0028

4.3 Q2: Key Factors Influencing Dribble Success

To better understand the contribution of individual features to the model's predictions, SHAP values were computed across all features. Figure 2 presents the SHAP values for the 14 features used for predicting dribble success. The sign and magnitude of these values indicate the direction and strength of each feature's effect on the predicted probability of a successful dribble. Specifically, features with higher SHAP values concentrated on the right suggest that increased feature values enhance the likelihood of a successful dribble, whereas those skewed to the left indicate the opposite.

Among all features, maximum speed emerges as a key determinant, both for the attacker and defender. This finding is consistent with prior models such as Brink et al. [4], which emphasize speed and acceleration as fundamental predictors. However, somewhat counterintuitively, a higher maximum speed corresponds with a reduced probability of a successful dribble. This suggests that while speed is important, other factors such as ball control may moderate its positive effect, aligning with previous observations from isolated experiments.

A similar counterintuitive effect is observed for acceleration. While explosive acceleration is typically associated with beating a defender, our results show that higher maximum acceleration actually correlates with a lower likelihood of dribble success. One possible explanation is that when a player accelerates very rapidly, it becomes harder to maintain close control of the ball, increasing the risk of losing possession. This again highlights that dribble success depends not only on physical attributes, but also on technical control.

Additionally, spatial context matters: dribbles performed further from the sideline have a higher likelihood of success, underscoring the importance of positional factors in outcome prediction.

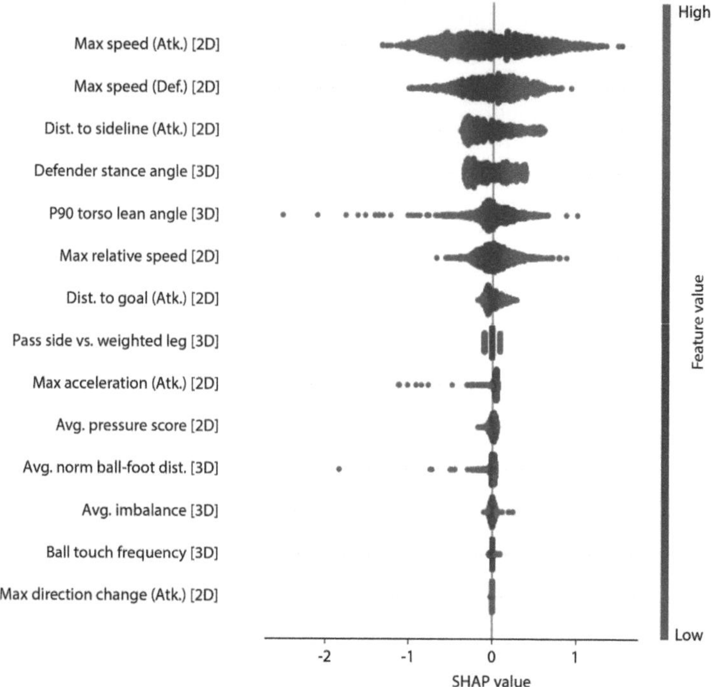

Fig. 2. SHAP values for the 2D and 3D features used for predicting dribble success. Positive SHAP values (right) indicate features that increase the probability of a successful dribble, while negative values (left) decrease it.

In contrast, features capturing attacker-defender interaction appear less influential overall. This stands in contrast to the finding by Oonk et al. [13] that only interactive features significantly affect dribble outcomes. Nevertheless, the two interactive features identified highlight critical aspects of attacker-defender interaction. Notably, elevated average defensive pressure during the dribble exerts a negative influence on success probability. Conversely, moments when the attacker exhibits a substantial relative speed advantage over the defender coincide with increased chances of dribble success, corroborating findings from Oonk et al. [13].

Among the most impactful 3D features, the defender's posture is paramount. A larger angle between the torso vectors of attacker and defender (Defender stance angle) signals a greater chance of a successful dribble, highlighting the role of defensive orientation. Similarly, the torso lean angle significantly affects model predictions; large lean angles measured during the dribble are associated with a higher likelihood of failure. These insights emphasize the importance of balance and posture. Finally, average normalized ball control, ball touch frequency and the imbalance metric appear to have a minimal effect on the model's predictions.

5   Conclusions

This paper aimed to analyze dribbling in professional football using 3D pose tracking data from Hawk-Eye, focusing on identifying relevant 3D features that describe dribbles and their impact on success. A methodology was developed to extract meaningful 3D features related to ball control, balance and attacker-defender interactions. The analysis showed that the attacker's torso lean angle and the alignment with the defender's posture strongly correlate with dribble success, while ball control had limited impact. Incorporating these 3D features into a logistic regression model alongside classic 2D features such as player speed, field position, and defensive pressure yielded a modest but clear improvement in predictive performance. These findings demonstrate that 3D pose data provides valuable new insights for understanding and predicting dribble outcomes in football.

Acknowledgements. JD received support from the KU Leuven Research Fund (iBOF/21/075, C14/24/091) and the Flemish government under the "Onderzoeksprogramma Artificiële Intelligentie (AI) Vlaanderen" programme.

A   Feature Definitions and Formulae

This appendix lists every feature used in our analysis, together with a brief explanation and the mathematical expression employed in the implementation. The following notations are used:

- T—dribble duration; N—number of frames.
- $j.$—3D joint coordinates returned by pose tracking.
- Subscripts "att", "def", "bf" denote attacker, defender, ball–foot.
- All spatial norms $\| \cdot \|$ are Euclidean distances in metres.

All integrals are evaluated numerically from frame-wise samples, i.e. $\int_0^T x(t)\, dt \approx \frac{1}{N} \sum_{k=1}^N x_k\, \Delta t$.

A.1   2D Spatial Features

These features describe the location of the dribble on the pitch, which impacts how aggressively the defense is played. For dribbles occurring far from the goal or close to the sideline, a defender is less compelled to defend aggressively than for dribbles close to the goal.

Distance to Sideline

$$d_{\text{side}} = \min\big(|y(t) - y_{\min}|,\ |y(t) - y_{\max}|\big)$$

where $y(t)$ is the lateral position of the attacker at time t, and $y_{\min}, y_{\max}$ are the y-coordinates of the two sidelines.

Distance to Goal

$$d_{\text{goal}} = \|\mathbf{p}(t) - \mathbf{g}\|,$$

where $\mathbf{p}(t) = (x(t), y(t))$ is the attacker's position at time t, and $\mathbf{g} = (x_{\text{goal}}, y_{\text{goal}})$ is the fixed 2-D coordinate of the center of the opponent's goal.

A.2   2D Kinematic Features

These features describe the speed and acceleration of a player during the dribble. They are computed both for the attacker and defender, independently of each other.

Average Speed

$$\bar{v} = \frac{1}{T} \int_0^T v(t)\, dt$$

Maximum Speed

$$v_{\text{max}} = \max_{t \in [0,T]} v(t)$$

Average Acceleration

$$\bar{a} = \frac{1}{T} \int_0^T a(t)\, dt$$

Maximum Acceleration

$$a_{\text{max}} = \max_{t \in [0,T]} a(t)$$

Maximum Change of Direction This feature quantifies the attacker's change of direction during the dribble. From the position coordinates, the player's speed, acceleration, and jerk (the time derivative of acceleration) are computed. When the acceleration exceeds a threshold $a_{\text{thresh}} = 3\,m/s^2$, it indicates the initiation of a directional turn. By analyzing the jerk $j(t) = \frac{da}{dt}$, specifically the moments when acceleration increases (positive jerk) and then decreases (negative jerk), the start and end points of the turn, t_{start} and t_{end}, are identified as:

$$a(t) > a_{\text{thresh}}, \quad j(t_{\text{start}}) > 0, \quad j(t_{\text{end}}) < 0.$$

The movement direction at time t is defined by the angle

$$\theta(t) = \arctan 2\big(v_y(t), v_x(t)\big),$$

where $v_x(t) = \frac{dx}{dt}$ and $v_y(t) = \frac{dy}{dt}$ are the velocity components. The degree of directional change is then quantified as the angular difference

$$\Delta\theta = |\theta(t_{\text{end}}) - \theta(t_{\text{start}})|.$$

This approach follows the method introduced by Kai et al. [10]. Finally, the maximum change of direction is computed as

$$\theta_{\text{max}} = \max_t |\theta(t + \delta t) - \theta(t)|.$$

A.3   2D Interactive Features

The interactive features focus on the relationship between the attacker and the defender(s). According to Oonk et al. [13], these features also represent the group of variables that have the greatest impact on distinguishing successful from unsuccessful dribbles.

Relative Speed. This feature describes the difference in speed between the attacker and the primary defender during the dribble. We consider both the average and maximal difference.

$$\Delta v_{\max} = \max_{t \in [0,T]} \left[v_{\text{att}}(t) - v_{\text{def}}(t) \right]$$

$$\overline{\Delta v} = \frac{1}{T} \int_0^T \left[v_{\text{att}}(t) - v_{\text{def}}(t) \right] dt$$

Pressure Score. The pressure exerted by nearby defenders on the attacker is determined using the pressure model of Andrienko et al. [1]. Given this pressure score $P(t)$, we compute the average and maximum defensive pressure during the dribble as

$$\bar{P} = \frac{1}{T} \int_0^T P(t)\, dt, \qquad P_{\max} = \max_{t \in [0,T]} P(t).$$

A.4   3D Ball Control

Normalized Ball-Foot Distance. Ball control describes how well a player keeps the ball within reach during the dribble. This feature is determined by measuring the average Euclidean distance between the ball and the foot that is closest to the ball.

$$d_{\text{bf}} = \frac{1}{T} \int_0^T \left\| \mathbf{b}(t) - \mathbf{f}_{\min}(t) \right\| dt,$$

where $\mathbf{b}(t)$ is the ball position and $\mathbf{f}_{\min}(t)$ is the toe joint closest to the ball.

How far a player can play the ball ahead of them is highly situation-dependent. When a player has a lot of space to dribble, they can play the ball further ahead without losing control of it. Therefore, we use the average pressure P exerted on the attacker during the dribble to normalize the ball control as follows:

$$d_{\text{bf}}^* = d_{\text{bf}}\, P^\alpha, \qquad \alpha = 0.1.$$

Ball Touch Frequency. The frequency of ball contact was identified as a determinant of dribbling in sports science research [20]. It also provides insight into the dribbling style employed: a higher frequency of ball contact generally points to a more technical dribbling style, whereas a lower frequency suggests players who tend to beat their opponent with speed.

The touch frequency can be derived from pose tracking data by analyzing the Euclidean distance between the ball and the big toe joint of the attacker's nearest foot in each frame. A ball contact is detected when:

- the distance is a local minimum, i.e., smaller than the distance in the preceding and following frame;
- the distance is smaller than a chosen threshold of 0.15 m;
- at least 0.25 s have passed since the previous detected ball contact, to avoid double-counting due to tracking noise.

The touch frequency is then calculated by dividing the number of ball contacts N_{touch} by the total duration of the dribble T, yielding a value expressed in touches per second:

$$f_{\text{touch}} = \frac{N_{\text{touch}}}{T}.$$

A.5 3D Balance Metrics

Several studies have already shown that balance plays an important role in the technical skills of football players [8,19]. In addition, Zago et al. [20] conclude that the centre of mass of players is also a determinant of dribbling

Centre-of-Mass Estimate. Two approaches to determine a player's centre of mass (CoM) based on the pose tracking data were implemented. A first, rather naïve, way to determine a player's centre of mass is simply to use the location of the *midHip* joint. This joint is located just below the navel, which is generally considered representative of the CoM of the human body.

$$\mathbf{CoM}_{\text{naive}} = \mathbf{j}_{\text{midHip}}.$$

A second method estimates a player's CoM using the anthropometric model of Winter [18], which assigns each body segment a percentage of the total body weight. In addition, it specifies where the CoM is located along each segment. Since these segments are defined by joints from the pose tracking data, their location is known, allowing us to estimate the CoM of a segment i as:

$$\mathbf{CoM}_i = (1 - r_i)\,\mathbf{j}_{1,i} + r_i\,\mathbf{j}_{2,i},$$

where $\mathbf{j}1,i$ and $\mathbf{j}2,i$ are the coordinates of the joints defining the segment and r_i its CoM ratio. The total CoM of the player is then computed as:

$$\mathbf{CoM} = \sum_{i=1}^{n} m_i\,\mathbf{CoM}_i,$$

Imbalance. This feature measures how centrally the player's CoM is positioned above the base of support and is defined as the distance in the XY-plane between the player's CoM and the midpoint between the two feet.

$$I = \left\lVert \mathbf{CoM}_{x,y} - \mathbf{FMP}_{x,y} \right\rVert,$$

where **FMP** denotes the midpoint between the left and right foot joints.

Torso Lean Angle. This feature indicates how much a player leans in a certain direction relative to their vertical axis, determined by defining a torso vector connecting the neck joint and the midpoint between the hips. The position of this vector in the vertical direction is then compared to its total length. The precise calculation is given by the formula:

$$\theta_{\text{lean}} = \arccos\left(\frac{z_{\text{neck}} - z_{\text{midHip}}}{\|\mathbf{v}_{\text{torso}}\|}\right), \quad \mathbf{v}_{\text{torso}} = \mathbf{j}_{\text{neck}} - \mathbf{j}_{\text{midHip}}.$$

where $\mathbf{j}_{\text{neck}}$ and $\mathbf{j}_{\text{midHip}}$ denote the 3-D coordinates of the neck and midHip joints, respectively, and z_{neck} and z_{midHip} represent the vertical (z-axis) components of these joint coordinates

A.6   3D Attacker–Defender Interaction

Pass Side vs. Weighted Leg. At a given moment in a dribble, the attacker must choose to pass the defender on the left or right side. We hypothesize that it's easier to pass the defender on the opposite side of his weight-bearing leg. Therefore, we first identify the defender's weight-bearing leg as based on the distances from his CoM to each heel joint. The leg with the shortest distance bears the most weight. Next, using 2D positional data, we infer the passing side by connecting the defender's position to the center of their own goal and constructing a perpendicular boundary line. When the attacker crosses this line, the defender is considered passed. The attacker's crossing relative to the defender's left or right side determines the passing side. This leads to a binary feature

$$\text{SidePass} = \begin{cases} 1, & \text{attacker passes opposite the defender's support leg,} \\ 0, & \text{otherwise.} \end{cases}$$

Defender Stance Angle. We define a vector for both the attacker and the defender, starting at the left hip joint and ending at the right hip joint. By calculating the angle between these two vectors at the moment when the attacker passes the defender, we determine the defender's posture as follows:

$$\theta_{\text{defender-attacker}} = \arccos\left(\frac{\mathbf{v}_{\text{defender}} \cdot \mathbf{v}_{\text{attacker}}}{\|\mathbf{v}_{\text{defender}}\| \cdot \|\mathbf{v}_{\text{attacker}}\|}\right)$$

where $\mathbf{v}_{\text{defender}}$ and $\mathbf{v}_{\text{attacker}}$ are the hip vectors of the defender and attacker, respectively.

Based on this angle (ranging between $90°$ and $180°$), three defender postures are distinguished:

$$\begin{cases} \text{side-on} & (90° - 120°) \\ \text{intermediate} & (120° - 150°) \\ \text{squared-up} & (150° - 180°) \end{cases}$$

References

1. Andrienko, G., et al.: Visual analysis of pressure in football. Data Min. Knowl. Disc. **31**(6), 1793–1839 (2017). https://doi.org/10.1007/s10618-017-0513-2
2. Arbués Sangüesa, A.: A journey of computer vision in sports: from tracking to orientation-based metrics. Ph.D. thesis, Universitat Pompeu Fabra, Barcelona, Spain (2021). https://repositori.upf.edu/items/835e902c-e861-4dcb-a02f-4fbcc332bc4e, phD thesis
3. Benjamin, I.: Top 10 fastest players in the world (2025). https://www.zonalsports.com/ranking/fastest-football-players
4. Brink, L., et al.: Measuring skill via player dynamics in football dribbling. Sci. Rep. **13** (2023). https://doi.org/10.1038/s41598-023-45914-6
5. Chapra, S.C., Canale, R.P., et al.: Numerical Methods for Engineers. Mcgraw-Hill Education (2011)
6. Decroos, T., Bransen, L., Van Haaren, J., Davis, J.: Actions speak louder than goals: Valuing player actions in soccer. In: Proceedings of the 25th ACM SIGKDD International Conference on Knowledge Discovery & Data Mining, pp. 1851–1861. Association for Computing Machinery (2019). https://doi.org/10.1145/3292500.3330758
7. Defazio, A., Bach, F., Lacoste-Julien, S.: SAGA: a fast incremental gradient method with support for non-strongly convex composite objectives. In: Proceedings of the 28th International Conference on Neural Information Processing Systems, pp. 1646—-1654. MIT Press, Cambridge, MA, USA (2014)
8. Evangelos, B., Georgios, K., Konstantinos, A., Gissis, I., Papadopoulos, C., Aristomenis, S.: Proprioception and balance training can improve amateur soccer players' technical skills. J. Phys. Educ. Sport **12**(1), 81–89 (2012)
9. FIFA: Semi-automated offside technology (2023). https://inside.fifa.com/innovation/world-cup-2022/semi-automated-offside-technology
10. Kai, T., Hirai, S., Anbe, Y., Takai, Y.: A new approach to quantify angles and time of changes-of-direction during soccer matches. PLoS ONE **16**(5) (2021). https://doi.org/10.1371/journal.pone.0251292
11. Kempe, M., Memmert, D.: "good, better, creative": the influence of creativity on goal scoring in elite soccer. J. Sports Sci. **36**(21), 2419–2423 (2018). https://doi.org/10.1080/02640414.2018.1459153
12. Meerhoff, L.A., Goes, F.R., De Leeuw, A.-W., Knobbe, A.: Exploring successful team tactics in soccer tracking data. In: Cellier, P., Driessens, K. (eds.) ECML PKDD 2019. CCIS, vol. 1168, pp. 235–246. Springer, Cham (2020). https://doi.org/10.1007/978-3-030-43887-6_18
13. Oonk, A., Buurke, T., Kempe, M., Lemmink, K.A.: Dribble like Robben: what determines successfulness in 1-vs-1 actions in elite soccer? (2024). presented at the 29th Annual Congress of the European College of Sport Science (ECSS)
14. Pedregosa, F., et al Édouard Duchesnay: Scikit-learn: machine learning in Python. J. Mach. Learn. Res. **12**(85), 2825–2830 (2011). http://jmlr.org/papers/v12/pedregosa11a.html
15. Rahimian, P., Toka, L.: Optical tracking in team sports: a survey on player and ball tracking methods in soccer and other team sports. J. Quant. Anal. Sports **18**(1), 35–57 (2022). https://doi.org/10.1515/jqas-2020-0088
16. Sony group corporation: Hawk-Eye: the evolution of sports officiating and analysis. https://www.sony.com/en/SonyInfo/technology/stories/entries/20240411/hawkeye/

17. Stats perform: opta event definitions (2024). https://www.statsperform.com/opta-event-definitions/
18. Winter, D.A.: Biomechanics and Motor Control of Human Movement, 4th edn. Wiley (2009)
19. Yusuf, M.Z., Rumini, R., Setyawati, H.: The effect of agility and balance training on dribbling speed in soccer games. J. Phys. Educ. Sports **11**(1), 125–133 (2022). https://doi.org/10.15294/jpes.v11i1.54044
20. Zago, M., et al.: Dribbling determinants in sub-elite youth soccer players. J. Sports Sci. **34**(5), 411–419 (2016)

Other Team Sports

Multidimensional Heterogeneity Learning for Field Goal Attempt Analysis of NBA Players

Guanyu Hu[1], Yishu Xue[2], and Weining Shen[3(✉)]

[1] Michigan State University, East Lansing, MI 48824, USA
`huguanyu@msu.edu`
[2] Mountain View, CA 94043, USA
[3] University of California, Irvine, CA 92697, USA
`weinings@uci.edu`

Abstract. We propose a multidimensional tensor clustering approach for studying how professional basketball players' shooting patterns vary over court locations and game time. Unlike most existing methods that only study continuous-valued tensors or have to assume the same cluster structure along different tensor directions, we propose a Bayesian nonparametric model that deals with count-valued tensors and projects the heterogeneity among players onto tensor dimensions while allowing cluster structures to be different over directions. Our method is fully probabilistic; hence allows simultaneous inference on both the number of clusters and the cluster configurations. We present an efficient posterior sampling method and establish the large-sample convergence properties for the posterior distribution. Simulation studies have demonstrated an excellent empirical performance of the proposed method. Finally, an application to shot chart data collected from 191 NBA players during the 2017–2018 regular season is conducted and reveals several interesting insights for basketball analytics.

Keywords: Basketball analytics · Bayesian nonparametrics · Tensor clustering

1 Introduction

There is a rapid growth in sports analytics over the recent years thanks to the fast development in game tracking technologies [1]. New statistics and machine learning methods are largely needed to address a range of questions from game outcome prediction to player performance evaluation [3,4,8], and to in-game strategy planning [7,30].

Our focus in this paper is to study the National Basketball Association (NBA) players' *shooting patterns*, in particular, how they change over shooting locations and game time (e.g., first quarter versus clutch time). In professional basketball research, shooting pattern (or field goal attempt) is a fundamental metric since

H. Rios-Neto et al. (Eds.): MLSA 2025, CCIS 2833, pp. 139–157, 2026.
https://doi.org/10.1007/978-3-032-15165-0_10

it often provides valuable insights to players, coaches and managers, e.g., players and coaches will be able to obtain a better understanding of their current shooting choices and hence develop further offensive/defensive plans accordingly, while managers can make better data-informed decisions on player recruitment. In the literature, it is common to employ spatial and spatial-temporal models [19,22,28] to study the spatial and temporal dependence in the field goal attempt data. The key novelty of our paper is to introduce a new Bayesian tensor multidimensional clustering method that studies the heterogeneity of shooting patterns among players.

Our starting point is to recognize that the field goal attempt data in basketball games enjoys a natural *tensor structure*. For example, we can divide the basketball half court into regions under the *polar coordinate* system and then summarize the number of field goal attempts over each region during each of the four quarters of the game as entries in a three-way tensor, where each tensor direction corresponds to the shooting distance, angle, and game time (quarter). One advantage of considering a tensor representation is that the spatial-temporal dependence structure is automatically considered as part of the tensor structure. Compared to the most existing works that rely on Cartesian coordinate system [17,19,22,37,38], our approach certainly makes more sense since shooting angle and distance are two important factors that affect the shooting selection of professional players [28]. Studying the change of shooting patterns over time is also meaningful, e.g., Stephen Curry has made a comparable fewer number of attempts in fourth quarter during regular season simply because Golden State Warriors has often established a significant lead at the end of the third quarter during the 2017–2018 regular season.

Related Work on Tensor Methods: Tensor models have received a great deal of attention in machine learning and statistics literature [2,15,20,33]. For tensor clustering problems, most existing work [5,14,21,34] either works with a single tensor or assumes that the clustering structure is the same across different tensor directions. It is also common that they only consider tensors with entries that take continuous or binary values. In terms of model estimation, clustering is often based on solving a regularized optimization problem, which requires pre-specifying the number of clusters or choosing the cluster number based on certain *ad hoc* criteria. There are some recent papers on Bayesian tensor models, e.g., [12,13,32]. However, all of them are in the regression context, hence cannot be directly applied to solve our problem. Our proposed approach differs with aforementioned methods in several ways. First, we consider a flexible multidimensional tensor clustering problem, which allows different clustering structures over tensor directions. We believe this is a meaningful relaxation in many applications, e.g., basketball players' shooting choice may differ significantly in terms of shooting distance, angle and game time depending on players' position, shooting preference and role in the team. Moreover, we focus on count-valued tensors (rather than continuous-valued tensors) for the obvious reason that the number of shot attempts is the main outcome of interest in our application. Thirdly, our model is fully probabilistic, which allows an easier interpretation compared to optimization-based methods. In particular, we consider a Bayesian nonparametric model under the mixture of finite mixtures framework (MFM) [23], which allows simultaneous estimation and inference for the number of clusters and the associated clustering configuration for each direction (e.g. distance, angle, and quarter).

Related Work on Spatial Analysis and Sports Analytics: In the literature, it is common to view sports data (especially basketball shooting chart) as a special type of spatial data and then consider spatial and spatiotemporal models [19,22,28]. However, there are still some notable differences between these two types of data. For example, most of the spatial data would assume dependent regions to be close to each other, i.e., neighboring effect. This is not necessarily the case in basketball analytics, e.g., shooting preference/accuracy for 3-point shots over two corners are often strongly correlated despite these two locations being far apart. This is one motivation to consider the tensor approach as an alternative to classical spatial methods.

Main Contributions and Broad Impact: (1) In sports analytics literature, very few papers have considered tensor approaches, e.g., [25] proposed an optimization-based tensor decomposition approach for learning latent factor representation of basketball shooting patterns, [29] studied basketball shooting strategies by estimating transition probability tensors, and [24] proposed a tensor decomposition framework that incorporates spatio-temporal patterns in basketball games. It is our hope that this paper can contribute to promoting more use of tensor methods in different sport applications. (2) We develop a novel multidimensional tensor clustering approach that allows different clustering structures over tensor directions and handles count-valued data. The proposed method is fully Bayesian, which renders convenient inference on the number of clusters and the clustering structure. (3) We provide a large-sample theoretical justification for our method by showing posterior consistency for the cluster number and contraction rate for the mixing distributions. These results are new for Bayesian tensor models.

2   Method

2.1   Probabilistic Multi-dimensional Tensor Clustering

We treat the number of shots as a three-way tensor and discuss a multidimensional clustering approach in this section. Note that each direction of the tensor represents the shooting angle, distance to the basket, and one of the four quarters in the game. Our proposed method can be conveniently extended to study general multi-way tensor data as well. Let Y be a $p_1 \times p_2 \times p_3$ tensor with each element Y_{ijk} only taking count values for $i = 1, \ldots, p_1; j = 1, \ldots, p_2; k = 1, \ldots, p_3$. It is natural to consider a Poisson distribution with a mean parameter represented as a rank-one tensor, that is,

$$Y \sim \text{Poisson}(\gamma_1 \circ \gamma_2 \circ \gamma_3), \tag{1}$$

where $\circ$ denotes the outer product between two vectors, and $\gamma_1 \in \mathbb{R}_+^{p_1}, \gamma_2 \in \mathbb{R}_+^{p_2}, \gamma_3 \in \mathbb{R}_+^{p_3}$. Model (1) can also be viewed as a Poisson regression model where the mean parameter corresponds to an analysis of variance (ANOVA) model with main effects only, that is, $\log \mathrm{E}(Y_{ijk}) = \log \gamma_{1,i} + \log \gamma_{2,j} + \log \gamma_{3,k}$ for $1 \leq i \leq p_1, 1 \leq j \leq p_2, 1 \leq k \leq p_3$. By ignoring the interaction effects (at this stage), the number of parameters is effectively reduced from $p_1 p_2 p_3$ to $(p_1 + p_2 + p_3)$. This enables parsimonious parameter estimation and easy interpretation in our NBA application study, i.e., the main effects $\log \gamma_1, \log \gamma_2, \log \gamma_3$ correspond to the additive effect of shooting distance, angle, and game time (quarter).

Our next step is to adopt a mixture model framework to learn the multidimensional heterogeneity pattern among players. Note that by doing so, the main effects corresponding to shooting angles, shooting distances, and game quarters are *no longer independent marginally* because of the mixture model component. In particular, we consider three independent mixture of finite mixtures (MFM) [23] priors on $\gamma_1, \gamma_2, \gamma_3$ such that the clustering pattern in those three directions can be learned separately. Here we present a brief introduction to MFM without getting into more details. Given n observations, we consider $z_1, \ldots, z_n$ as their clustering labels, e.g., $z_1 = z_2 = z_4$ would mean that observations $1, 2, 4$ belong to the same cluster. Then the MFM prior can be expressed as

$$K \sim p(\cdot), \quad (\pi_1, \ldots, \pi_K) \mid K \sim \mathrm{Dir}(\gamma, \ldots, \gamma),$$
$$z_i \mid K, \pi \sim \sum_{h=1}^{K} \pi_h \delta_h, \quad i = 1, \ldots, n, \tag{2}$$

where K is the number of clusters, $(\pi_1, \ldots, \pi_K)$ are associated cluster weights and $\sum_{h=1}^{K} \pi_h \delta_h$ is the mixture distribution with δ_h being a point-mass at h. Under the Bayesian framework, all those three quantities are random and hence are assigned with prior distributions, i.e., we use $p(\cdot)$, which is a proper probability mass function on $\mathbb{N}_+$, as a prior on K, and a Dirichlet distribution on the mixture weights. Our model is related to but different from the classical Chinese restaurant process (CRP) [10], where the probability of introducing a new table (cluster) for MFM is slowed down by a factor of $V_n(t+1)/V_n(t)$, which allows for a model-based pruning of the tiny extraneous clusters. Here the coefficient $V_n(t)$ is defined as

$$V_n(t) = \sum_{n=1}^{+\infty} \frac{k_{(t)}}{(\gamma k)^{(n)}} p(k),$$

where $k_{(t)} = k(k-1)\ldots(k-t+1)$, and $(\gamma k)^{(n)} = \gamma k(\gamma k+1)\ldots(\gamma k+n-1)$, and γ is the hyperparameter in the Dirichlet prior for the weights. The conditional distributions of $z_i, i = 2, \ldots, n$ under (2) can be defined in a Pólya urn scheme similar to CRP:

$$P(z_i = c \mid z_1, \ldots, z_{i-1}) \propto$$
$$\begin{cases} |c| + \gamma, & \text{at an existing table labeled } c \\ V_n(t+1)/V_n(t)\gamma, & \text{if } c \text{ is a new table} \end{cases} \tag{3}$$

with t being the number of existing clusters.

Now back to the shooting chart data, as we propose to use three independent MFM priors for clustering shooting distance, angle, and game time, our final model can be presented in the following hierarchical structure,

$$
\begin{aligned}
&K_\ell \overset{\text{i.i.d.}}{\sim} p_K, \quad \ell = 1, 2, 3, \\
&\boldsymbol{\pi}_\ell = (\pi_{\ell,1}, \ldots, \pi_{\ell,K_\ell}) \mid K_\ell \sim \text{Dir}(\nu, \ldots, \nu), \nu > 0, \\
&\log \boldsymbol{\gamma}_{\ell,1}, \ldots, \log \boldsymbol{\gamma}_{\ell,K_\ell} \overset{\text{i.i.d.}}{\sim} \text{MVN}_{p_\ell}(\mathbf{0}, \Sigma_\ell), \quad \ell = 1, 2, 3, \\
&\Sigma_\ell = \sigma_\ell^2 (I_\ell - \rho_\ell \boldsymbol{W}_\ell), \quad \ell = 1, 2, 3, \\
&\sigma_\ell^2 \sim \text{Gamma}(a, b), \quad \ell = 1, 2, 3, \\
&\rho_\ell \sim \text{Unif}(c_{1\ell}, c_{2\ell}), \quad \ell = 1, 2, 3, \\
&P(z_{i\ell} = j \mid \boldsymbol{\pi}_\ell, K_\ell) = \pi_{j\ell}, \quad \ell = 1, 2, 3, \quad j = 1, \ldots, K_\ell, \\
&\boldsymbol{Y}_i \sim \text{Poisson}(\boldsymbol{\gamma}_{1,z_{i1}} \circ \boldsymbol{\gamma}_{2,z_{i2}} \circ \boldsymbol{\gamma}_{3,z_{i3}}), \quad i = 1, \ldots, n,
\end{aligned}
\tag{4}
$$

where the main effects for distance, angle, and period are modeled by multivariate normal distributions and their covariance matrices involve adjacency matrices, denoted by $\boldsymbol{W}_l$'s, that are used for incorporating the potential spatial and temporal correlation information ($\boldsymbol{W}_l$ is a binary matrix where an entry equals to one only if two corresponding shooting locations or quarters are next to each other). To ensure those covariance matrices Σ_ℓ are positive definite, we introduce $c_{1\ell}$ and $c_{2\ell}$ as the reciprocals of minimum and maximum eigenvalues of $\boldsymbol{W}_l$, respectively. For the prior p_K on the number of clusters, we consider a truncated Poisson(1) following the recommendations in [9, 23].

Our multidimensional clustering model in (4) sits between two extremes. One is the usual tensor clustering model that assumes the same cluster structure across different directions, which certainly is more restrictive compared to ours. The other is to marginally cluster over each of the tensor directions and solve multiple clustering problems independently, which does not fully utilize the tensor structural information. Our method combines the attractive features from both sides by allowing cluster structures to be different over directions while borrowing information to improve the estimation efficiency.

Our model in (4) can be viewed as a Bayesian mixture of rank-one tensor models. Compared to the frequentist work on tensor clustering [5, 34], where a Tucker decomposition is usually utilized and the choice of the rank relies heavily on pre-specification or certain model selection criteria, our approach is capable of automatically determining the rank while quantifying the uncertainty in rank selection. Moreover, our method is fully probabilistic; hence each mixture component is easy to interpret in practice.

2.2 Theoretical Properties

Next we study the theoretical properties for the posterior distribution obtained from model (4). For convenience, we define three mixing measures $G_\ell = \sum_{i=1}^{K_\ell} \pi_{\ell,i} \delta(\gamma_{\ell,i})$ for $\ell = 1, 2, 3$, where $\delta(\cdot)$ is the point mass measure. In other words, G_1, G_2, G_3 represent the clustering structures and associated parameters along each of the three directions in the tensor. In order to establish the posterior contraction results, we consider a refined parameter space $\boldsymbol{\Theta}^*$ defined as $\cup_{k_1,k_2,k_3=1}^{\infty} \boldsymbol{\Theta}_{\boldsymbol{k}}^*$ for $\boldsymbol{k} = (k_1, k_2, k_3)$, where $\boldsymbol{\Theta}_{\boldsymbol{k}}^*$ is a compact parameter space for all model parameters including mixture weights and main effects given a fixed cluster number for each direction, i.e., $K_1 = k_1, K_2 = k_2$, and $K_3 = k_3$. More precisely, we define $\boldsymbol{\Theta}_{\boldsymbol{k}}^*$ as

$$\left\{ \pi_{\ell,i} \in [\epsilon, 1 - \epsilon] \ \text{ for every } i = 1, \ldots, k_\ell, \ell = 1, 2, 3, \right.$$

$$\sum_{j}^{k_\ell} \pi_{\ell,j} = 1 \ \text{ for every } \ell = 1, 2, 3,$$

$$\left. \gamma_{\ell,i} \in [\epsilon, M] \ \text{ for every } i = 1, \ldots, k_\ell, \ell = 1, 2, 3, \right\},$$

where ϵ and M are some pre-specified positive constants. For any two mixing measures $G_1 = \sum_{i=1}^{k} p_i \delta(\gamma_i)$ and $G_2 = \sum_{j=1}^{k'} p'_j \delta(\gamma_j)$, we define their Wasserstein distance as $W(G_1, G_2) = \inf_{q \in \mathcal{Q}} \sum_{i,j} q_{ij} |\gamma_i - \gamma_j|$, where $\mathcal{Q}$ denotes the collection of joint discrete distribution on the space of $\{1, \ldots, k\} \times \{1, \ldots, k'\}$ and q_{ij} is the probability being associated with (i, j)-element and it satisfies the constraint that $\sum_{i=1}^{k} q_{ij} = p'_j$ and $\sum_{j=1}^{k'} q_{ij} = p_i$, for every $i = 1, \ldots, k$ and $j = 1, \ldots, k'$.

For $\ell = 1, 2, 3$, let K_ℓ^0 and G_ℓ^0 be the true number of clusters and true mixing measure along direction ℓ. Also let P_0 be the associated joint probability measure. Then the following theorem establishes the posterior consistency and contraction rate for the cluster number and mixing measure. The proof is given in the Appendix; and it is based on the results for Bayesian mixture models in [11].

Theorem 1. *Let $\Pi_n(\cdot \mid \boldsymbol{Y}_1, \ldots, \boldsymbol{Y}_n)$ be the posterior distribution obtained from (4) given i.i.d. observations $\boldsymbol{Y}_1, \ldots, \boldsymbol{Y}_n$. Suppose that the true parameters belong to $\boldsymbol{\Theta}^*$. Then for each of $\ell = 1, 2, 3$, we have*

$$\Pi_n \left\{ K_\ell = K_\ell^0 \mid \boldsymbol{Y}_1, \ldots, \boldsymbol{Y}_n) \right\} \to 1, \ and$$

$$\Pi_n \left\{ (W(G_\ell, G_\ell^0) \lesssim (\log n / n)^{-1/4} \mid \boldsymbol{Y}_1, \ldots, \boldsymbol{Y}_n) \right\} \to 1,$$

almost surely under P_0 as $n \to \infty$.

Theorem 1 shows that as sample size $n \to \infty$, our proposed Bayesian model is capable of correctly identifying the unknown number of clusters along each of the tensor directions with posterior probability tending to one. Moreover, the latent clustering structure (e.g., cluster membership) can also be consistently recovered. The contraction rate for G_ℓ is agrees with the rate obtained in [11]. The assumption of a compact parameter space $\boldsymbol{\Theta}^*$ is needed to rule out extreme scenarios, for example, when some mixture probabilities are extremely close to 0, for which it becomes very challenging to distinguish between our model and a sub-model without these small mixture components. In practice, this assumption is often satisfied since we can always restrict the modeling parameters to take values within a pre-specified range, e.g., assuming cluster probability to be at least ϵ for some small ϵ values such as .0001%. Our results can also be extended to general multi-way tensors as long as the independent MFM priors are used for each direction.

2.3 Bayesian Inference

We discuss the posterior sampling scheme for our model. For the MFM prior, we use the stick-breaking [31] approximation to reconstruct

$$K_\ell \sim p_K, \boldsymbol{\pi}_\ell = (\pi_{1\ell}, \dots, \pi_{K_\ell \ell}) \mid K_\ell \sim \mathrm{Dir}(\nu, \dots, \nu)$$

as follows for each of $\ell = 1, 2, 3$,

- **Step 1.** Generate $\eta_1, \eta_2, \cdots \overset{\text{iid}}{\sim} \mathrm{Exp}(\psi_\ell)$,
- **Step 2.** Let $K_\ell = \min\{j : \sum_{k=1}^{j} \eta_k \geq 1\}$,
- **Step 3.** Set $\pi_{h\ell} = \eta_h$, for $h = 1, \cdots, K_\ell - 1$,
- **Step 4.** Set $\pi_{h\ell} = 1 - \sum_{h=1}^{K_\ell - 1} \pi_h$,

where we choose $(K_\ell - 1) \sim \mathrm{Poisson}(\psi_\ell)$ and $\nu = 1$. Based on the stick-breaking reparameterization, we obtain a similar hierarchical model as the Dirichlet process mixture model in [18] when we choose a sufficiently large dimension T for $\boldsymbol{\pi}_\ell$ and set the last $T - K_\ell$ elements to be zero. Due to the lack of available analytical form for the posterior distribution of γ's, we employ the MCMC sampling algorithm to sample from the posterior distribution, and then obtain the posterior estimates of the unknown parameters. Computation is facilitated by the **nimble** [35] package in R [26].

To determine the final clustering configuration based on post-burn-in iterations, we use the Dahl's method [6]. The main idea is to obtain a clustering configuration that best represents the posterior samples based on comparing the "pairwise similarity" between different cluster structures. The procedure can be described as follows. First, at MCMC iteration t, based on the n-dimensional vector $(z_1^{(t)}, \dots, z_n^{(t)})$ for the latent clusters, a membership matrix $M^{(t)}$ consisting of 0 and 1's can be obtained, where $M^{(t)}(i,j) = M^{(t)}(j,i) = 1(z_i^{(t)} = z_j^{(t)})$. Next, the membership matrices are averaged over all post-burn-in iterations to get a matrix of pairwise similarity, $\overline{M} = \sum_{t=1}^{T} M^{(t)}/T$, where T denotes the total number of iterations. Finally, the iteration that has the smallest element-wise Euclidean distance from $\overline{M}$ is taken as the inferred clustering configuration, i.e., with t^* being

$$t^* = \arg\min_t \sum_{i=1}^{n} \sum_{j=1}^{n} \left(M^{(t)}(i,j) - \overline{M}(i,j) \right)^2,$$

and the final inferred configuration is obtained as $(z_1^{t^*}, \dots, z_n^{t^*})$.

3   NBA Data Analysis

We consider the shot attempts made by players during the 2017–2018 NBA regular season excluding the overtime period. Rookie year players who started their NBA career in 2017 are excluded. We also exclude players who made very few number of shots in that season, e.g., due to long-term injury. Shots that were made at negative degrees (under the polar coordinate system) are also excluded. At the end, the dataset that we study consists of 122,001 shot attempts made by 191 players, with Aron Baynes bottoming the list with 317, and Russell Westbrook topping the list with 1356 shot attempts.

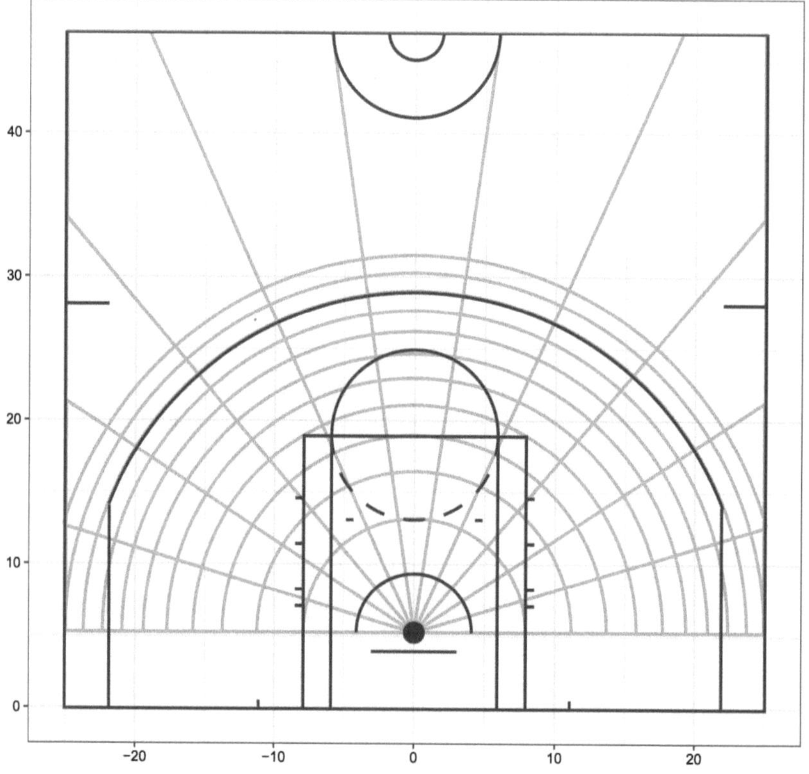

Fig. 1. Illustration of the partition scheme imposed on the court.

We consider the polar coordinate representation of shot attempts in a similar way with [28]. We treat the basket as origin and partition the angle (from 0 to π) into 11 equal sections. In terms of the shooting distance, we partition it into 12 sections, with the first 11 be designed so that the areas of all sectors and annular sectors are the same. The remaining 9 areas correspond to the remaining areas on the offensive half court. The partition scheme is illustrated in Fig. 1.

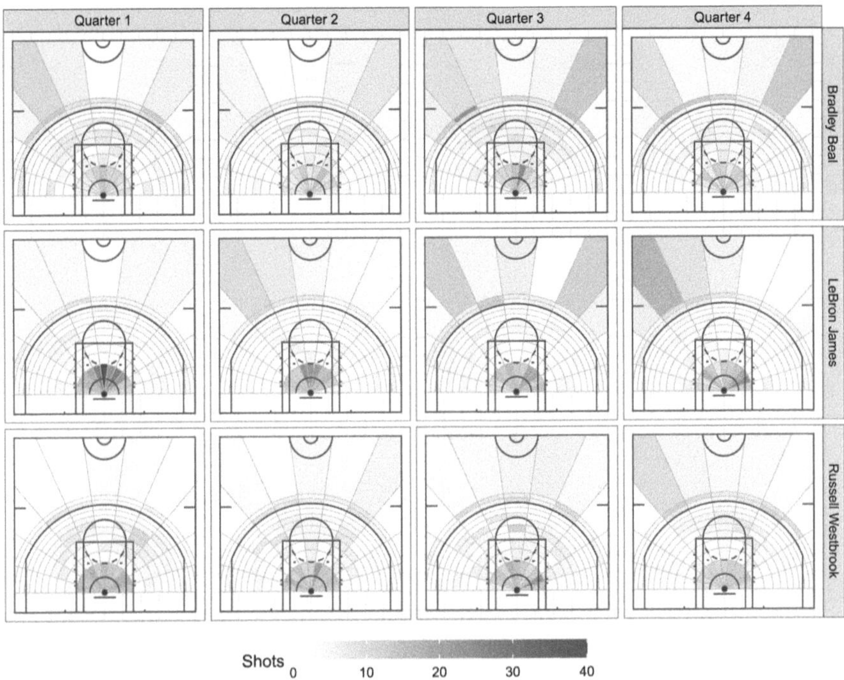

Fig. 2. Visualization of shot count tensors for Bradley Beal, LeBron James, and Russell Westbrook.

Compared to the partition scheme in Fig. 2 of [28], where the annular sectors only covered the regions near the three-point line, we extend the annular sectors because of the current trend of making three-point shots among NBA players, e.g., Stephen Curry and Damian Lillard. For each player, we further divide the number of shot attempts by four game quarters for each court partition, and end up with a $11 \times 12 \times 4$-dimensional tensor. In Fig. 2, we choose three players, Bradley Beal, LeBron James, and Russell Westbrook, and present their shot charts for demonstration. Some interesting patterns can be observed from the plots, e.g., LeBron James makes more shots facing the basket, and Russell Westbrook makes fewer shot attempts in the fourth quarter on average.

We apply the proposed multidimensional heterogeneity learning approach on the collected tensor data from 191 players. The same neighborhood matrices W_1, W_2, and W_3 from the simulation studies are used. We consider a MCMC chain of length 10,000 and and a thinning interval of 2, resulting in a total of 5,000 posterior samples. We then discard the first 2,000 as burn-in and use the rest of 3,000 samples to obtain the final clustering configuration using Dahl's method as described in Sect. 2.3.

We obtain two clusters of sizes 71 and 120 over the angle direction as shown in Fig. 3. While it can be seen that players in both clusters make more shots when facing the basket, those in cluster 1 also make a fair amount of shots at

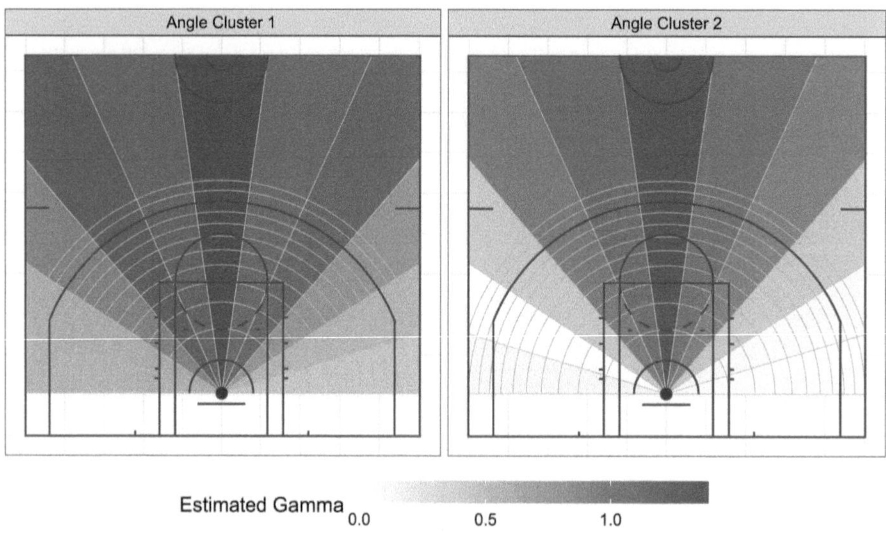

Fig. 3. Visualization of γ_1 estimates for two shooting angle clusters.

the two wings, as well as the corners. Players in cluster 2, however, mostly shoot in the region facing the basket and its immediate neighbors. Compared to those in cluster 1, they make less corner shots, as the estimated γ_1 is almost 0 in the two regions on each side. Representative players for the two clusters are, respectively, James Harden and John Wall. Their shot charts are given in Fig. 4. Compared to John Wall, James Harden has a wider range of shooting angle hot spots.

Shooting patterns in terms of distance to basket have been clustered into three groups as visualized in Fig. 5. Players in the cluster 1 have two hot regions: near the basket, and beyond the three point line. Point guards and shooting guards (small forwards) make the majority of this cluster (75 players), with representative players such as Kyrie Irving and Stephen Curry. Compared with cluster 1, the 90 players in cluster 2 tend to shoot less beyond the three point line, but make more perimeter shots. A representative player for this cluster is Russell Westbrook. Finally, in cluster 3, most of the 26 players only shoot in regions that are closest to the basket, such as DeAndre Jordan and Clint Capela. Most of their shots are slam dunks and alley-oops. Some other players (e.g., Fred VanVleet and Jonas Valanciunas) in cluster 3, although also making perimeter shots and three-pointers, rely heavily on lay-ups. We pick one representative player from each cluster and present their shooting charts in Fig. 6. It shows that Curry most often makes three-pointers, or lay-ups, while Russell Westbrook, in addition to three-pointers and lay-ups or slam dunks, also make a fair amount of perimeter shots. DeAndre Jordan, however, rarely shoots outside the 3-second zone.

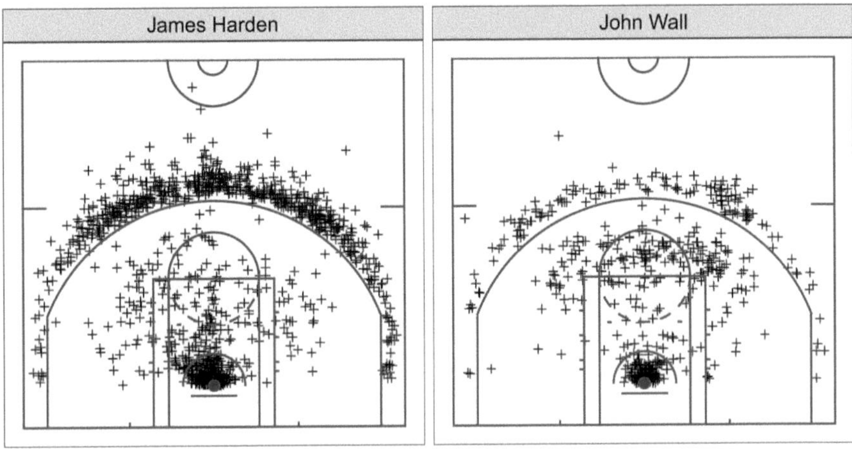

Fig. 4. Shot charts for representative players from the two angle clusters.

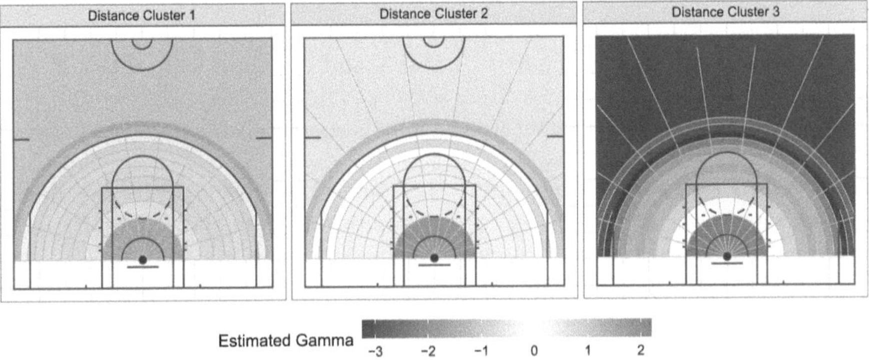

Fig. 5. Visualization of γ_2 estimates for the three shooting distance clusters.

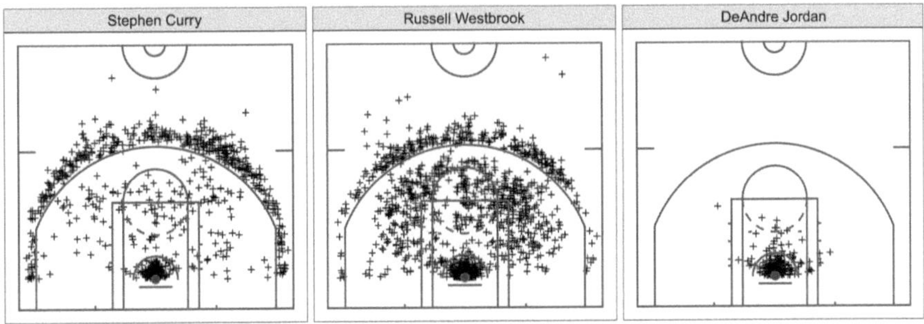

Fig. 6. Shot charts for representative players from the three distance clusters.

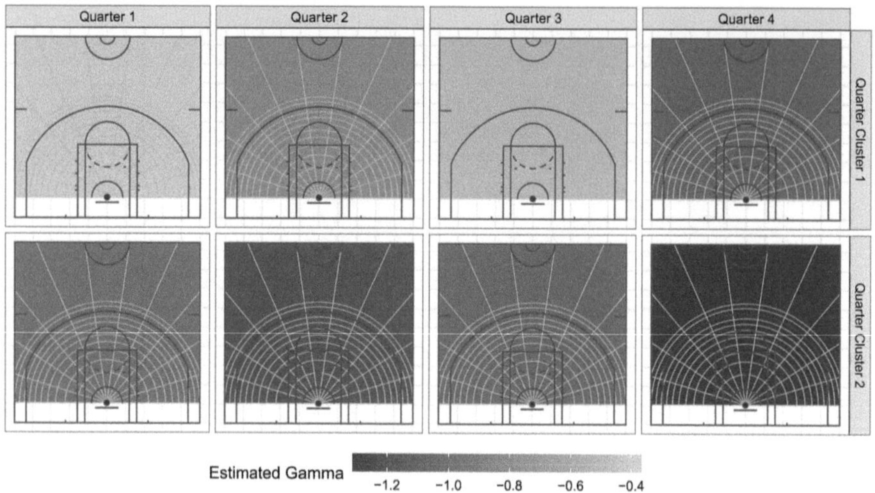

Fig. 7. Visualization of γ_3 estimates for two game quarter clusters.

Finally, the two clusters for quarters are visualized in Fig. 7. In cluster 1, players make more shots in quarters 1 and 3, and less shots in quarters 2 and 4. Most players in this cluster are leading players in their teams, and they often take breaks during the second quarter. In the fourth quarter, leading players may also take breaks if their teams lead or fall behind by wide margins. Stephen Curry, Kevin Durant and Paul George are in this cluster. In cluster 2, the distribution of shots across four quarters is more even than that in cluster 1, and on average the estimated γ_3 is relatively smaller. The cluster sizes are 91 and 100, which indicate these two patterns are similarly prevalent among the players that we studied. We pick Anthony Davis and Chris Paul as two representative players from two clusters and present their shooting charts over four quarters in Fig. 8. It can be seen that Anthony Davis makes more shots in quarters 1 and 3, while the distribution of shots of Chris Paul is more even across the four quarters.

Please see the Appendix for the simulation study results.

4   Discussion

We propose a new multidimensional tensor clustering method in this paper and demonstrate its utility by studying how shooting patterns distribute over court locations and game time among different players. Our method is applicable to many other sports such as football and baseball, where it is natural to formulate and model the multi-way array data. The proposed method also applies to other applications such as imaging analysis and recommender systems.

Several future work directions remain open. First, our method is based on Poisson distribution for outcomes in the tensor; and it is of interest to generalize this assumption by considering other types of distributions such as zero-inflated

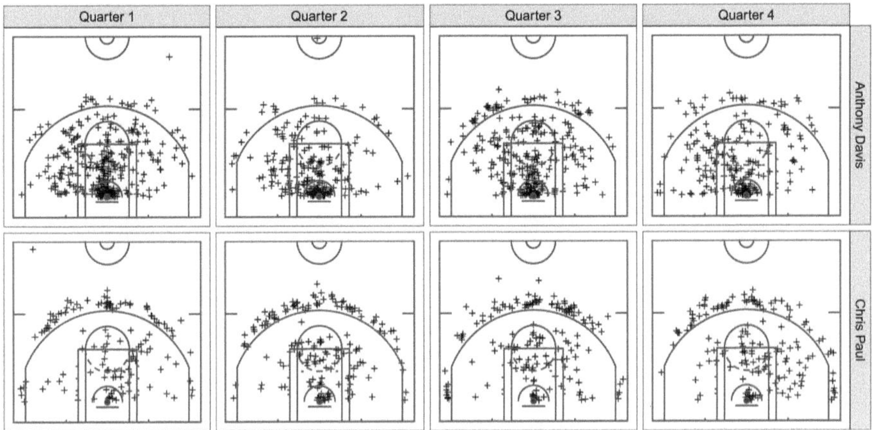

Fig. 8. Shot charts for representative players from the two quarter clusters.

Poisson and continuous distributions. Incorporating sparsity in tensor models is another interesting direction that will allow us to deal with high-dimensional tensors. We adopt Dahls' method for summarizing the posterior samples on the clustering allocation. It will be of interest to adopt other approaches such as [36]. From applications point of view, it is of interest to analyze and compare the shooting patterns between different periods of games/seasons, e.g., regular season versus playoff games, and before-pandemic versus 2020 NBA bubble seasons.

Appendix

Simulation

To evaluate the performance of the proposed model, simulation studies are performed on generated data sets with a total of 150 players. We consider two simulation settings. For the first setting, we consider a three-angle pattern and three-distance partition of the court, i.e., the court is divided into 9 parts based on combinations of distance and angle. Two clusters of size 75 are set for angle, distance, and quarter, respectively. The patterns for angle and group are visualized in Fig. 9. For quarter group 1, we choose $\gamma_3 = (-1, -1, -1, -1)^\top$; and for quarter group 2, $\gamma_3 = (-0.5, -2, -0.5, -2)^\top$. For the second simulation setting, we consider a finer partition of the court, including 11 angles, 12 distances, and again two quarter patterns in the same way as design 1. The true number of clusters is 3 (each cluster cluster of size 50) for the angle, 3 (each cluster of size 50) for the distance, and 2 (each of size 75) for the quarter. The angle and group patterns are visualized in Fig. 10. Under both settings, for each piece of the partitioned court, the corresponding number of shots is generated using the associated γ_1, γ_2 and γ_3 based on the last line of Eq. 4. The proposed multidimensional clustering approach is then applied to fit the generated data; and this procedure is repeated for 100 times for each setting. All the computations were performed on a computing server (256GB RAM, with 8 AMD Opteron 6276 processors, operating at 2.3 GHz, with 8 processing cores in each) and the running time was within twelve hours.

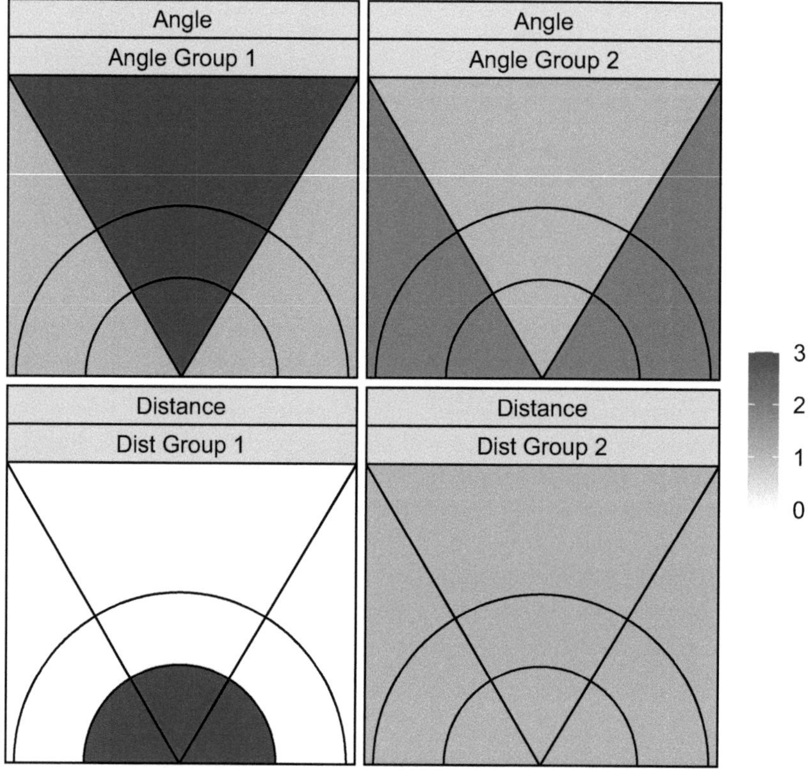

Fig. 9. Visualization for γ_1 and γ_2 in the first simulation setting.

To evaluate the clustering performance on each of the tensor directions, we use the Rand index (RI) [27], which is a commonly used metric that measures the concordance between two clustering schemes. Taking values between 0 and 1, a larger value of RI indicates a higher agreement. To evaluate whether the true number of clusters is correctly inferred, we also examine the total number of clusters inferred in each replicate over each of the three directions.

We consider two competing methods, K-means (function kmeans() in R) and density-based spatial clustering (DBSCAN; implemented in **fpc** [16]). To make a fair comparison, we use the number of clusters obtained by our method for K-means. For DBSCAN, as the method depends on a pre-specified "reachability distance", we use four candidate values, 25, 50, 75, and 100; and we denote the methods as DBSCAN-25,..., DBSCAN-100 for the rest of this paper. Both methods are applied to each of the three directions in an independent manner.

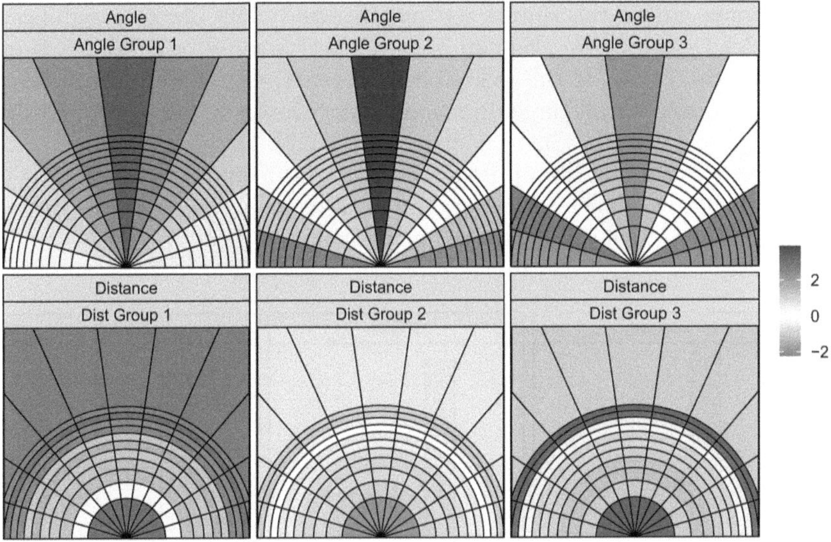

Fig. 10. Visualization for γ_1 and γ_2 in the second simulation setting.

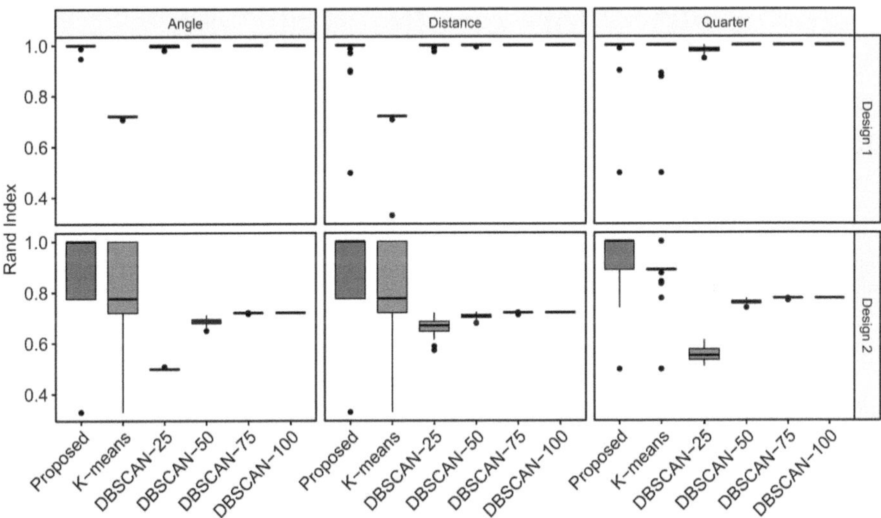

Fig. 11. Simulation results: Rand index boxplots for angle, distance, and quarter over 100 Monte-Carlo replicates.

In other words, for 150 simulated players, we sum out the distance and quarter directions, and obtain 150 11-dimensional count vectors for clustering.

We summarize the rand indexes from 100 replicates as boxplots in Fig. 11 and also report the average RI in Table 1. From the results, we find a clear advantage of our method over K-means. Compared to DBSCAN, our advantage is not obvious under the simple setting, Design 1; but becomes significantly better under Design 2. We also note that the performance of DBSCAN is quite sensitive to the choice of the reachability distance, e.g., DBSCAN-25 has the worst performance for all three directions under Design 2, but not for Design 1. Our method, on the other hand, manages to achieve a reasonably high average Rand Index for different tensor directions under both simulation designs. These results highlight the benefit of incorporating the tensor structure and borrowing information from other directions by our method.

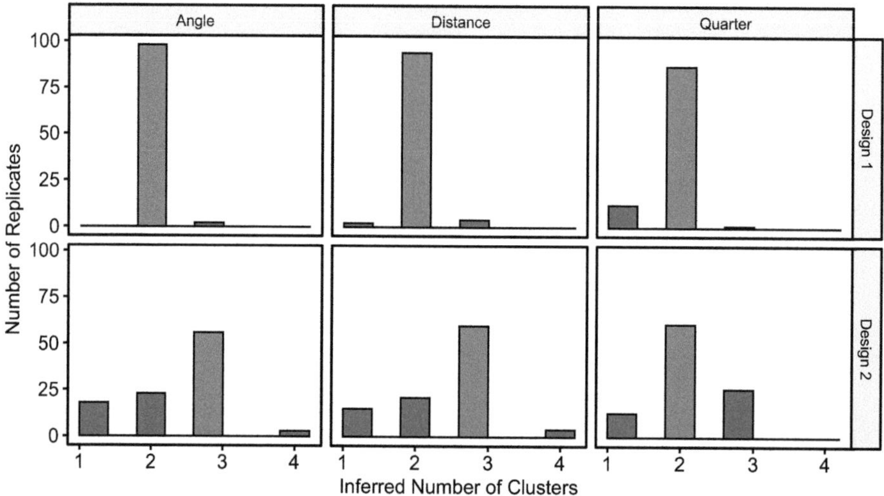

Fig. 12. Simulation results: Histograms of cluster numbers over 100 Monte-Carlo replicates for angle, distance, and quarter under two designs. Correct estimate of K is marked in orange color. (Color figure online)

We also present the histogram of the estimated number of clusters from 100 replicates in Fig. 12. Under Design 1, where there are only two clusters on each direction, the proposed method manages to correctly estimate the cluster number 98%, 94%, and 87% of times for angle, distance, and quarter, respectively. In Design 2, with a finer partition of the court, it becomes harder to infer the number of clusters, and the percentage of correct estimation reduces to 56%, 60%, and 61%. All these findings confirm the excellent performance of method in terms of recovering the unknown number of clusters and the results match the asymptotic results provided in the previous section.

Table 1. Simulation results: Average Rand Index over 100 Monte-Carlo replicates under two simulation designs for the proposed method and two competing methods.

Design	Method	Angle	Distance	Quarter
1	Proposed	0.999	0.987	0.938
	K-means	0.720	0.712	0.985
	DBSCAN-25	0.996	0.998	0.982
	DBSCAN-50	1.000	1.000	1.000
	DBSCAN-75	1.000	1.000	1.000
	DBSCAN-100	1.000	1.000	1.000
2	Proposed	0.826	0.851	0.903
	K-means	0.773	0.786	0.851
	DBSCAN-25	0.499	0.667	0.554
	DBSCAN-50	0.687	0.706	0.759
	DBSCAN-75	0.720	0.720	0.776
	DBSCAN-100	0.720	0.720	0.776

Proof sketch of Theorem 1

The proof proceeds by using the Theorem 3.1 of [11]. Note that our tensor mixture model can be viewed as a mixture of marginally independent Poisson distributions. Therefore it suffices to consider a mixture of univariate Poisson distributions. We need to verify Conditions (P.1)–(P.4) in [11] for mixtures $\sum_{k=1}^{K} \pi_k \mathrm{Poi}(\gamma_k)$ where both π_k's and γ_k's are taking values in bounded intervals. Condition (P.1) is satisfied since we restrict our parameters of interest to a compact space Θ^* and the Poisson kernel is indeed first-order identifiable. Condition (P.2) also holds since we assign a non-zero continuous distribution on the parameters within a bounded support. Condition (P.4) holds since we use a Poisson distribution (excluding 0) on K. Finally, for Condition (P.3), consider $G_0 = \sum_{i=1}^{k_0} \pi_i \delta(\gamma_i)$ and $G = \sum_{j=1}^{k_0} \pi'_j \delta(\gamma'_j)$. Given $W_1(G_0, G) \le \epsilon_0$ for sufficiently small ϵ_0, since we restrict the mixture weights and γ's to be both lower and upper bounded by finite constants, we have $|\pi_i - \pi'_i| \le C\epsilon_0$ and $|\gamma_i - \gamma'_i| \le C\epsilon_0$ for every $i = 1, \ldots, k_0$ and some constant $C > 0$. Therefore (P.3) holds. This completes the proof.

References

1. Albert, J., Glickman, M.E., Swartz, T.B., Koning, R.H.: Handbook of Statistical Methods and Analyses in Sports. CRC Press (2017)
2. Bi, X., Tang, X., Yuan, Y., Zhang, Y., Qu, A.: Tensors in statistics. Ann. Rev. Stat. Appl. **8**, 345–368 (2021)
3. Cervone, D., D'Amour, A., Bornn, L., Goldsberry, K.: Pointwise: predicting points and valuing decisions in real time with NBA optical tracking data. In: Proceedings

of the 8th MIT Sloan Sports Analytics Conference, Boston, MA, USA, vol. 28, p. 3 (2014)

4. Cervone, D., D'Amour, A., Bornn, L., Goldsberry, K.: A multiresolution stochastic process model for predicting basketball possession outcomes. J. Am. Stat. Assoc. **111**(514), 585–599 (2016)

5. Chi, E.C., Gaines, B.R., Sun, W.W., Zhou, H., Yang, J.: Provable convex co-clustering of tensors. J. Mach. Learn. Res. **21**(214), 1–58 (2020)

6. Dahl, D.B.: Model-based clustering for expression data via a Dirichlet process mixture model. In: Kim-Anh Do, Peter Müller, M.V. (ed.) Bayesian Inference for Gene Expression and Proteomics, vol. 4, pp. 201–218. Cambridge University Press (2006)

7. Fernandez, J., Bornn, L.: Wide open spaces: a statistical technique for measuring space creation in professional soccer. In: Sloan Sports Analytics Conference, vol. 2018 (2018)

8. Franks, A., Miller, A., Bornn, L., Goldsberry, K., et al.: Characterizing the spatial structure of defensive skill in professional basketball. Ann. Appl. Stat. **9**(1), 94–121 (2015)

9. Geng, J., Bhattacharya, A., Pati, D.: Probabilistic community detection with unknown number of communities. J. Am. Stat. Assoc. **114**(526), 893–905 (2019)

10. Ghosal, S., van der Vaart, A.W.: Fundamentals of Nonparametric Bayesian Inference, vol. 44. Cambridge University Press (2017)

11. Guha, A., Ho, N., Nguyen, X.: On posterior contraction of parameters and interpretability in Bayesian mixture modeling. Bernoulli **27**(4), 2159–2188 (2021)

12. Guhaniyogi, R.: Bayesian methods for tensor regression. Wiley StatsRef: Statistics Reference Online, pp. 1–18 (2020)

13. Guhaniyogi, R., Qamar, S., Dunson, D.B.: Bayesian tensor regression. J. Mach. Learn. Res. **18**(1), 2733–2763 (2017)

14. Han, R., Luo, Y., Wang, M., Zhang, A.R.: Exact clustering in tensor block model: statistical optimality and computational limit. J. R. Stat. Soc. Ser. B Stat Methodol. **84**, 1666–1698 (2022)

15. Han, R., Willett, R., Zhang, A.R.: An optimal statistical and computational framework for generalized tensor estimation. Ann. Stat. **50**(1), 1–29 (2022)

16. Hennig, C.: FPC: Flexible Procedures for Clustering (2020). https://CRAN.R-project.org/package=fpc, R package version 2.2-9

17. Hu, G., Yang, H.C., Xue, Y.: Bayesian group learning for shot selection of professional basketball players. Statistics, e324 (2020)

18. Ishwaran, H., James, L.F.: Gibbs sampling methods for stick-breaking priors. J. Am. Stat. Assoc. **96**(453), 161–173 (2001)

19. Jiao, J., Hu, G., Yan, J.: A Bayesian joint model for spatial point processes with application to basketball shot chart. J. Quant. Anal. Sports (2020). forthcoming

20. Kolda, T.G., Bader, B.W.: Tensor decompositions and applications. SIAM Rev. **51**(3), 455–500 (2009)

21. Mai, Q., Zhang, X., Pan, Y., Deng, K.: A doubly-enhanced EM algorithm for model-based tensor clustering. J. Am. Stat. Assoc. (just-accepted), 1–44 (2021)

22. Miller, A., Bornn, L., Adams, R., Goldsberry, K.: Factorized point process intensities: a spatial analysis of professional basketball. In: Xing, E.P., Jebara, T. (eds.) Proceedings of the 31st International Conference on Machine Learning. Proceedings of Machine Learning Research, vol. 32, pp. 235–243. PMLR, Bejing, China (2014)

23. Miller, J.W., Harrison, M.T.: Mixture models with a prior on the number of components. J. Am. Stat. Assoc. **113**(521), 340–356 (2018)

24. Papalexakis, E.E., Pelechrinis, K.: THOOPS: a multi-aspect analytical framework for spatio-temporal basketball data. In: CIKM, pp. 2223–2232 (2018). https://doi.org/10.1145/3269206.3272002
25. Park, J.Y., Carr, K., Zheng, S., Yue, Y., Yu, R.: Multiresolution tensor learning for efficient and interpretable spatial analysis. In: International Conference on Machine Learning, pp. 7499–7509. PMLR (2020)
26. R Core Team: R: A Language and Environment for Statistical Computing. R Foundation for Statistical Computing, Vienna, Austria (2013). http://www.R-project.org/
27. Rand, W.M.: Objective criteria for the evaluation of clustering methods. J. Am. Stat. Assoc. **66**(336), 846–850 (1971)
28. Reich, B.J., Hodges, J.S., Carlin, B.P., Reich, A.M.: A spatial analysis of basketball shot chart data. Am. Stat. **60**(1), 3–12 (2006)
29. Sandholtz, N., Bornn, L.: Markov decision processes with dynamic transition probabilities: an analysis of shooting strategies in basketball. Ann. Appl. Stat. **14**(3), 1122–1145 (2020)
30. Sandholtz, N., Mortensen, J., Bornn, L.: Measuring spatial allocative efficiency in basketball. J. Quant. Anal. Sports **16**(4), 271–289 (2020)
31. Sethuraman, J.: A constructive definition of Dirichlet priors. Statistica Sin., 639–650 (1994)
32. Spencer, D., Guhaniyogi, R., Prado, R.: Bayesian mixed effect sparse tensor response regression model with joint estimation of activation and connectivity. arXiv preprint arXiv:1904.00148 (2019)
33. Sun, W.W., Hao, B., Li, L.: Tensors in modern statistical learning. Wiley StatsRef: Statistics Reference Online, pp. 1–25 (2014)
34. Sun, W.W., Li, L.: Dynamic tensor clustering. J. Am. Stat. Assoc. **114**(528), 1894–1907 (2019)
35. de Valpine, P., Turek, D., Paciorek, C.J., Anderson-Bergman, C., Lang, D.T., Bodik, R.: Programming with models: writing statistical algorithms for general model structures with NIMBLE. J. Comput. Graph. Stat. **26**(2), 403–413 (2017)
36. Wade, S., Ghahramani, Z.: Bayesian cluster analysis: Point estimation and credible balls (with discussion) (2018)
37. Yin, F., Hu, G., Shen, W.: Analysis of professional basketball field goal attempts via a Bayesian matrix clustering approach. J. Comput. Graph. Stat. **32**, 49–60 (2023)
38. Yin, F., Jiao, J., Hu, G., Yan, J.: Bayesian nonparametric estimation for point processes with spatial homogeneity: a spatial analysis of NBA shot locations. In: International Conference on Machine Learning (2022)

Evaluating Movement Initiation Timing in Ultimate Frisbee via Temporal Counterfactuals

Shunsuke Iwashita[1], Ning Ding[2], and Keisuke Fujii[1,3]

[1] Graduate School of Informatics, Nagoya University, Nagoya, Japan
`fujii@i.nagoya-u.ac.jp`
[2] Graduate School of Engineering, Nagoya Institute of Technology, Nagoya, Japan
[3] Center for Advanced Intelligence Project, RIKEN, Osaka, Japan

Abstract. Ultimate is a sport where points are scored by passing a disc and catching it in the opposing team's end zone. In Ultimate, the player holding the disc cannot move, making field dynamics primarily driven by other players' movements. However, current literature in team sports has ignored quantitative evaluations of when players initiate such unlabeled movements in game situations. In this paper, we propose a quantitative evaluation method for movement initiation timing in Ultimate Frisbee. First, game footage was recorded using a drone camera, and players' positional data was obtained, which will be published as UltimateTrack dataset. Next, players' movement initiations were detected, and temporal counterfactual scenarios were generated by shifting the timing of movements using rule-based approaches. These scenarios were analyzed using a space evaluation metric based on soccer's pitch control reflecting the unique rules of Ultimate. By comparing the spatial evaluation values across scenarios, the difference between actual play and the most favorable counterfactual scenario was used to quantitatively assess the impact of movement timing. We validated our method and show that sequences in which the disc was actually thrown to the receiver received higher evaluation scores than the sequences without a throw. In practical verifications, the higher-skill group displays a broader distribution of time offsets from the model's optimal initiation point. These findings demonstrate that the proposed metric provides an objective means of assessing movement initiation timing, which has been difficult to quantify in unlabeled team sport plays. (The code is available at https://github.com/shunsuke-iwashita/VTCS)

Keywords: space evaluation · tracking data · invasion sports

1 Introduction

Ultimate Frisbee (hereafter "Ultimate") is a field sport played by two teams of seven athletes on a rectangular pitch that comprises a central zone flanked by two end zones. A point is scored when a player catches the flying disc in the opponent's end zone. Since the thrower must establish a pivot and cannot run with the disc, territorial gain arises from passes directed into space created by the movements of off-ball (i.e., without the disc) teammates. In contrast with invasion games such as football, basketball, and American football, where extensive event and tracking data have provided a large analytics literature [6], empirical work on Ultimate has still been scarce. One of the key obstacles is the lack of publicly available player-tracking datasets, leaving many tactical questions unexplored.

Pioneering work of Ultimate tactics is Weiss and Childers's paper [37], which introduced location-based completion and scoring probability maps derived from location data to quantify the tactical value of each field region. This work was extended to the player contribution metric in [38], but the tracking data was not published. Lam et al. [22] modelled passes and turnovers as zone-to-zone state transitions, and Eberhard et al. [5] combined four seasons of professional tracking to build completion-probability and field-value models that jointly capture throw difficulty and positional value. Most previous work in Ultimate has used only discrete event data, including the time and coordinates of each pass, catch, or turnover, without continuous xy trajectories for all players, because acquiring full-field tracking remains costly. Even in team sports that routinely collect tracking data, such as soccer and basketball, evaluating the optimal timing of unlabeled movement initiations poses two challenges. First, the onset of a run or cut must be detected in dense, overlapping trajectories (see also a specific play case in basketball [13]). Second, such a moment must be linked to a motion model and a value function that can be trained with limited samples. Recently, the only study that has combined space valuation in Ultimate exists [20]; their 3-vs-3 game tracking data modified an existing spatial metric [31] but did not address the timing problem.

In this paper, we propose VTCS (Valuing Timing by Counterfactual Scenarios), a framework that quantifies how much earlier or later a receiver should have initiated a movement. VTCS first detects each initiation frame for each player from player-tracking data, then generates a family of counterfactual plays by systematically shifting that frame forward and backward with a rule-based motion model. For every real and counterfactual sequence, it computes a framewise field value inspired by a pitch control model [31] but adapted to Ultimate's mechanics. Then the timing score is defined as the gap between the realized trajectory and the best counterfactual. We model and evaluate VTCS on UltimateTrack, a drone-captured, frame-level dataset of 64 possessions of practice matches. VTCS is therefore the first approach to provide an objective, data-driven estimate of optimal movement-initiation timing in invasion sports where such unlabeled decisions were previously impossible to measure.

The main contributions of our paper are as follows. (1) We introduce the VTCS framework together with the open UltimateTrack dataset, enabling fine-grained timing evaluation in Ultimate for the first time. (2) We propose a rule-based counterfactual motion model, a sport-specific field-value formulation and a timing-effect metric defined as the gap between actual and optimal scenarios. (3) Experiments show that thrown sequences score higher than non-throw sequences and that elite players exhibit a wider, reasonable spread around the model-optimal initiation time. In the following sections, we describe our methods in Sect. 2 and the experimental results in Sect. 3, and conclude this paper in Sect. 4. Ultimate frisbee rules and related work are in Appendices A and B.

2 Methods

In this study, we propose VTCS (Valuing Timing by Counterfactual Scenarios), a framework for quantitatively evaluating the optimality of a player's initiation timing. This section describes each component of the VTCS framework. We begin by introducing the dataset and the motion model used to generate counterfactual scenarios. We then define the space evaluation metric. Finally, we present the timing evaluation metrics based on frame-level and scenario-level spatial values, which together measure how effective the actual initiation timing was.

2.1 UltimateTrack Datasets

This study constructs and publishes a new tracking dataset called Ultimate-Track, aimed at evaluating counterfactual scenarios and spatial control.

The dataset was created based on aerial footage captured by a drone (DJI, Mavic 3) during a scrimmage conducted by the Nagoya University Flying Disc Team. Player positions were manually tracked for every frame. The dataset is provided in its final processed form, incorporating unified representations of position, velocity, and acceleration, as described in the following section. It comprises 18,075 frames at 15 FPS and includes 64 possessions. The tracked objects consist of 15 entities: 7 offense players, 7 defense players, and 1 disc. All positional data are expressed in a normalized field coordinate system of $94 \times 37\,\mathrm{m}$. The data is formatted as a CSV file, where each row records the state of one object at one frame. The variables are listed in Appendix C. An example video is given here. To the best of our knowledge, this is the first publicly available dataset in Ultimate Frisbee that provides continuous positional data for all players. The preprocessing procedure is described in Appendix D.

In this study, we target the receiver's first decisive cut, defined as the moment a receiver accelerates for a potential pass. See Appendix E for details. In short, candidate initiations are detected automatically by simple kinematic rules that look for a sudden burst of acceleration aligned with the current velocity and preceded by a period in which the player has not possessed the disc. Subsequently, 455 sequences in total were visually reviewed to filter out movements toward crowded areas or those lacking a clear spatial objective. As a result, 310 sequences were retained for further analysis.

While the present dataset was collected from a single team in a limited match-like setting, future work will include expanding data collection to a wider range of competitive environments and tactical contexts. We also plan to explore methods for streamlining annotation and scaling up data acquisition, potentially leveraging advances in computer vision. Although these extensions are not covered in this paper, we recognize them as important next steps for broadening the applicability and robustness of our approach.

2.2   Motion Model to Generate Counterfactual Scenarios

To quantitatively evaluate the impact of a receiver's initiation timing on the unfolding of gameplay, we construct **temporally counterfactual scenarios**. In these scenarios, only the initiation timing of the target player and their corresponding defender is altered, while all other conditions remain identical to those of the actual play. This framework enables the analysis of the causal effect that the timing of initiation has on spatial control. In designing our framework, we deliberately adopt a rule-based approach for generating counterfactual scenarios, rather than relying on fully data-driven [9,10,33] or reinforcement learning-based models [11,27,43]. This choice allows explicit manipulation of the target player's initiation timing while keeping all other variables fixed, making the causal effect both intuitive and interpretable. Furthermore, rule-based modeling is advantageous for providing actionable and comprehensible feedback to coaches and players, such as indicating "a better outcome could have been achieved if initiation had occurred at this timing". This interpretability is especially important under data constraints and in practical sports analysis.

A series of counterfactual scenarios is constructed by altering the initiation timing of the detected player and considering the corresponding defender marking them. Specifically, based on the original initiation frame t_0, a set of temporally shifted position sequences $\{\mathbf{p}_i^{(\xi)}(t)\}$ is generated by applying a shift parameter $\xi \in [-15, 15]$, where $\xi < 0$ denotes an earlier and $\xi > 0$ denotes a delay initiation.

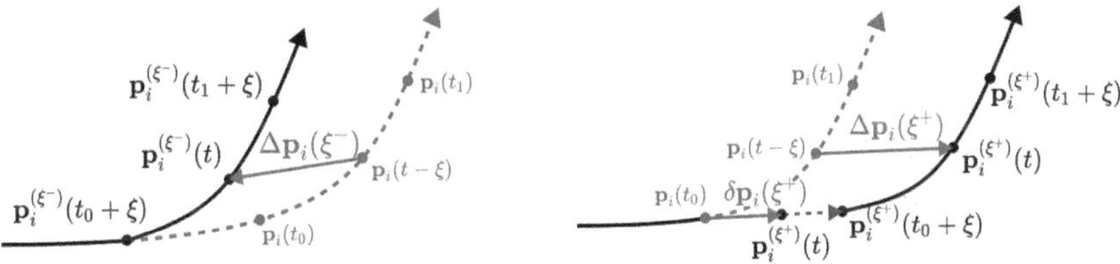

(a) Initiation is brought forward ($\xi < 0$): The trajectory is shifted earlier and corrected by $\Delta\mathbf{p}_i(\xi^-)$

(b) Initiation is delayed ($\xi > 0$): The gap is filled with $\delta\mathbf{p}_i(\xi^+)$ and corrected by $\Delta\mathbf{p}_i(\xi^+)$

Fig. 1. Visualization of temporally counterfactual scenarios (solid lines) by shifting the initiation timing of the target player (dashed line).

First, when $\xi < 0$ (see Fig. 1 (a)), the player's original movement is replayed $|\xi|$ frames earlier, and the trajectory is translated to ensure continuity at the initiation point. The position sequence is defined as follows:

$$\mathbf{p}_i^{(\xi^-)}(t) = \begin{cases} \mathbf{p}_i(t) & \text{for } t \leq t_0 + \xi \\ \mathbf{p}_i(t - \xi) + \Delta\mathbf{p}_i(\xi^-) & \text{for } t > t_0 + \xi \end{cases} \tag{1}$$

To ensure continuity of the trajectory at the initiation point, a correction vector $\Delta\mathbf{p}_i(\xi^-) = \mathbf{p}_i(t_0 + \xi) - \mathbf{p}_i(t_0)$ is added after time $t_0 + \xi$. This adjustment ensures that the earlier-shifted trajectory connects smoothly with the original movement.

On the other hand, when $\xi > 0$ (see Fig. 1 (b)), the player first undergoes a hypothetical linear motion $\delta\mathbf{p}_i(\xi^+)$ based on the average velocity $\bar{\mathbf{v}}_i$, and then follows the original trajectory delayed by ξ frames. The corresponding position sequence is defined as:

$$\mathbf{p}_i^{(\xi^+)}(t) = \begin{cases} \mathbf{p}_i(t) & \text{for } t \leq t_0 \\ \mathbf{p}_i(t_0) + \delta\mathbf{p}_i(\xi^+) & \text{for } t_0 < t \leq t_0 + \xi \\ \mathbf{p}_i(t - \xi) + \Delta\mathbf{p}_i(\xi^+) & \text{for } t > t_0 + \xi \end{cases} \tag{2}$$

The hypothetical movement term $\delta\mathbf{p}_i(\xi^+)$ represents a linear motion initiated from the original position $\mathbf{p}_i(t_0)$, proceeding at the average velocity $\bar{\mathbf{v}}_i$. This term is introduced to fill the temporal gap caused by the delayed initiation and to ensure continuity of motion in the counterfactual trajectory. The associated hypothetical movement and correction terms are defined as:

$$\delta\mathbf{p}_i(\xi^+) = \bar{\mathbf{v}}_i \cdot (t - t_0), \quad \Delta\mathbf{p}_i(\xi^+) = \bar{\mathbf{v}}_i \cdot \xi \tag{3}$$

The average velocity vector over the one-second period (15 frames) prior to initiation is computed as: $\bar{\mathbf{v}}_i = \frac{1}{15} \sum_{k=1}^{15} \mathbf{v}_i(t_0 - k)$.

For all other players $j \neq i$, the position sequence remains identical to that of the original play: $\mathbf{p}_j^{(\xi)}(t) = \mathbf{p}_j(t)$. This setup ensures that the only factor affecting spatial control in each counterfactual scenario is the initiation timing ξ of the target player. The linear motion model provides a tractable baseline, but incorporating richer defensive dynamics is left for future research.

2.3   Space Evaluation Metric

To evaluate the impact of initiation timing on spatial advantage, we build upon the pitch control framework [31], which defines the original Potential Pitch Control Field (PPCF). We adopt an Ultimate-specific extension of it, UPPCF [20], with a modified reaction time estimation derived from players' velocity direction. Furthermore, we propose a weighted version, wUPPCF, which accounts for practical gameplay factors such as pass difficulty and defensive pressure. The definitions of PPCF and UPPCF are provided in Appendix F.

Weighted Extension: wUPPCF. To further account for the difficulty of passing in Ultimate, we apply a distance-based weight w_d, which penalizes locations that are farther from the disc holder. Specifically, w_d decreases as the distance from the disc increases, reflecting the decreased feasibility of successful long passes due to throwing limitations. This weighting encourages the evaluation to prioritize reachable and tactically viable spaces. The spatial distribution of w_d is visualized in Appendix F.3, where warmer colors indicate higher feasibility.

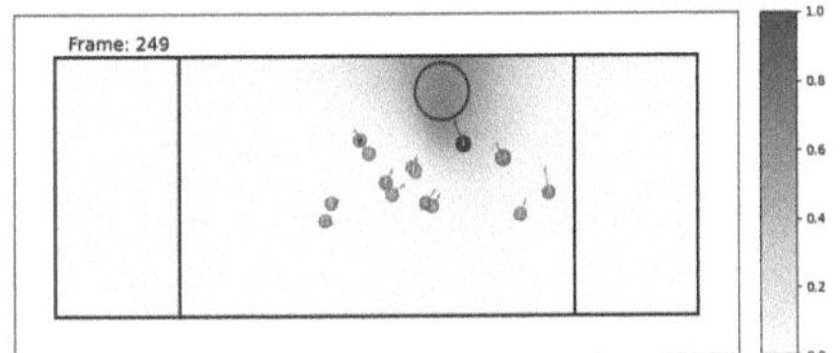

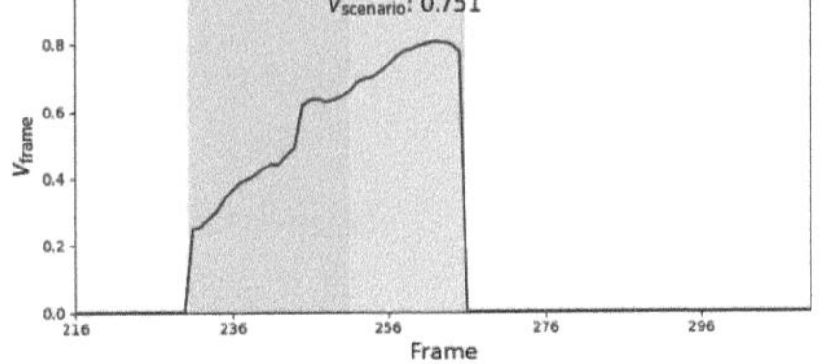

Fig. 2. An example of frame-wise evaluation value V_{frame}, defined as the average wUPPCF within the predicted reachable area (blue circle) of the target receiver.

Fig. 3. Temporal transition of V_{frame}. The scenario-wise evaluation value V_{scenario} is defined as the maximum value of a 15-frame moving average applied to V_{frame}.

We also model the obstruction caused by a marker's blocking motion by defining a pair of virtual arms extending laterally from the defender and evaluating whether they intersect with the intended disc trajectory. The virtual arm length r is defined as a function of the distance between the disc and the target:

$$r = 1 - \min\left(\frac{\|\mathbf{p}_t - \mathbf{p}_d\|}{30}, 1\right) \tag{4}$$

Here, $\mathbf{p}_d$ denotes the position of the disc, and $\mathbf{p}_t$ denotes the target location of the intended pass. If an intersection occurs between the virtual arms and the disc's intended path, the obstruction weight by the marker's blocking motion w_s is calculated based on the normalized distance from the defender to the intersection point. A shorter distance results in a stronger obstruction effect (lower weight), while a longer distance has less impact. If no intersection occurs, the weight is set to 1.

Finally, the weighted spatial control metric for player i is defined as:

$$\mathrm{wUPPCF}_i = \mathrm{UPPCF}_i \cdot w_d \cdot w_s \tag{5}$$

wUPPCF is a practical spatial evaluation metric that extends PPCF for Ultimate by incorporating pass feasibility and defensive interference. It is computed individually for each player and is used in the following section to evaluate the effectiveness of initiation timing (V_{timing}).

2.4   Timing Evaluation Metric

To evaluate the impact of initiation timing on spatial advantage, we propose a novel metric called VTCS. VTCS evaluates how effective a player's actual timing decision is by applying spatial control-based evaluation to a series of counterfactual scenarios constructed using the motion model (see Sect. 2.2). VTCS is computed through the following three steps: frame-level evaluation metric V_{frame}, scenario-level evaluation metric V_{scenario}, and the final differential metric V_{timing} (Figs. 2 and 3).

V_{frame}. The frame-wise value $V_{\text{frame}}(t)$ is defined as the average of wUPPCF (see Sect. 2.3) within the area $\Omega(t)$, where the target player is likely to receive the disc:

$$V_{\text{frame}}(t) = \frac{1}{|\Omega(t)|} \sum_{\mathbf{r} \in \Omega(t)} \text{wUPPCF}_i(t, \mathbf{r}) \tag{6}$$

Here, $\Omega(t)$ denotes the region where the target player and the disc can arrive simultaneously. Specifically, we solve the following equations to find the intersection time τ, based on the target player's position and velocity $\mathbf{p}_i(t), \mathbf{v}_i(t)$, the disc's position $\mathbf{p}_{\text{disc}}(t)$, and its known speed v_{disc} with directional angle θ:

$$\begin{cases} p_{i,x}(t) + \tau \cdot v_{i,x}(t) = p_{\text{disc},x}(t) + \tau \cdot v_{\text{disc}} \cdot \cos\theta \\ p_{i,y}(t) + \tau \cdot v_{i,y}(t) = p_{\text{disc},y}(t) + \tau \cdot v_{\text{disc}} \cdot \sin\theta \end{cases} \tag{7}$$

Using the solution τ, we define the predicted position of the player as:

$$\mathbf{c}(t) = \mathbf{p}_i(t) + \tau \cdot \mathbf{v}_i(t) \tag{8}$$

The region $\Omega(t)$ is then defined as a circle centered at $\mathbf{c}(t)$ with a radius of $\frac{1}{2}\|\mathbf{v}_i(t)\|\tau$, representing the area where the player is expected to be able to receive the disc. See Appendix G for an illustration.

V_{scenario}. For each counterfactual scenario with a timing shift ξ, the scenario-wise evaluation value $V_{\text{scenario}}^{(\xi)}$ is defined as the maximum of the moving average of $V_{\text{frame}}(t)$ over a 15-frame window:

$$V_{\text{scenario}}^{(\xi)} = \max_t \frac{1}{15} \sum_{k=1}^{15} V_{\text{frame}}(t + k) \tag{9}$$

This allows us to identify the frame at which the target player gained the most spatial advantage, depending on the initiation timing.

V_{timing}. V_{timing} quantifies the effectiveness of the actual initiation timing as the difference between the scenario score of the actual case ($\xi = 0$) and the best counterfactual.

$$V_{\text{timing}} = V_{\text{scenario}}^{(0)} - \max_{\xi \in [-15,15], \, \xi \neq 0} V_{\text{scenario}}^{(\xi)} \tag{10}$$

Here, $V_{\text{scenario}}^{(0)}$ denotes the evaluation score of the actual scenario, while $\max V_{\text{scenario}}^{(\xi)}$ represents the highest score among all counterfactual scenarios. A large V_{timing} value implies that the actual initiation timing led to significantly greater spatial advantage compared to any alternative timing, suggesting that the decision was highly effective. Conversely, a small V_{timing} indicates that a better initiation timing may have existed, indicating room for improvement.

3   Results

We conducted experiments using the UltimateTrack dataset introduced in Sect. 2.1 to evaluate the effectiveness of our proposed method. First, we validate the frame-wise evaluation metric V_{frame}, and then the timing evaluation metric V_{timing}. The use case of evaluating the initiation timing of a receiver and an optimal alternative is presented in Appendix H, with a video demonstration available here.

3.1   Validation of Frame-Wise Evaluation Metric V_{frame}

Here we evaluate whether the proposed metric V_{frame} provides a valid assessment that aligns with actual passing decisions. Specifically, we statistically analyze the relationship between V_{frame} values and whether a pass was thrown to the detected player. Importantly, this comparison was conducted exclusively on the held-out test data from the same five-fold Group K-Fold cross-validation procedure, ensuring that no data leakage occurred.

Construction of Evaluation Data via Target Prediction Model. In the context of temporally counterfactual scenarios, the timing of a player's initiation of movement is altered to generate multiple hypothetical trajectories. Consequently, whether a pass is thrown to the player in each scenario may vary, making it impossible to define a single ground truth for pass occurrence. To address this issue, we construct a classifier that estimates the probability that a detected player is the intended pass target in each frame, and use this prediction as a proxy for ground truth. Specifically, we train an XGBoost model using spatial and kinematic features derived from the scenario data. A 5-fold Group-KFold cross-validation is employed to assess generalization performance. The model achieved a mean RMSE of approximately 0.316 and a mean coefficient of determination (R^2) of approximately 0.163, indicating moderate predictive performance. Given the inherent uncertainty near the decision boundary, we exclude ambiguous cases and retain only those instances where the predicted probability was clearly high (≥ 0.55) or low (≤ 0.30). This filtering enables a more reliable comparison of V_{frame} values in relation to pass occurrence.

Comparison of V_{frame} Based on Pass Outcome. Based on the target prediction results, we compared the V_{frame} values of the detected player between cases where the pass was directed to the detected player ("target") and cases where it was directed to another player ("others") (Fig. 4 (a) and (b). The distributions exhibited clear separation, as confirmed by the Kolmogorov–Smirnov (KS) test. For all data, the KS D-value was 0.3147 with $p = 0$, indicating a substantial difference between the two groups. When analyzed by skill group (Group 1 and Group 2; the specific criteria for group classification are described in a later section), the KS D-value was 0.3159 ($p = 0$) for Group 1 and 0.3120 ($p = 0$) for Group 2, both reflecting significant distributional differences.

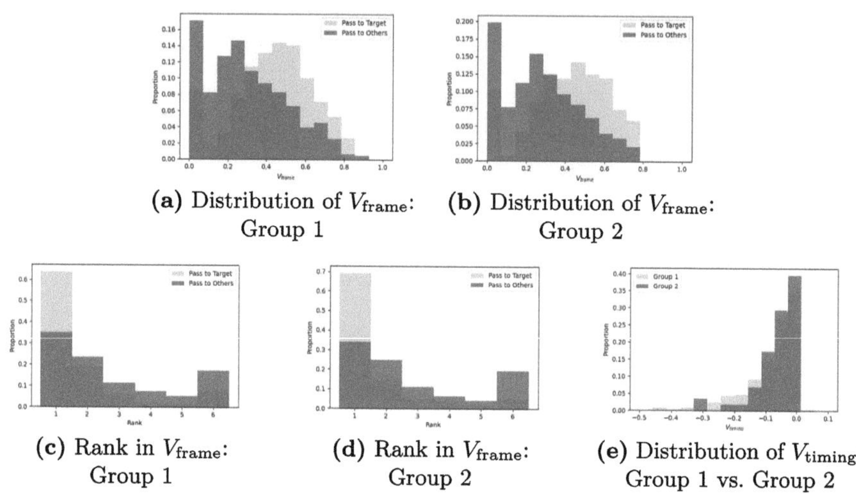

(**a**) Distribution of V_{frame}:
Group 1

(**b**) Distribution of V_{frame}:
Group 2

(**c**) Rank in V_{frame}:
Group 1

(**d**) Rank in V_{frame}:
Group 2

(**e**) Distribution of V_{timing}:
Group 1 vs. Group 2

Fig. 4. Comparison of spatial and temporal evaluation metrics across skill groups and pass outcomes. Distributions of V_{frame} values (a, b) and team-relative ranks (c, d) in V_{frame} for detected players when the pass was actually directed to them (orange) versus to another player (blue). Distribution of V_{timing} scores (e) across skill groups, where Group 1 (intermediate-to-advanced) and Group 2 (novice-to-intermediate). Higher V_{frame} values, higher ranks, and smaller deviations in V_{timing} (closer to zero) support the validity of the proposed metrics.

The D-value in the KS test represents the maximum difference between the cumulative distribution functions (CDFs) of the two groups; for example, a D-value of 0.1 indicates that the two cumulative distributions differ by at most 10% at any point [17]. The D-values observed in this study (all above 0.31) therefore indicate a pronounced separation between the V_{frame} distributions for the two pass outcome groups. These results suggest that V_{frame} tends to be higher when the detected player is the actual pass recipient, and this trend is consistent across different skill groups.

Relative Ranking Within the Offensive Team. We further computed the V_{frame} values for all non-possessing offensive players within each frame and ranked the detected player accordingly. This allows us to evaluate the relative spatial advantage of the detected player within the team (Fig. 4 (c) and (d)). The Mann–Whitney U test indicated a statistically significant difference between cases where the detected player was the actual pass recipient and when they were not ($p = 0$), and the effect size, as measured by Cliff's Delta, was -0.339, which corresponds to a medium magnitude according to the interpretation criteria in [25].

When analyzing the data by skill group, the trend remained consistent. For Group 1, Cliff's Delta was -0.329 (small magnitude), while for Group 2 it was -0.382 (medium magnitude), with both comparisons yielding $p = 0$. These results indicate that, across all groups, detected players tended to rank higher in V_{frame} when they were the actual pass recipient, although the effect was slightly more pronounced in Group 2.

Comparison Across Skill Groups. To examine whether the V_{frame} values are robust across different skill levels, we stratified the data into two groups:

Group 1: Male players with 1–3 years of experience (intermediate to advanced)
Group 2: Female players with up to 3 years and male players with less than 1 year of experience (novice to intermediate)

Figure 4 (a) and (b) show similar distributional patterns of V_{frame} values across the two groups, and Fig. 4 (c) and (d) further demonstrate that the relative ranking of target players remains consistent. These parallel trends suggest that the proposed metric maintains consistent behavior regardless of player experience, indicating robustness to differences in skill level.

However, the data used in this study were collected from a single team under limited match-like conditions. The diversity of player demographics and tactical contexts (e.g., man-to-man vs. zone defense) remains limited. Future validation across different competition levels (e.g., club team, national tournaments) and varied tactical environments would provide further evidence of the generalizability and practical utility of V_{frame}.

3.2   Validation of Timing Evaluation Metric V_{timing}

This section examines the distribution of V_{timing} (a score indicating the deviation from optimal timing) scores and explores differences in the effectiveness of initiation timing between skill groups. Figure 4 (e) illustrates the V_{timing} distributions for two groups categorized by experience: Group 1 (intermediate to advanced players) and Group 2 (novice to intermediate players). The initial hypothesis anticipated that higher-skilled players in Group 1 would be more likely to select near-optimal initiation timings, thereby achieving higher V_{timing} values. Contrary to this expectation, the results indicated that Group 2 had a distribution concentrated closer to zero, indicating a tendency toward higher V_{timing} values. Several interpretations are possible for this result. One plausible explanation is that players in Group 2 exhibit limited variability in their playing style and movement patterns. This homogeneity may constrain the range of counterfactual scenarios, thereby reducing the gap between the actual initiation and the optimal timing. Another possibility is that players in Group 1, who tend to attempt more advanced plays, are subject to stronger defensive pressure. As a result, they may find it more difficult to initiate movement at the optimal moment, leading to greater deviations and thus lower V_{timing} values despite their higher skill level. These considerations suggest that V_{timing} does not merely reflect individual skill but also captures the quality of context-adaptive decision-making, taking into account the available offensive options and situational constraints such as defensive intensity. Future work should aim to refine the interpretation of V_{timing} by incorporating contextual variables, such as defender proximity and marking status, into the counterfactual evaluation framework.

4   Conclusions

In this study, we proposed a novel framework called VTCS (Valuing Timing by Counterfactual Scenarios) to quantitatively evaluate how the timing of a receiver's movement initiation affects spatial advantage in Ultimate Frisbee. VTCS constructs a series of temporally counterfactual scenarios that alter only the initiation timing of the target player and evaluates each scenario using a spatial control-based metric to assess the effectiveness of the actual decision.

These findings collectively enable the quantitative assessment of movement initiation timing: an unlabelled yet tactically crucial movement that has been difficult to evaluate. While developed for Ultimate, the VTCS framework can be applied to other invasion sports where tracking data is available, thus the applications to other invasion sports as well as various competitive levels in Ultimate will be future work.

Acknowledgments. This study was financially supported by JSPS KAKENHI 23H03282, JP24K23889.

Appendix

A   Ultimate Frisbee Rules

Ultimate Frisbee (commonly referred to as "Ultimate") is an invasion-type team sport played with a flying disc. Each team consists of seven players on the field. The game is played on a rectangular field with end zones at both ends (typically 100 m in total length, 37 m in width, and 20-meter end zones). The offensive team aims to score one point by successfully completing a series of passes that culminate in a teammate catching the disc in the opposing end zone.

A player holding the disc (the thrower) must establish a pivot foot and is not allowed to move from that spot while in possession of the disc until the disc is released. There is also a time limit on holding the disc, referred to as "stalling". A defensive player within three meters of the thrower (the marker) initiates a stall count by audibly counting "one, two, ..." up to ten seconds. If the disc is not thrown before the count reaches ten, a turnover is called due to a "stall out". Stalling functions not only as a temporal constraint but also as a defensive tactic. By controlling their positioning and stance, the marker can restrict the thrower's viable angles and limit available passing lanes. This tactical constraint reduces the offensive team's passing options and narrows their strategic choices.

Turnovers also occur due to dropped discs, out-of-bounds throws, or interceptions, resulting in an immediate change of possession. When a point is scored, the scoring team earns one point and begins the next point on defense by performing a "pull"—a throw that initiates play.

Ultimate is fundamentally non-contact and is governed by a unique ethos known as the "Spirit of the Game", which emphasizes self-officiating and fair play. This principle contributes to Ultimate's distinctive combination of strategic depth and ethical sportsmanship.

B Related Work

B.1 Space Evaluation Methods

Since off-ball actions (in this case, disc receiver actions) are seldom logged as discrete events, space evaluation metrics using all players' locations are important. Early work relied on rule-based heuristics: basketball research incorporated player profiles when rating off-ball movements in passing sequences [40] and similar rule-driven "dangerosity" scores have been proposed for soccer [23], but a variety of off-ball options makes general evaluation difficult.

A parallel line of research models space mathematically. Dominant-region approaches use Voronoi diagrams based on minimum arrival time [16,32], later refined with player-specific kinematics [1,24] and distance-weighted fields [28]. The probabilistic Off-Ball Scoring Opportunity (OBSO) framework [31] inspired indices that quantify how attackers pull defenders apart.OBSO has since been adapted to soccer (attackers [33,42], defenders [34]), basketball [21], and Ultimate [20]. Purely data-driven variants also exist, such as a neural-network estimator for badminton doubles [4].

B.2 Counterfactual Analysis

From [6], machine-learning approaches investigate "what-if" questions by conditioning generative models on altered game states. In basketball, recurrent networks and diffusion models have been conditioned on teammate and opponent positions to synthesise alternative player trajectories, clarifying how specific role changes shape future movement patterns [2,9,41]. In soccer, several frameworks have been proposed to address counterfactual scenarios: the Player Action Value Estimation framework [3], which quantifies the value of player actions by comparing predicted possession values between actual and counterfactual scenarios generated by replacing a player's trajectory; the Shooting Payoff Computation framework [42], which combines deep learning with game-theoretic reasoning to compare hypothetical shot and pass decisions; and TacticAI [36], which advises corner-kick positioning by generating counterfactual setups. However, these data-driven methods inherit the biases of their training samples and capture correlation rather than true causality when the data are sparse or unbalanced.

Causal inference techniques seek stronger guarantees by estimating treatment effects from observational data. Propensity-score matching has been applied to questions such as timeout effectiveness in basketball [18], crossing pressure in soccer [39], and pitch selection in baseball [26]. These methods can yield more valid counterfactual estimates but demand large, representative datasets and careful modeling of confounders.

A third strand employs explicit mathematical models that embed sport-specific rules and physical constraints. Voronoi-based dominant-region approaches and their probabilistic successors, such as OBSO model [31], provide closed-form tools for simulating positional adjustments. Building on OBSO, Umemoto and Fujii generated counterfactual defensive alignments to identify optimal soccer defender positions [34]. Because the governing equations are pre-defined, such models remain interpretable and data-efficient, offering a principled complement to purely statistical or learning-based counterfactual frameworks.

B.3   Evaluation of Movement Initiation Timing

Early evidence on the evaluation of movement initiation comes from tightly controlled (and simulated) 1-on-1 basketball experiments. A series of biomechanical studies showed that defenders output earlier movement initiation when better preparatory states based on the ground reaction forces before an attacker cuts [7,8,12,14,15]. Although these works isolate timing effects with laboratory precision, they involve only two actors and omit the spatiotemporal complexity of full team play.

Field-based studies remain sport and situation specific. In soccer, dive initiation during penalty kicks has been timestamped by expert video annotation and, more recently, markerless pose estimation [29]. Beyond goalkeeping, [19] detected the instant an attacker's run created decisive separation, highlighting off-ball timing as a neglected performance factor. Comparable efforts in basketball are just emerging: OBTracker mines NBA tracking data to label and score the timing of off-ball cuts and screens, providing one of the first data-driven baselines for temporal analysis in professional settings [40]. Ultimate Frisbee has virtually no timing studies, with wearable-sensor work focusing on biomechanics rather than tactical optimisation [30], and existing state-transition models relying on discrete pass events (e.g., [22], see also Introduction Section).

Counterfactual timing frameworks are even scarcer. G-computation has been used to estimate the effect of taking versus swinging at a 3-0 pitch in baseball [35], yet the analysis ignores spatial interactions. Another basketball work employed counterfactual recurrent networks to gauge the benefit of an extra basketball pass [10]; however, that causal approach requires large, balanced training sets and still treats timing indirectly via sequence modelling. By contrast, our study integrates full-field tracking with a rule-based motion model to compute spatially explicit counterfactuals, delivering the first objective estimate of optimal movement-initiation timing in Ultimate.

C   Structure of the CSV File in UltimateTrack Dataset

See Table 1.

Table 1. Structure of each row in the dataset CSV file

Variable	Description
`frame`	Frame index
`id`	Object ID (1–15)
`class`	Object type (`offense`, `defense`, `disc`)
`x, y`	Position on the field [m]
`vx, vy`	Velocity [m/s]
`ax, ay`	Acceleration [m/s^2]
`closest`	ID of the closest opposing player
`holder`	Boolean indicating whether the object holds the disc

D   Preprocessing

The dataset was processed through the following preprocessing steps. First, the four corners of the field were manually annotated in the footage to define a coordinate system in which the offensive direction is consistently from left to right. Then, the position of each player was manually recorded frame by frame. The disc holder was annotated for each possession, and the disc position was inferred accordingly. Specifically, the disc was assumed to be at the same position as the holder during possession, and its position during passes was linearly interpolated between the previous and next known points.

The image coordinates were transformed into field coordinates in meters based on the annotated reference points. The resulting position data was smoothed to estimate velocity and acceleration. Each object was then classified as offense, defense, or disc, and for each offensive player, the closest defensive player was identified and paired one-to-one.

These preprocessing steps produced a high-quality tracking dataset with consistent position, velocity, and acceleration data, ready for direct use in evaluating counterfactual scenarios and conducting quantitative spatial analysis.

E   Detection of Initiation of Movement

In this study, the receiver's initiation of movement is defined as the onset of rapid acceleration with the intention of receiving a pass. We detect this event automatically using rule-based criteria. The frame where this initiation is detected becomes the starting point of a movement sequence, which is defined as the entire span of motion from that frame until the player either receives a pass or ceases the attempt. The extracted sequence is then verified via manual video inspection to eliminate false positives.

E.1   Definition of Initiation of Movement

A player is deemed to initiate movement if they satisfy all of the following conditions (Condition 1), and the corresponding frame is treated as the beginning of the movement sequence.

Condition 1 (Criteria for detecting initiation of movement):

(i) Acceleration magnitude is at least $4\,m/s^2$.
(ii) The player has not held the disc for the past 2 s (30 frames).
(iii) The angle between the velocity and acceleration vectors is $90°$ or less.

(i) A high acceleration magnitude typically reflects a decision to change movement direction. (ii) However, players also tend to accelerate after throwing the disc from a stationary state; to exclude such cases, we add the condition that the player has not held the disc for the preceding 2 s. (iii) Since large acceleration can also result from deceleration, we include a directional condition to ensure consistency.

E.2   Expansion of the Movement Sequence

A movement sequence is defined as the segment of motion that begins with the initiation of movement and continues until the player either receives the disc or abandons the cut. To identify the full sequence, we extend the segment forward and backward by including additional frames based on the following criteria.

Condition 2 (Forward extension of the movement sequence):

(i) The player was part of the movement sequence in the previous frame.
(ii) The player is not holding the disc.
(iii) Velocity magnitude is at least $3\,m/s$.
(iv) Directional change in velocity from the previous frame is $20°$ or less.
(v) Deviation from the average velocity direction in the current sequence is $90°$ or less.

Condition 3 (Backward extension of the movement sequence):

(i) The player is included in the movement sequence in the next frame.
(ii) Velocity magnitude is at least $0.05\,m/s$.
(iii) Velocity magnitude in the next frame has not decreased by more than $0.05\,m/s$.

Condition 2 is applied iteratively to propagate the movement sequence forward, capturing frames where the player maintains sufficient speed and directional consistency. Condition 3 is used to incorporate frames before the initiation frame, in cases where acceleration may have started earlier.

E.3   Exclusion Criteria

Among the extracted movement sequences, those satisfying the following condition are excluded from evaluation, as they are unlikely to represent attempts to receive a pass.

Condition 4 (Exclusion criteria):
At the end of the movement sequence, one or more of the following holds:

(i) Two or more offensive players are within a 5-meter radius at the end of the movement sequence.

(ii) Two or more offensive players are located within a 90° cone in the forward direction.

These conditions are designed to filter out movements toward crowded areas or those lacking a clear spatial objective. Additionally, all detected sequences are reviewed in video form, and those without a clear intent to receive a pass are also excluded.

F   Definition of Space Evaluation Metric

F.1   PPCF

PPCF defines the probability density that player i controls location r at time t within time T as:

$$\frac{d\mathrm{PPCF}_i}{dT}(t, r, T) = \left(1 - \sum_k \mathrm{PPCF}_k(t, r, T)\right) f_i(t, r, T)\lambda_i \qquad (11)$$

where $f_i(t, r, T)$ is the probability that player i can reach location r within time T, and λ_i is a control ability constant (set to 4.3 for both offense and defense in this study). The final control probability field $\mathbf{PPCF}_i(t, r)$ is obtained by numerically integrating the above expression over $T \in [0, \infty)$.

F.2   UPPCF

In adapting PPCF to ultimate, we incorporate domain-specific characteristics. In ultimate, the player holding the disc is not allowed to move, and defenders positioned within 3 m—typically engaged in stalling—also tend to remain stationary. Iwashita et al. (2024) proposed excluding these players from pitch control calculations, and we follow this approach to better reflect actual player dynamics. Additionally, we introduce a direction-dependent reaction time, assuming that reaction latency depends on the alignment between a player's movement and the disc or their marking target. The reaction angle and reaction time are defined as follows:

$$\theta_{\text{reaction}} = \begin{cases} \theta_{d-\mathbf{v}} & \text{(offense)} \\ \min(\theta_{d-\mathbf{v}}, \theta_{d-\mathbf{o}}) & \text{(defense)} \end{cases}, \quad \mathrm{RT} = 0.1 + \frac{\theta_{\text{reaction}}}{\pi} \qquad (12)$$

Here, $\theta_{d-\mathbf{v}}$ is the angle between the disc direction and the player's velocity vector, and $\theta_{d-\mathbf{o}}$ is the angle to the marked offensive player.

F.3   Distance Weight

See Fig. 5.

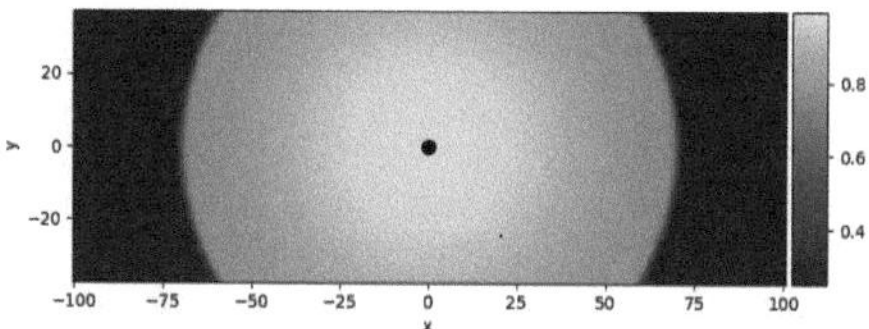

Fig. 5. Spatial distribution of the distance-based weight w_d. The weight decreases as the distance from the disc (black dot) increases, reflecting the decreasing likelihood of successful long passes in ultimate frisbee. Warmer colors indicate higher weights.

G   Reachable Area

See Fig. 6.

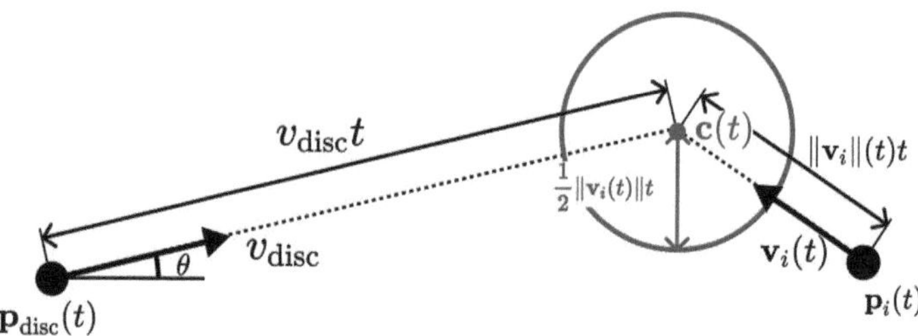

Fig. 6. Geometric illustration of the predicted reachable area $\Omega(t)$, defined as a circle centered at the predicted reception point $\mathbf{c}(t)$, with a radius proportional to the player's velocity. The disc and player trajectories are used to solve for the expected interception point.

H   Application

VTCS quantitatively evaluates how the timing of movement initiation influences spatial advantage by comparing actual plays with temporally counterfactual scenarios. In this section, we demonstrate its applicability through a specific example in which the initiation timing of a receiver is analyzed, and a more optimal alternative is identified.

Figure 7 (a) illustrates the actual play. At the moment the receiver initiated movement, the marker (a defensive player near the thrower) was already approaching the thrower and limiting the passing lane, preventing the receiver from gaining sufficient open space. The scenario evaluation value at this point was $V_{\mathrm{scenario}} = 0.407$.

In contrast, Fig. 7 (b) shows a counterfactual scenario in which the receiver initiated movement 15 frames (i.e., 1 s) earlier. In this scenario, the receiver was able to cut into the open space before the marker could effectively restrict the passing lane, resulting in a significantly improved spatial advantage. The scenario evaluation value in this case increased to $V_{\text{scenario}} = 0.751$, demonstrating a clear improvement over the actual play.

These results highlight how VTCS enables the visualization of lost spatial opportunities caused by suboptimal initiation timing. Moreover, VTCS can function not only as a diagnostic tool that provides concrete suggestions–such as how much earlier (or later) the movement should have been initiated. This insight is valuable for players and coaches seeking to improve timing decisions through data-informed feedback.

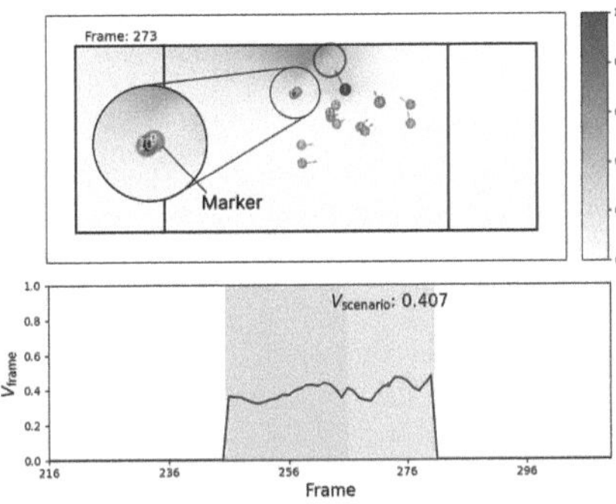

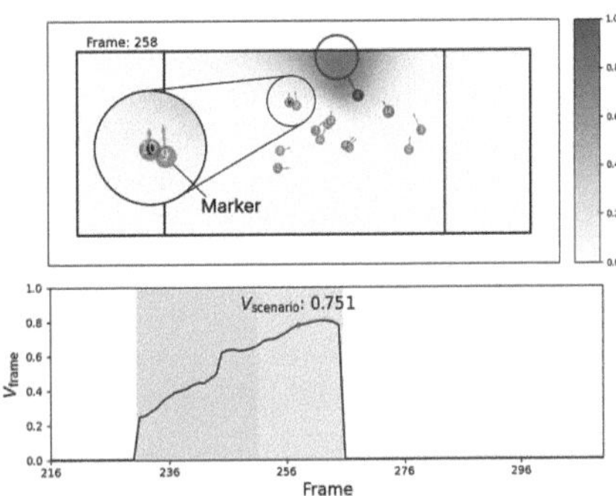

(a) Actual play

The receiver has already initiated movement, but the marker is closely guarding the thrower, severely limiting the passing lane. As a result, the spatial control within the reachable area is low, and the receiver is unable to secure sufficient open space. The scenario evaluation value is $V_{\text{scenario}} = 0.407$.

(b) Optimal scenario

In the counterfactual scenario where the receiver initiates movement 15 frames earlier, they can reach open space before the marker obstructs the passing lane, thereby achieving a higher spatial advantage. The scenario evaluation value improves to $V_{\text{scenario}} = 0.751$.

Fig. 7. Comparison between the actual play (left) and the counterfactual scenario with 15-frame earlier initiation (right). The top panels show the player positions and spatial control at the respective moments; the blue circles represent the receiver's reachable area. The bottom panels present the time series of spatial evaluation values V_{frame}, where the gray region indicates the evaluation window and the yellow region shows the averaging window used to compute V_{scenario}. The red dot marks the frame shown in the corresponding top panel. The comparison suggests that earlier initiation leads to a higher spatial advantage ($0.407 \rightarrow 0.751$). (Color figure online)

References

1. Brefeld, U., Lasek, J., Mair, S.: Probabilistic movement models and zones of control. Mach. Learn. **108**(1), 127–147 (2019)
2. Chen, X., et al.: Professional basketball player behavior synthesis via planning with diffusion. arXiv preprint arXiv:2306.04090 (2023)
3. Dick, U., Tavakol, M., Brefeld, U.: Rating player actions in soccer. Front. Sports Active Living **3**, 682986 (2021)
4. Ding, N., Takeda, K., Jin, W., Bei, Y., Fujii, K.: Estimation of control area in badminton doubles with pose information from top and back view drone videos. Multimedia Tools Appl. **83**(8), 24777–24793 (2024)
5. Eberhard, B., Miller, J., Sandholtz, N.: A machine learning approach to player value and decision making in professional ultimate frisbee. In: MIT Sloan Sports Analytics Conference (2025)
6. Fujii, K.: Machine learning in sports: open approach for next play analytics (2025)
7. Fujii, K., Isaka, T., Kouzaki, M., Yamamoto, Y.: Mutual and asynchronous anticipation and action in sports as globally competitive and locally coordinative dynamics. Sci. Rep. **5** (2015). https://doi.org/10.1038/srep16140
8. Fujii, K., Shinya, M., Yamashita, D., Oda, S., Kouzaki, M.: Superior reaction to changing directions for skilled basketball defenders but not linked with specialised anticipation. Eur. J. Sport Sci. **14**(3), 209–216 (2014). https://doi.org/10.1080/17461391.2013.780098
9. Fujii, K., Takeishi, N., Kawahara, Y., Takeda, K.: Decentralized policy learning with partial observation and mechanical constraints for multi-person modeling. Neural Netw. **171**, 40–52 (2024)
10. Fujii, K., Takeuchi, K., Kuribayashi, A., Takeishi, N., Kawahara, Y., Takeda, K.: Estimating counterfactual treatment outcomes over time in complex multi-agent scenarios. IEEE Trans. Neural Netw. Learn. Syst., 1–15 (2024)
11. Fujii, K., Tsutsui, K., Scott, A., Nakahara, H., Takeishi, N., Kawahara, Y.: Adaptive action supervision in reinforcement learning from real-world multi-agent demonstrations. In: 16th International Conference on Agents and Artificial Intelligence (ICAART 2024), vol. 2, pp. 27–39 (2024)
12. Fujii, K., Yamashita, D., Kimura, T., Isaka, T., Kouzaki, M.: Preparatory body state before reacting to an opponent: short-term joint torque fluctuation in real-time competitive sports. PLoS ONE **10**(5), e0128571 (2015)
13. Fujii, K., Yokoyama, K., Koyama, T., Rikukawa, A., Yamada, H., Yamamoto, Y.: Resilient help to switch and overlap hierarchical subsystems in a small human group. Sci. Rep. **6** (2016)
14. Fujii, K., Yoshioka, S., Isaka, T., Kouzaki, M.: Unweighted state as a sidestep preparation improve the initiation and reaching performance for basketball players. J. Electromyogr. Kinesiol. **23**(6), 1467–1473 (2013)
15. Fujii, K., Yoshioka, S., Isaka, T., Kouzaki, M.: The preparatory state of ground reaction forces in defending against a dribbler in a basketball 1-on-1 dribble subphase. Sports Biomech. **14**(1), 28–44 (2015)
16. Fujimura, A., Sugihara, K.: Geometric analysis and quantitative evaluation of sport teamwork. Syst. Comput. Jpn. **36**(6), 49–58 (2005)
17. Gibbons, J.D., Chakraborti, S.: Nonparametric Statistical Inference: Revised and Expanded. CRC press (2014)
18. Gibbs, C.P., Elmore, R., Fosdick, B.K.: The causal effect of a timeout at stopping an opposing run in the NBA. Ann. Appl. Stat. **16**(3), 1359–1379 (2022)

19. Herold, M., et al.: Off-ball behavior in association football: a data-driven model to measure changes in individual defensive pressure. J. Sports Sci. **40**(12), 1412–1425 (2022)
20. Iwashita, S., Scott, A., Umemoto, R., Ding, N., Fujii, K.: Space evaluation based on pitch control using drone video in ultimate. arXiv preprint (2024)
21. Kono, R., Fujii, K.: Mathematical models for off-ball scoring prediction in basketball. In: International Workshop on Machine Learning and Data Mining for Sports Analytics. Springer (2024). https://doi.org/10.1007/978-3-031-86692-0_4
22. Lam, H., Kolbinger, O., Lames, M., Russomanno, T.G.: State transition modeling in ultimate frisbee: adaptation of a promising method for performance analysis in invasion sports. Front. Psychol. **12**, 664511 (2021)
23. Link, D., Lang, S., Seidenschwarz, P.: Real time quantification of dangerousity in football using spatiotemporal tracking data. PLoS ONE **11**(12), e0168768 (2016)
24. Martens, F., Dick, U., Brefeld, U.: Space and control in soccer. Front. Sports Active Living **3**, 676179 (2021)
25. Meissel, K., Yao, E.S.: Using cliff's delta as a non-parametric effect size measure: an accessible web app and R tutorial. Pract. Assess. Res. Eval. **29**(1) (2024)
26. Nakahara, H., Takeda, K., Fujii, K.: Pitching strategy evaluation via stratified analysis using propensity score. J. Quant. Anal. Sports **19**(2), 91–102 (2023)
27. Nakahara, H., Tsutsui, K., Takeda, K., Fujii, K.: Action valuation of on-and off-ball soccer players based on multi-agent deep reinforcement learning. IEEE Access **11**, 131237–131244 (2023)
28. Narizuka, T., Yamazaki, Y., Takizawa, K.: Space evaluation in football games via field weighting based on tracking data. Sci. Rep. **11**(1), 5509 (2021)
29. Reddy, C., Jeon, W.: Identifying goalkeeper movement timing from single-camera broadcast footage through pose estimation: a pilot study. Appl. Sci. **14**(13), 5961 (2024)
30. Slaughter, P.R., Adamczyk, P.G.: Tracking quantitative characteristics of cutting maneuvers with wearable movement sensors during competitive women's ultimate frisbee games. Sensors **20**(22), 6508 (2020)
31. Spearman, W.: Beyond expected goals. In: Proceedings of the 12th MIT SloanSports Analytics Conference, pp. 1–17 (2018)
32. Taki, T., Hasegawa, J., Fukumura, T.: Development of motion analysis system for quantitative evaluation of teamwork in soccer games. In: Proceedings of 3rd IEEE International Conference on Image Processing, vol. 3, pp. 815–818. IEEE (1996)
33. Teranishi, M., Tsutsui, K., Takeda, K., Fujii, K.: Evaluation of creating scoring opportunities for teammates in soccer via trajectory prediction. In: International Workshop on Machine Learning and Data Mining for Sports Analytics. Springer (2022). https://doi.org/10.1007/978-3-031-27527-2_5
34. Umemoto, R., Fujii, K.: Evaluation of team defense positioning by computing counterfactuals using statsbomb 360 data. In: StatsBomb Conference (2023)
35. Vock, D.M., Vock, L.F.B.: Estimating the effect of plate discipline using a causal inference framework: an application of the g-computation algorithm. J. Quant. Anal. Sports **14**(2), 37–56 (2018)
36. Wang, Z., et al.: TactiCAI: an ai assistant for football tactics. Nat. Commun. **15**(1), 1906 (2024)
37. Weiss, J., Childers, S.: Maps for reasoning in ultimate. In: International Workshop on Machine Learning and Data Mining for Sports Analytics, pp. 21–27 (2013)
38. Weiss, J.C., Childers, S.: Spatial statistics to evaluate player contribution in ultimate. MIT Sloan Sports Analytics Conference (2014)

39. Wu, L.Y., Danielson, A.J., Hu, X.J., Swartz, T.B.: A contextual analysis of crossing the ball in soccer. J. Quant. Anal. Sports **17**(1), 57–66 (2021)
40. Wu, Y., et al.: OBTracker: visual analytics of off-ball movements in basketball. IEEE Trans. Visual Comput. Graphics **29**(1), 929–939 (2023). https://doi.org/10.1109/TVCG.2022.3209373
41. Yeh, R.A., Schwing, A.G., Huang, J., Murphy, K.: Diverse generation for multi-agent sports games. In: Proceedings of the IEEE Conference on Computer Vision and Pattern Recognition, pp. 4610–4619 (2019)
42. Yeung, C., Fujii, K.: A strategic framework for optimal decisions in football 1-vs-1 shot-taking situations: an integrated approach of machine learning, theory-based modeling, and game theory. Complex Intell. Syst., 1–20 (2024)
43. Yeung, C., Ide, K., Someya, T., Fujii, K.: OpenStarLb: open approach for spatio-temporal agent data analysis in soccer. arXiv preprint arXiv:2502.02785 (2025)

Author Index

If you have any concerns about our products,
you can contact us on
ProductSafety@springernature.com

In case Publisher is established outside the EU,
the EU authorized representative is:
Springer Nature Customer Service Center GmbH
Europaplatz 3, 69115 Heidelberg, Germany

Printed by Libri Plureos GmbH
in Hamburg, Germany